$\dfrac{acc}{\times a^2}$ 25 F 16

HISTORY OF THE

CLAY-WORKING INDUSTRY

IN

THE UNITED STATES

BY

HEINRICH RIES, Ph.D.

PROFESSOR OF ECONOMIC GEOLOGY IN CORNELL UNIVERSITY, AUTHOR OF
" ECONOMIC GEOLOGY OF THE UNITED STATES," AND "CLAYS:
THEIR OCCURRENCE, PROPERTIES AND USES"

AND

HENRY LEIGHTON, A.B.

ASSISTANT ECONOMIC GEOLOGIST, NEW YORK GEOLOGICAL SURVEY

FIRST EDITION
FIRST THOUSAND

NEW YORK
JOHN WILEY & SONS
London: CHAPMAN & HALL, Limited
1909

Stanhope Press
F. H. GILSON COMPANY
BOSTON, U.S.A.

PREFACE.

THE materials for this work were collected for the Department of Economics and Sociology of the Carnegie Institution of Washington for use in a projected series of "Contributions to the Economic History of the United States." This advance publication is by the permission of the late Carroll D. Wright (who was the Director of the Department) with the understanding that any of the data herein contained may be used in that series. Mr. Edward W. Parker, of the United States Geological Survey, a collaborator of Dr. Wright, has had the more immediate supervision of the present work and has approved the manuscript for this volume.

In the preparation of this work the authors have consulted all available magazines, private publications and government and state reports. Those which have served as sources of information are listed at the end of the work, but they do not represent more than one quarter of all the works consulted. When reference is made to these in the text, a number is given in parenthesis, corresponding to that of the reference in the list, and this number is followed by the volume or page number, the former being given in Roman numerals and the latter in Arabic figures.

The data obtained from these publications have been supplemented by inquiries addressed to the different State geologists, and a very large number of producers, as well as private individuals who it was thought might be able to supply any of the desired facts. The replies to many of these communications developed such a startling lack of knowledge of the subject in nearly all quarters that the authors venture to hope that the gathering together of what scattered information there is may prove of value. In some cases it was hardly possible to get any data on important States especially in the case of Illinois and Kentucky, for there appears to be very little literature on the subject according to our own searches and the statement of State officials; moreover most of the manufacturers to whom requests for information were sent did not even reply to the inquiries. And this failure on the part of many producers to respond to inquiries, is responsible for the occasional omission of references to works of which one might reasonably expect a mention.

In the arrangement of the subject matter the main treatment of the subject is by products, but as this leaves gaps here and there, it has been followed by a discussion by States.

It has of course been impossible to refer to every deposit or factory in the country, only the more important ones being mentioned, and this chiefly for pointing out the development of the industry at different points. For this purpose it has also been necessary to mention some of the smaller plants as well. Developments in manufacturing methods are sometimes referred to, but it should be understood that the discussion of technologic details is not one of the main objects of the work.

Since the primary object of the work is a discussion of the history of the industry, details relating to the mode of occurrence and distribution of the clays are omitted; moreover, such details have already been published elsewhere in Geological Survey and private publications.

The statistics in nearly all cases are taken from the United States Geological Survey reports on Mineral Resources, and the earlier ones are to be regarded as only approximate. Those for the years 1850, 1860, 1870, 1880 and 1890 are from the reports of the Census Bureau.

The authors take this opportunity of thanking most heartily all those who have aided them in the collection of this material, but special thanks are due to Messrs. E. C. Stover, Trenton, N. J.; F. W. Walker, Beaver Falls, Pa.; R. R. Hice, Beaver, Pa.; J. H. Burgess, Hockessin, Del.; E. Mayer, Beaver Falls, Pa.; B. W. Robinson, Akron, Ohio; L. Parker, St. Louis, Mo.; H. N. Harker, East Liverpool, Ohio; J. N. McClave, Toronto, Ohio; Wm. Walker, Pittsburg, Pa.; W. D. Richardson and Prof. Edward Orton, Jr., Columbus, Ohio, and Messrs. C. B. Stowe, Cleveland, Ohio, and Jefferson Middleton, United States Geological Survey.

CORNELL UNIVERSITY,   HEINRICH RIES.
    Ithaca, N.Y.   HENRY LEIGHTON.

CONTENTS.

PART I.

RÉSUMÉ OF THE CLAY-WORKING INDUSTRY BY PRODUCTS.

CHAPTER I.

CHAPTER II.

PART II.

HISTORY OF THE CLAY-WORKING INDUSTRY BY STATES.

CHAPTER III.

Alabama to Iowa.

CHAPTER IV.

Kansas to New Hampshire.

CHAPTER V.

New Jersey to Ohio.

CHAPTER VI.

Oregon to Wyoming.

CONTENTS.

LIST OF ILLUSTRATIONS.

Plates.

Figures.

ix

History of the Clay-Working Industry in the United States.

PART I.

CHAPTER I.

INTRODUCTION.

IT is probable that clay working represents one of the oldest established industries in the United States, for the early colonists who were used to houses of brick or stone in the countries whence they came, took steps to construct equally durable ones in the new land to which they had migrated. It is not surprising, therefore, to find many references in the early histories to the establishment of brick yards and potteries, accompanied sometimes by interesting data and quaint anecdotes relating to their operation. Unfortunately such detailed chronicling of events has not been carried on up to the present time, and the collection of facts bearing on the development of the clay-working industry in the United States has been beset with difficulties. The making of clay products on this continent did not, however, begin with the white settlers, for the Indians had long before that been active in the production of pottery, and the molding of these wares, often of unique design and characteristic decorations, has persisted up to the present time.

Clay, unlike gold and silver, is not a substance commanding a high market value either in its raw or refined state, and has not, therefore, been eagerly sought for in all parts of the country to such an extent that it became an important factor in civilization like the nobler metals. For this reason partly, the discovery of new deposits and their development has not always been widely advertised or intelligently described in the magazines and newspapers.

Then too, the methods of mining and treatment have been simple as compared with those of the metals, so that they have attracted but little attention in the technical literature in this country.

Added to this is the fact that journals devoted to the clay industry are of comparatively recent establishment and the only Ceramic Society of the United States in which matters of technical interest are discussed, is but 11 years old. The State Geological Surveys, though in many cases organized at an early date, gave but passing mention to their plastic resources, and the first report, the classic work of Dr. Cook of New Jersey, did not appear until 1878.

This was followed after an interval by the appearance of clay reports in many other States, New York, Ohio, and Missouri being among the earliest, followed later by a number of others. But nearly every one of these reports was devoted primarily and mainly to a consideration of the properties and occurrence of the raw materials, and the status of the industry at the time it was prepared. Few of them made any reference to the past history of the ceramic art in their respective States.

It will, therefore, be easily seen that all of these factors combined have made the recorded history of the clay-working industry in the United States a somewhat imperfect one. Nor is this all. The earlier writers, and indeed, unfortunately, some of the later ones, have been careless in their choice of descriptive terms, so that difficulty is sometimes encountered in telling the exact nature of the products referred to.

In following out the history of the industry in each State, a chronological arrangement has been maintained as far as possible, although in some cases this has been temporarily departed from in order to trace out the development in some particular district. Moreover in States like Pennsylvania, Ohio, New Jersey, etc., where the industry is varied, a subdivision by products has seemed advisable.

RÉSUMÉ OF THE HISTORY OF THE CLAY-WORKING INDUSTRY BY PRODUCTS.

As explained in the Introduction the history of the clay-working industry has been discussed first by products, in order to review the development in each branch. This is then followed by a discussion of the development in each State. This necessitates more or less repetition, but it permits the presentation of a more connected chain of events for each district, as well as the incorporation of details of local interest.

In tracing out the development of the ceramic industry it will be seen that it began at a very early date in the eastern part of the country and that it gradually spread westward until it covered the entire United States, becoming most highly developed in those regions where there was usually a supply of the proper raw materials, large population, large and thriving towns and cities, and numerous industries.

The dependence of man upon burned clay is certainly emphasized by a parallel study of the history of the clay-working industry and the development of the country, and while the recital of the more important details of clay-working history may serve to impress us with the extent and variety of its development, nevertheless it does not bring out clearly and forcibly its value.

In order therefore to be able to regard the subject from the latter viewpoint we must make use of statistics, though they are at times incomplete. This incompleteness, however, shows that the figures are not overstated, though they may at times appear large. They may, therefore, be regarded as conservative estimates.

From the smallest beginning the clay-working industry has gradually crept up to the foremost ranks of the mineral industry, being at present only exceeded in the value of its production by iron, coal and copper. This slow but steady growth, with but few relapses, can be well seen by reference to the Census Bureau figures which are compiled every ten years. To these are also added the figures compiled by the United States Geological Survey for 1907.

The table (from Ref. 172) given below is a comparative summary of the statistics for the clay industry in its entirety as returned at the censuses of 1850 to 1905, with percentages of increase.

Several points in the table (see p. 5) are worthy of mention. The decrease since 1900 in the number of establishments was caused by the consolidation of a number of plants under a single management. "Notwithstanding this decrease in the number of establishments, the capital increased $82,844,654 or 56 per cent between 1900 and 1905. Of this increase, $44,974,133 or 54.3 per cent was in the pottery, terra-cotta and fire-clay products branch of the industry, and $37,870,521 or 45.7 per cent in the brick and tile branch. The increase in the former over 1900 was 68.2 per cent, and in the latter 46.1 per cent."

"The concentration of the industry is further indicated by the increase of 37.5 per cent in the average number of employees per establishment between 1900 and 1905, and by the fact that the total value of products from the 5,507 establishments in 1905 exceeds that from the 6,423 establishments reported in 1900 by $39,818,992 or 41.7 per cent. This increase during five years is largely in excess of that shown for any ten-year period since 1850, with the single exception of that of $48,016,865 between 1880 and 1890. The steady increase in the price of lumber, the growing demand of builders and investors for building material that affords the greatest protection against fires, and the increasing appreciation of the products of American potteries, are conditions favorable to a rapid growth of the manufacture of clay products."

Large as are the figures for 1905 given in the census table below those for the two following years are even larger, amounting to $161,032,722 in 1906 and $158,942,369 in 1907, according to the statistics compiled by the United States Geological Survey. Although 1907 shows a slight decrease from 1906, in part attributable to financial conditions, it was, nevertheless, considerably greater than 1905, which was a year of unusual prosperity.

Looking over the production of the individual products during the past ten years, we find that in practically every case there has been a steady increase.

COMPARATIVE SUMMARY OF CLAY PRODUCTS, WITH PER CENT OF INCREASE FROM 1850 TO 1905.

	Census.							Per cent of Increase					
	1850	1860	1870	1880	1890	1900	1905	1850 to 1860	1860 to 1870	1870 to 1880	1880 to 1890	1890 to 1900	1900 to 1905
Number of establishments....	2,121	2,240	3,950	6,383	6,535	6,423	5,507	5.6	76.7	61.2	2.4	1.7*	14.3*
Capital........................	$5,217,231	$9,707,952	$26,776,011	$35,039,939	$108,705,670	$148,038,333	$230,882,977	86.1	175.8	30.9	210.2	36.2	56.
Number of salaried officials...	(a)	(a)	(a)	(a)	6,291†	5,203	7,442	......	......	......	......	17.3*	43.0
Salaries....................	(a)	(a)	(a)	(a)	$4,254,043†	$5,036,195	$8,158,213	......	......	......	......	18.4	62.0
Wage earners, average number	19,801	24,569	50,167	76,576	123,156	105,693	118,449	24.1	104.2	52.6	60.8	14.2*	12.1
Total wages...................	$4,890,422	$5,224,859	$13,332,547	$17,044,250	$38,578,389	$39,575,070	$53,823,670	6.8	155.2	27.8	126.3	2.6	36.0
Miscellaneous expenses........					$7,111,776	$6,845,040	$14,625,214	......	......	......	......	3.8*	113.7
Cost of materials used.........	$1,768,374	$2,930,547	$9,531,162	$12,683,897	$18,257,098	$22,921,384	$32,907,961	65.7	225.2	33.1	43.9	25.5	43.6
Value of products.............	$8,180,359	$13,987,828	$36,368,151	$41,810,920	$89,827,785	$95,533,862	$135,352,854	70.8	160.0	15.0	114.8	6.4	41.7

(a) Not reported separately.

* Decrease.

† Includes proprietors and firm members with their salaries; number only reported in 1900 and 1905, but not included in this table.

All of these figures then show a wonderful increase in the production of burned-clay wares in the United States, although unfortunately those collected for the Census Bureau prior to 1890 were not as detailed as those gathered after that date, and, moreover, since 1890 was a year of great prosperity, and the year 1899[1] one of incomplete recovery from the depression of 1893, there will be in some cases a decrease from 1890 to 1899 in the Census reports. Still, in most instances, there is a strong advance. This is especially emphasized by such products as architectural terra cotta, hollow brick, conduits, and paving brick, as well as some lines of pottery whose use expanded at a phenomenal rate in this decade.

Considering the causes leading to the development of the clay-working industry in any State, we find that in the case of every grade of clay product, except those made from the finer grades of clay, the presence of raw materials is the controlling factor, and in the case of the lower grades a market near at hand.

Common bricks and tiles are not only made close to the clay deposit, but will not, as a rule, bear the cost of long shipment. Fire brick, sewer pipe, pressed brick, and stoneware can often be shipped long distances, partly because they command a higher price, and partly because the necessary raw materials are not to be found everywhere.

White ware and wall tile, being made from a mixture of raw materials derived usually from widely separated sources, require the factory to be located where in- and out-shipping facilities are good, and fuel and labor easily obtained.

It must be admitted, however, that in the cases of many isolated plants, it is sometimes difficult without more detailed knowledge, to explain satisfactorily the reason for their location.

A strong factor in the development of the technology of the clay-working industry in any country, must be the presence of skilled ceramic technologists in responsible positions. Their duty, it is, to detect errors and remedy them, to improve the methods in use, and by their knowledge also to better the quality of the wares. In pottery works they may even, and often do, have more or less

---

[1] It should be remembered that the figures given in the 1900 census are those for the year 1899.

opportunity to express their artistic ability in the designing of new forms.

Men of this character are rarely self-trained, but are the product of ceramic schools, and the establishment of such institutions cannot fail to have a beneficial effect on the industry. Schools of this character are common in Germany and have abundantly proved their value, but there are few of them in the United States.

The first of these schools of ceramics was that of the Ohio State University, started in 1894, well equipped with clay-working machinery and other appliances for the study and testing of clays. This school, which is under the direction of Prof. Edward Orton, Jr., gives considerable attention to the engineering side of ceramics, and has been highly successful.

A second one to be established was the New York State College of Ceramics, founded by the State Legislature in 1901, and located at Alfred University. Prof. Charles F. Binns is director. This school not only contains appliances and apparatus for testing clays, but also a well equipped department of Ceramic Arts.

The New Jersey School of Clay-working and Ceramics, the third to be organized, is located at the State College, New Brunswick, N. J. It was started in 1902 and is under the directorship of Dr. C. W. Parmelee. Like the other schools it is well equipped with testing machinery and apparatus for the practical and scientific study of clays.

A fourth school was organized at the University of Illinois in 1905, under the direction of Prof. C. W. Rolfe, and in 1907 the Iowa State Legislature made provision for a similar school to be located at Iowa State College, Ames, Ia., under the directorship of Prof. I. A. Williams. Instruction in Ceramics had however been given there since 1900.

During the past year the United States Geological Survey has equipped and located a laboratory at Pittsburg for testing clay products, and the study of problems which affect the interests of the clay worker.

There is probably no kind of clay product which is not made in the United States at the present day, but the production of some of these, such as high-grade porcelain and art pottery, is very small,

RANK OF TWELVE LEADING STATES AS PRODUCERS OF CLAY PRODUCTS FROM 1890-1907.

1890	1894	1895	1896	1897	1898	1899	1900	1901	1902	1903	1904	1905	1906	1907	30 mill. dollars
Pa.	O.	O.	O.	O.	O.	O.	O.	O.	O.	O.	O.	O.	O.	O.	
O.	Ill.	Pa.	Pa.	Pa.	Pa.	Pa.	Pa.	Pa.	Pa.	Pa.	Pa.	Pa.	Pa.	Pa.	20
N.Y.	Pa.	Ill.	N.Y.	N.J.	N.J.	N.J.	N.J.	N.J.	N.J.	N.J.	N.J.	N.J.	N.J.	N.J.	
N.J.	N.Y.	N.Y.	Ill.	N.Y.	Ill.	N.Y.	Ill.	Ill.	Ill.	Ill.	Ill.	N.Y.	N.Y.	Ill.	
Ill.	N.J.	N.J.	N.J.	Ill.	N.Y.	Ill.	N.Y.	N.Y.	N.Y.	N.Y.	N.Y.	Ill.	Ill.	N.Y.	10
Mo.	Ind.	Ind.	Mo.	Ind.	Ind.	Ind.	Ind.	Mo.	Ind.	Ind.	Ind.	Ind.	Ind.	Mo.	
Ind.	Mo.	Mo.	Ind.	Mo.	Mo.	Mo.	Mo.	Ind.	Mo.	Mo.	Mo.	Mo.	Mo.	Ind.	
Mass.	Ia.	Mass.	Mass.	Mass.	Ia.	Ia.	Ia.	Ia.	Ia.	Ia.	Calif.	Calif.	Calif.	Calif.	
Calif.	Mass.	Ia.	Ia.	Ia.	Mass.	Mass.	W. Va.	W. Va.	W. Va.	Calif.	Ia.	Ia.	Ia.	Ia.	5
Colo.	Mich.	Calif.	Md.	Conn.	Md.	Wis.	Mass.	Mass.	Mass.	W. Va.	Ky.	Ky.	W. Va.	W. Va.	
Neb.	Md.	Mich.	Conn.	Md.	Minn.	Md.	Md.	Calif.	Calif.	Ky.	W. Va.	Md.	Ky.	Ky.	
Md.	Wis.	Minn.	Mich.	Tex.	Calif.	Calif.	Ky.	Tex.	Colo.	Mass.	Ga.	Ga.	Kas.	Tex.	1

large quantities of these being still imported.   That these importations will slowly decrease would cause no surprise, but the falling off will be exceedingly slow, for the production of such ware in the United States is surrounded by many difficulties, such as cost of labor, lack of workmen trained for making this kind of product, and prejudice against American wares of this grade on the part of the purchasing public.   While the United States produces practically every type of clay product known, and in the total value of these leads the world, still it is doubtful if any one of the kinds made has originated in this country.

Looking over the statistics of the past fourteen years we find that there has been comparatively little change in the rank of the leading States.   Ohio has held the first position throughout this period, while Pennsylvania has been second except in 1894.

The position of the twelve leading States during the period above mentioned is shown on the accompanying table, the heavy lines representing a certain value of output, being drawn under those States which had a value of production equal to or greater than that indicated by the respective lines.

COMMON BRICK.

It can, perhaps, be truthfully said that brickmaking represents the earliest form of clay working in this country, some of the Indian tribes of the southwest having constructed their dwellings of adobe brick before the white men reached these shores, but of their work we have practically few chronological data.

That the early colonists lost no time in making use of the brick clays is shown by the numerous records, which mention the erection of brick kilns at many points, so that early in the 17th century the common-brick clays were being utilized.

In Virginia they were made as early as 1611, in Massachusetts by 1629, and about the same date in New York.   All brick used prior to that date in the last-named State were probably imported.   The earliest records found for Maine were 1635; for North Carolina 1663; Rhode Island, 1681; and Pennslyvania, 1683.   There are no early records for Connecticut, but brick yards no doubt were established at about the same time brickmaking began in New York and Massachusetts. The industry had begun in western Pennsylvania in 1750, and by 1776 the brick clays around Trenton, N. J., were sought after. Brickmaking was known to be under way in New Hampshire shortly after that date. By 1792, the industry had taken a foothold in the Hudson River valley, destined to become the greatest brickmaking district in the United States. Other early records show that the brickmolders were at work in South Carolina by 1797.

Curiously enough, the colonies were also doing some export business at this early date.

Bishop (Ref. 1, I, 221), states that bricks were included among the exports from the Port of Piscataqua, Me., in the years 1789–90.

New Hampshire in 1789 exported 129,000 bricks to the West Indies, and the whole country is said to have exported 787,764 bricks in 1790, as well as 157 crates of yellow Queensware and 55 dozen of stoneware. In 1791 the brick exports amounted to 743,000 and were chiefly from Massachusetts and New Hampshire (Ref. 1, I, p. 231.)

There has been some dispute among historians as to whether there was any importation of bricks from England. Some claim that there was, while others assert the contrary, explaining that the references to " English brick," meant that the brick were of the same size as those made in England.

In the Mississippi Valley States, the industry developed at a later date. Common brick are said to have been made in Chicago by 1812; in Cincinnati, Ohio, by 1829; and at Indianapolis, Ind. by 1822. At New Cumberland, W. Va., bricks were molded in 1839.

In the Lake Superior States the records do not appear to go very far back, the earliest dates noted being about 1810 for Michigan, 1842 for Wisconsin, and 1844 for Minnesota. Small plants no doubt existed prior to those dates.

While the industry began at an early date in eastern New York, it does not seem to have become firmly established in the western part much before 1837. The great brick clay deposits at Sayreville, N. J., are known to have been opened up in 1851.

In the western States the industry, as might have been expected, seems to have been developed at a much later date. The brick clays were worked around Dubuque, Ia., by 1837, and at Iowa City by 1840. By 1870 yards were scattered all over Illinois. This was also probably true of Ohio, Indiana and Missouri.

Texas in 1870 had 24 yards, which number had increased to 113 by 1880. The clays of Nebraska are also known to have been utilized for brickmaking in 1870, there being 17 yards in the State at that date.

FIG. 1. — Small common brick yard, typical of many of the earlier works, and also of small plants of the present time.

It is not known just when the industry began in Colorado, although it was no doubt earlier than in North Dakota, where bricks were made in the seventies, or in Nevada which had one yard by the same date. California supported one plant at Sutterville in 1847, but the industry expanded rapidly after that, as by 1852 there were many plants running.

For many years the raw materials used for common brick manufacture were the soft plastic surface clays.   Indeed these were the only materials that could be used with the methods then known and until better and stronger machinery was introduced.   With the development of improved manufacturing methods, brickmakers turned their attention to the shale deposits.   It is probable that they were drawn to these by observing the mellowed and plastic products of weathering which the hard rock-like shale yielded.   Evidence as to the first location where these shales were used is conflicting, but it is known that in New York State they were employed by L. G. Eisenhardt of Horseheads in 1880, while in Indiana they were not employed or their value even recognized until the early nineties.   Now they are used at numerous localities in many different States.

The early plants established in this country were small affairs, requiring little capital, and using the crudest forms of machinery, the bricks being molded by hand.   As the industry developed the plants became of more permanent character and of greater capacity.   There always were, and always will be small plants, using primitive methods, scattered all over the country, and run largely to supply a small local demand, while around the great markets many large concerns develop.

A significant industrial development has been the consolidation of the individual plants in some of the more important localities, one result of which has been to keep the price of bricks up to a reasonable figure.   Among these consolidations may be mentioned the formation of the Baltimore Brick Company of Baltimore, Md., in 1899, and of the New England Brick Company of Boston, Mass., and the Illinois Brick Company of Chicago in 1900.   Several attempts have been made to consolidate the Hudson River yards but they have not been successful.

The first bricks were made by hand, and burned in crude kilns. Later, horse-power machines were introduced for pugging and molding the clays.   The drying of the brick had to be carried on in the open air, so that in those parts of the country having freezing

PLATE I. — Brick yards at Sayreville, N. J.

weather in winter the yards could only be run in summer. As time went on the processes of manufacture were greatly improved by the introduction of steam-power machinery, driers using artificial heat, and kilns with permanent walls and roof, all contributing to a better regulation of the burning and a reduction of loss.

Methods of molding also changed. The old, soft-mud method was made to share honors with the dry-press process, and still later with the stiff-mud method. It should be added, however, that the dry-press process did not come into extensive use until after the stiff-mud machines were invented. All three of these are in use at the present day, some predominating in one region and others in another. Their selection is not always governed by the character of the clay.

The writers have endeavored to ascertain when the different methods of manufacture were introduced, but encountered some difficulty in doing so. According to information received from different sources the first steam-power soft-mud machine appears to have been the invention of a Mr. Adams of Philadelphia, and was used at that place previous to 1840. Another early form was introduced by Henry Martin and used around Perth Amboy, N. J. Patents for brick machines are known to have been granted as early as 1800, but they may have been hand-power ones. The stiff-mud process was in use prior to 1860, but it is not known who made the first machine, although one with an automatic cutter was put into operation by the Chambers Brothers Company, at Pea Shore near Camden, N. J., about 1862.

The greatest diversity of opinions exists with regard to the dry-press machine. We are informed by Mr. J. J. Koch of St. Louis, Mo., that a dry-clay press was built in Washington, D. C., in 1838, and that E. Rogers constructed an hydraulic press in Cleveland, Ohio, in 1856, which with added improvements is still in operation at Memphis, Tenn.

Another writer states (private communication) that dry-pressed bricks were being made at Cincinnati, Ohio, in 1829. Still a third machine, claimed by some to be the first, was unsuccessfully tried at Cleveland, Ohio, in 1865, but developed with improvements in Chicago at a later date.

Similar doubt exists as to the introduction of artificial drying, and while it is known that Mr. Cyrus Chambers, Jr., had a tunnel for drying stiff-mud bricks in the early sixties, the locality of operation is not known, and we have no definite information that it was the first artificial dryer introduced.

The introduction of these several types of machines for molding could not help having an important influence on the development of the industry, for while all decreased the cost of manufacture the stiff-mud process gave a greatly increased capacity, but the dry-press permitted the manufacture of a better looking and smoother product, not obtainable by the other methods of molding, until repressing was introduced.

Common brick are now made all over the United States by methods ranging from the crudest to the most highly developed ones, but there are several districts contiguous to great markets which are worthy of special mention.

According to the census of 1900, the leading common brick region of the United States is that of the Hudson Valley of New York including the Hackensack district of New Jersey. This region, which still leads, supplies the great markets of New York and adjoining cities. Cook County, Illinois, supplying Chicago and neighboring markets, was second, while Philadelphia County, Pennsylvania, was third. In addition to these there are other important though smaller districts around Washington, D. C.; Baltimore, Md.; St. Louis, Mo.; Kansas City, Mo.; Richmond, Va.; Detroit, Mich.; Milwaukee, Wis.; Cleveland, Ohio, etc. The value of common brick produced annually in the census years 1870, 1880, 1890, and annually since 1894 is given below.

VALUE OF COMMON BRICK PRODUCED IN THE UNITED STATES
FROM 1870 TO 1907.

Year.	Value.	Quantity (thousands).	Average price per thousand.
1870.............	$10,253,734	....	....
1880.............	32,833,587	....	....
1890.............	48,810,271	....	....
1894.............	35,062,538 [1]	6,152,420	$5.70
1895.............	31,569,126	6,017,965	5.25
1896.............	29,664,043	5,703,279	5.20
1897.............	26,430,207	5,292,532	4.99
1898.............	30,980,704	5,867,415	5.28
1899.............	39,887,522	7,695,305	5.18
1900.............	38,621,514	7,140,622	5.41
1901.............	45,503,076	8,038,579	5.66
1902.............	48,885,869	8,475,067	5.77
1903.............	50,532,075	8,463,683	5.97
1904.............	51,768,558	8,665,171	5.97
1905.............	61,394,383	9,817,355	6.25
1906.............	61,300,696	10,027,039	6.11
1907.............	58,785,461	9,795,698	6.00

[1] Includes front brick.

PRESSED BRICK AND ORNAMENTAL BRICK.

With improvements in the methods of manufacture it was possible, not only to produce bricks with a smooth surface and sharp edges suitable for the fronts of buildings, but by the dry-press process ornamental bricks could also be easily made.

It is somewhat difficult to trace the development of the pressed-brick industry proper, for the reason that many of the records found no doubt refer to the manufacture of a few pressed brick by some yard making chiefly common brick.

The earliest record of pressed brick indicates that dry-press machines were in use at Cincinnati in 1829. Seventeen years later pressed brick were being made in Baltimore, Md. In 1850 dry-press machines were in operation in Mississippi, and in 1856 in Florida. These, however, were only sporadic attempts, and did not represent the development of a permanent industry.

The red pressed-brick industry began around Trenton in 1865, and a hydraulic press was in operation at Louisville, Ky., in 1875. It is probable that pressed brick were also being made around

Philadelphia by this date. By 1882 some were made at Golden, Colo., and Minneapolis, Minn.

Some of the States which are now prominent in the manufacture of pressed brick were slow in developing the industry. Thus in Ohio the business was not highly developed up to 1884, at which time the Zanesville district was the most important. Indeed it may be said that in general the pressed-brick industry received its greatest impetus in the late eighties or early nineties, during which time the districts of Ohio, Pennsylvania, Illinois, Indiana and Missouri developed, these States being the most important producers.

During the early history of the pressed-brick industry red-burning clays were almost exclusively used, but these have been superseded to a large extent by fire clays, which alone yield a brick showing some shade of buff, or by the admixture of artificial colorants, give a speckled or gray product.

The wide use of fire clays for pressed brick manufacture has naturally tended to restrict the industry somewhat to those districts where such clays occur, for the factory is usually located near to the clay deposit. The product, however, is often shipped to a considerable distance.

A type of pressed brick extensively used for a period of years, although less so now, were the *Roman brick* which were about 12 inches long and 1½ inches thick. By many these are also called *Pompeiian brick*, but R. R. Hice[1] contends that the former term refers particularly to the size, while the latter correctly belongs to the flashed bricks of medium dark shade with a brownish body covered with iron spots. The manufacture of these seems to have been begun at two different localities within a year of each other. Mr. Wm. Walker informs the authors that in the spring of 1886 a Boston architect sent to Harbison and Walker part of a brick of the Roman size from Pompeii with a request that they manufacture them, which they did. At that time these were in the nature of a by-product, and made from clays that could not be employed for fire brick. In later years, however, more care was given to the selection of the raw materials, as the color of the product was

[1] Private communication.

often an important item. About the year 1886 or 1887 the Perth
Amboy Terra Cotta Company of New Jersey also commenced
the manufacture of Roman brick, the first ones being used in the
Tiffany residence at 72nd Street and Madison Avenue, New York
City.

The *Norman brick*, 12 inches long and 2⅝ inches thick were first
made in the east a few years later and in the Pittsburg district
about 1897.

The great centers of pressed brick production are east of the
Mississippi, but this type of product is also made in the Western
States particularly in Colorado, California and Washington.

With one exception the pressed-brick industry is not marked by
any consolidation of works comparable with those of the common-
brick industry.   This exception is the Hydraulic-press Brick Company, whose main works are in St. Louis, but which also owns
and operates plants at Collinsville, Ill., Kansas City, Mo.; Omaha,
Neb.; Memomonie, Wis.; Porter, Ind.; Dewitt Park, Ohio; Findlay, Ohio; Brazil, Ind.; Roseville, Ohio; Winslow Junction, N. J.;
and near Alexandria, Va.

The statistics of production as compiled by the United States
Geological Survey are given below.

VALUE OF FRONT BRICK PRODUCED IN THE UNITED STATES
FROM 1890 TO 1907.

Year.	Value.	Quantity (thousands).	Average price per thousand.
1890.............	$5,973,902	....	....
1895.............	4,399,367	339,204	$12.97
1896.............	3,390,941	270,335	12.54
1897.............	3,855,033	310,918	12.40
1898.............	3,572,385	295,833	12.08
1899.............	4,767,343	438,817	10.86
1900.............	3,864,670	344,516	11.09
1901.............	4,709,737	415,343	11.34
1902.............	5,318,008	458,391	11.60
1903.............	5,402,861	433,016	12.48
1904.............	5,560,131	434,351	12.80
1905.............	7,108,092	541,590	13.12
1906.............	7,895,323	617,469	12.79
1907.............	7,329,360	585,943	12.51

VALUE OF ORNAMENTAL BRICK PRODUCED IN THE UNITED
STATES FROM 1894 TO 1907.

Year.	Value.	Year.	Value.
1894.............	$1,128,608	1901.............	$372,131
1895.............	652,519	1902.............	335,290
1896.............	763,140	1903.............	328,387
1897.............	685,048	1904.............	300,233
1898.............	358,372	1905.............	293,907
1899.............	476,191	1906.............	207,119
1900.............	289,698	1907.............	361,243

ENAMELED BRICK.

The manufacture of enameled brick is a recent introduction.
Formerly those used in this country were imported, mainly from
England, but at the present time their manufacture is successfully
carried on at several points from domestic fire clays. The first
factory to be established was probably at Momence, Ill. (1893),
followed by that at Mount Savage, Md., and Saylorsburg, Pa.,
in 1896. About the same time their production was also begun by
Sayre & Fisher of Sayreville, N. J.

Although of promising growth the enameled brick industry has
suffered somewhat by competition with wall tile.

According to the census of 1900, there were produced in the
United States in 1899, 5,785,000 enameled brick, having a total
value of $329,969.

The census bulletin (Ref. 172, p. 67) of 1905 states that the
value of enameled brick in that year showed an increase of 35.2
per cent over 1900. New Jersey was the leading State, followed
by Illinois and Pennsylvania. Kentucky, Missouri, Iowa, Ohio,
and Michigan are included in the list of producers, but the authors
know of no steady output from those States.

The statistics of production have been given separately by the
United States Geological Survey only since 1898, and these are
given below.

VALUE OF ENAMELED BRICK PRODUCED IN THE UNITED STATES
FROM 1898 TO 1904.

Year.	Value.	Year.	Value.
1898.............	$279,993	1903.............	$569,689
1899.............	329,969	1904.............	545,397
1900.............	323,630	1905.............	636,279
1901.............	463,709	1906.............	773,104
1902.............	471,163	1907.............	918,173

ARCHITECTURAL TERRA COTTA.

Useful terra cotta, such as garden vases, statuary, etc., was made as early as 1765 by A. Hews & Co. in Massachusetts from local clays, but the making of true architectural terra cotta not only began at a late date, as compared with many other clay products, but its introduction was accompanied by difficulties.

The first serious attempt at using it was made by James Renwick, the well known New York architect. The following letter, written by Mr. Renwick in 1886, is of interest.

"In 1853 I conceived the idea of introducing terra cotta as a building material and substitute for cut-stone work in New York. I went to Mr. Young, who had a factory for making glazed and other earthen sewer pipe in 40th Street, told him what I proposed doing, and asked him if he would manufacture it from my designs and under my supervision. I supposed it would be a source of large profits to him, as it would be more durable and ornamental and less expensive than the free-stones which were then in use. I made a contract with him for the belt courses and the cornice of the Tontine Building, and for the ornamental work of the St. Denis Hotel, and of three houses in 9th Street, between Fifth and Sixth Avenues. All these buildings are now standing, and the terra cotta is as good as when first put up. We tried to introduce it into general use, but were violently opposed by the stone cutters and builders who said it would not stand, and persuaded owners not to use it. The only other building it was used in, as far as I know, was the Lafarge Hotel Court. This building was destroyed by the fire which originated in Tripler Hall, which was in the rear part of the hotel. Mr. Young, finding it impossible to introduce it and having lost money in the attempt, gave up the manufacture and returned to making pipe. The fact is we were ahead of the times, and could find no one who understood or would venture to use it. The buildings above mentioned in which it was used belonged either to my family, or friends who had confidence in my judgment. About eight or ten years after this Mr. Greenough, the sculptor, came from Rome to New York for the express purpose of introducing the use of terra cotta. I happened to dine with him, and he broached the subject. The next morn-

PLATE II. — Original Plant of the Perth Amboy Terra Cotta Company, Perth Amboy, N. J. (Photo loaned by G. P. Putnam).

ing I took him to see the work on the St. Denis Hotel and related my experience, and he gave up the idea, being afraid of meeting the same difficulties I had experienced."

The late Richard Upjohn also did much towards encouraging the use of terra cotta in New York. About the year 1853 Mr. Upjohn prepared the designs for the Trinity Building on Broadway, just north of Trinity Church. He determined to use brick and terra cotta, and the work was made and burned at a drain-pipe factory on 17th Street near the North River. The terra-cotta work used in this building is still perfect, although it has been found necessary to recut the damaged and disintegrated faces of the brown-stone work in the building.

After the unsuccessful efforts noted above no further attempts were made to introduce the use of terra cotta in New York until 1877. In that year a residence was built on the north side of 36th Street, just west of Park Avenue, from designs of George B. Post, architect, in which terra cotta was quite extensively used, both for decorative and constructive purposes.

The next important New York building in which terra cotta was used was the Morse Building, corner of Beekham and Nassau Streets, erected in 1878.

A large increase in the number of brick buildings erected followed the great fires of Chicago and Boston. By these fires it was conclusively demonstrated that fireproof buildings could not be made of unprotected stone or iron, and that only brick and terra-cotta walls were practically fireproof. This increased use of brick work, and of terra cotta as constructive and decorative material in connection with brick work, revived the demand for the manufacture of this material in or near New York. At this time there was at Perth Amboy a yellow and Rockingham-ware and fire-brick factory known as the A. Hall & Sons' Fire-Brick Works. The proprietors of these works decided in 1877 to change the yellow and Rockingham-ware works into a plant for the manufacture of architectural terra cotta, continuing the manufacture of buff and fire bricks. The necessary changes were made and the manufacture of terra cotta was commenced. In 1879, the business was incorporated under the name of the Perth Amboy Terra Cotta Company. Two years later, Mr. Alfred Hall retired

PLATE III.—Modern plant of the Perth Amboy Terra Cotta Co., now owned by the Atlantic Terra Cotta Co. (N. J. Geol. Survey, Final Report VI).

from the company and started in Perth Amboy a new fire brick and architectural terra-cotta works under the name of the A. Hall Terra Cotta Company. After being in business for five years, the latter company went into liquidation in April, 1887, shortly after the death of the president, Mr. Alfred Hall.

After architects and others had begun to realize the usefulness and durability of this new form of burned clay, and its possibilities, the growing demand was naturally followed by the establishment of works in different parts of the country. A second factory was established at Perth Amboy in 1888 followed by several others.

Atlanta, Ga., saw the starting of a works in 1870, and San Francisco, Cal., in 1876. None was established in Missouri until the Winkle Terra Cotta Company began operations in 1883, and this was followed by the beginning of other works at Long Island City, 1885, and at Philadelphia in 1886. This latter was the firm of Stephens & Leach, changed in 1887 to Stephens, Leach & Conkling, and in 1890 to Stephens, Armstrong & Conklin. This was absorbed by the New York Architectural Terra Cotta Company of Long Island City in 1893. The Northwestern Terra Cotta Company of Chicago began operations in 1876, the Indianapolis Terra Cotta Company of Indianapolis, Ind., in 1884. Another terra-cotta works (Corning Terra Cotta Company) was started at Corning, N. Y., in 1896, at Crum Lyne, Pa. (O. W. Ketchan), in 1906, and at Bradford, Pa. (Northeastern Terra Cotta Company), in the same year. There are also scattered factories along the Pacific coast which have begun operations mostly in the last ten years. The clays used by these works are referred to under their respective States.

The methods of manufacture now used are similar to those in vogue years ago, although larger and more powerful machinery is now employed for mixing. Most of the earlier terra cotta did not have its surface covered with a coloring and protective slip, nor is all of it so treated now, although the practise became wide spread about 1884 (private correspondence).

Important developments in the terra-cotta industry in the last few years have been the introduction of matte glazes, and polychrome decorations. This last type of product is also put out by art potteries, such as the Grueby and Rookwood, as well as by the regular terra-cotta factories such as the Northwestern and Atlantic.

Other innovations are the production of full-glazed terra cotta, introduced commercially about 1897, and the decoration of the surface with markings and colorings to match the building stone that is to be used in conjunction with it. Foreign manufacturers had been producing the full glaze and polychrome ware for some years prior to its introduction into the United States, and its development in this country, although tardy, is most gratifying.

The tendency towards consolidation is shown in this branch of the industry as in others. One such combination has already been referred to, and more recently there has been a union of three New Jersey and one Staten Island works, the new corporation being the Atlantic Terra Cotta Company.

At the present time New Jersey is the leading producer of architectural terra cotta, followed by New York, Pennsylvania, Illinois and Missouri. The production of terra cotta in the United States by years since 1894 is given below.

VALUE OF ARCHITECTURAL TERRA COTTA PRODUCED IN THE UNITED STATES FROM 1894 TO 1907.

Year.	Value.	Year.	Value.
1894.............	$1,476,185	1901.............	$3,367,982
1895.............	2,512,193	1902.............	3,526,906
1896.............	2,359,983	1903.............	4,672,028
1897.............	1,841,422	1904.............	4,107,473
1898.............	2,043,325	1905.............	5,003,158
1899.............	2,027,532	1906.............	5,739,460
1900.............	2,372,568	1907.............	6,026,977

HOLLOW WARE FOR STRUCTURAL WORK.

Under this heading are included fireproofing, terra-cotta lumber, hollow blocks, and hollow bricks, but it is probable also that the terms have been sometimes loosely used in the literature and in a broad sense. Since the methods of manufacture of the three are essentially similar, and the raw materials required of much the same character, they are sometimes made at the same factory. At some works the production of one type may predominate, the others being made simply as a side line for the purpose of filling occasional orders.

The earliest record of hollow ware is in the New Jersey report for 1878, in which Dr. Cook speaks of the introduction of this new type of ware whose use would be watched with interest. Mr. J. A. Rossi, however, informs us that the manufacture of hollow ware had already begun in New Jersey in 1875.[1]

The production of the fireproofing was bound to increase as it formed an important part of the modern fireproof building, and the many disastrous conflagrations in recent years have served to emphasize its value. There has also been a great call for hollow blocks in the Central States, where they appear to have been in great favor as structural material in place of brick.

Although New Jersey appears to have been the first producer of fireproofing, the credit for the discovery of terra-cotta lumber is given by some to a man named Gilman, of Eldora, Iowa.[2] He was a clay manufacturer who in 1883 made the experiment of mixing prairie soil with clay and found that it burned to a light porous block. This was used for absorbing alcohol, which he sub-sequently fired and placed under a receptacle for heating coffee.

The attention of a New York architect being accidentally drawn to this porous block, he exclaimed: "This is what I have always been looking for, for fireproofing purposes." Mr. Gilman sought to carry out the idea and hit upon the use of sawdust as a desirable substitute for prairie soil.

Whether or not Mr. Gilman was the actual discoverer of the method of making this porous fireproofing, it is true that ever since the introduction of fireproofing in the New Jersey works there has been a steady and increasingly large demand for these hollow blocks, whether filled with sawdust or not, and now New Jersey stands as the leading producer.

Ohio was not far behind New Jersey, and in 1884 fireproofing was much used, being made at Toronto and Columbus. Hollow blocks at that time, however, were only being turned out at one locality, in Summit County. Terra-cotta lumber was made in Illinois as early as 1884.

---

[1] Hall (Ref. 172, p. 67) notes that on Dec. 9, 1856, a patent was issued to M. and J. H. Buck and F. A. Cushman of Lebanon, N.H., for a machine for pressing hollow building brick as building tile.

[2] A. W. Beidler, private correspondence.

In 1885 fireproofing manufacture began in Indiana, and has continued up to the present time, while a large local industry was started on the surface clays at Hobart, Ind., in 1887, and has there undergone great expansion. During the 90's factories for making fireproofing or hollow blocks sprang up at a number of points and became active and successful producers, those located near the great markets being often run to the limit of their capacity.

It is to be noted that the most important producing districts are not far from the large markets, as the cheapness of the ware does not permit long hauls. Clays of suitable character for hollow blocks, etc., are not hard to find, and almost every State contributes to the total production, and supplies a local demand.

An important step, in 1899, was the incorporation of the National Fireproofing Company of Pittsburgh, Pa., which took over a number of works located in Pennsylvania, Ohio, New Jersey, Massachusetts, and Maryland, most of which have continued in operation.

At the present day New Jersey, Ohio, Indiana, Illinois, and Pennsylvania are the more important producers of fireproofing, while Ohio, New Jersey, Indiana, and Iowa are the leading producers of hollow blocks and hollow building tile.

The following table shows the production of fireproofing and hollow blocks in the United States since 1894.

VALUE OF FIREPROOFING PRODUCED IN UNITED STATES FROM 1894 TO 1907.

Year.	Value.	Year.	Value.
1894	$ 514,637	1901	$1,860,269
1895	741,626	1902 [1]	3,175,593
1896	1,706,504	1903	2,708,143
1897	1,979,259	1904	2,502,603
1898	1,900,642	1905	3,004,526
1899	1,665,066	1906	3,652,181
1900	1,820,214	1907	3,162,453

[1] Includes hollow brick up to and including 1902.

Since 1902 the value of hollow block production has been given separately by the United States Geological Survey and these figures are as follows.

VALUE OF HOLLOW BLOCK PRODUCED IN THE UNITED STATES
FROM 1903 TO 1907.

Year.	Value.	Year.	Value.
1903............	$1,153,200	1906.............	$ 934,357
1904............	1,126,498	1907.............	1,088,165
1905............	1,094,267		

ROOFING TILE.

This product is not nearly so extensively used in the United States as it is in foreign countries. It is known that Hüster, a German tile maker, was manufacturing flat shingle roofing tile in Montgomery County, Pa., in 1735, and similar ones were made at Bethlehem, Pa., by the Moravians in 1740, but although such tiles were made in large quantities in Eastern Pennsylvania during the last century the United States industry did not assume a permanent character until 1875, when Merrill and Ewart established a factory at Akron, Ohio.[1] This in 1902 was changed to the Akron Roofing-Tile Company. The raw materials used are the Sharon shales which serve as the bases of so many clay-working industries in this district. The next works followed in 1876, when Bennett erected a tile works at Baltimore, Md. He did not continue making this line of wares. The work was subsequently taken up intermittently by another factory, the Baltimore Terra Cotta Company.

Some years later, in 1891, the Devonian shales were tried with success at Alfred Center, N. Y., for making an interlocking vitrified tile, and the industry there has continued to the present day. In the following year, 1892, roofing-tile manufacture was taken up at Montezuma, Ind., and about this time also at Chicago Heights, Ill., the latter by the Ludowici Company, using local calcareous clays. Up to 1892 most of the tile made were of the Spanish pattern and the only important factory was that at Akron, Ohio. This works also made some flat shingle tile, and some interlocking tile of French type.[2]

In 1893 the Carboniferous clays were being worked for roofing

---

[1] See further under Ohio.   [2] Private communication.

tile in Ohio at Akron, Bellaire and New Philadelphia. The last two are no longer in operation, but others have begun at Lima and New Lexington. A factory was also running in the middle nineties at Ottawa, Ill., but has gone over to paving-brick manufacture. An unsuccessful attempt was likewise made about 1896 to utilize the Carboniferous shales near St. Louis. No further developments occurred until 1899, when at Huntington, W. Va., the brick works was remodeled for making roofing tile, from the Conemaugh shale. Another eastern works was started in 1900 at Ludowici, Ga., where a red-burning surface clay is being employed, and a plant at Parkesburg, W. Va., in 1903. Some roofing tile are also made by the California factories.

The only consolidation of interests recorded is the merger of the Ludowici Roofing-Tile Company and Celadon Roofing-Tile Company in 1905. As can be seen from the above account, the factories are scattered mainly over the eastern half of the United States, their location being governed partly by the distribution or occurrence of the raw materials and partly with reference to markets and shipping facilities.

It is impossible to make any statement regarding the value of the domestic product, as the statistics are not given separately in the United States Geological Survey reports.

FLOOR AND WALL TILE.

The first floor and wall tiles made in the United States, were, no doubt, those made in the factory of A. Miller of Philadelphia, in 1845, and a few ornamental tiles for flooring were made at Bennington, Vt. in 1853 (Ref. 8, p. 344). The latter were molded by the plastic process. As early as 1872 Hyzer and Llewellen of Philadelphia had been experimenting with encaustic tile made from natural and artificially colored clays made by the dry-press process, after finding the plastic method unsatisfactory.

The first glazed wall-tile operations seem to have been the works of the Low Art Tile Company of Chelsea, Mass., which ran for a number of years. In 1875 the American Encaustic Tile Company was organized at Zanesville, Ohio, with a view to making floor tiles from the Ohio clays, but met at first with poor success. In 1880 this company added glazed tile to its products, which involved the bringing in of clays from other States. Since that time the industry has developed at a number of points, the location of the plants being decided by various commercial considerations other than the location of the clay, for in no case has the raw clay for wall tile been obtained near the works, nor for floor tile from one locality, the deposits of Ohio, Florida, Georgia, Pennsylvania, Kentucky, Tennessee, North Carolina and England having been drawn upon. Flint and spar also have to be used.

The development of the industry can be best indicated by a chronological table as follows:

1875. Zanesville, Ohio, American Encaustic Tile Company.   Floor and glazed tile.

1876. Pittsburg, Pa., Pittsburg Encaustic Tile Company, merged into Star Encaustic Tile Company in 1882.   Plain and encaustic floor tile.

1876. Indianapolis, Ind.   United States Encaustic Tile Works.   Floor, wall and fire-place tile.

1882. Trenton, N. J.   Harris Manufacturing Company, changed later to Trent Tile Company.   Floor and wall tile.

1884. West Philadelphia.   Park Porcelain works.   Glazed relief tiles.   No longer in operation.

1885. Trenton, N. J.   Providential Tile Works.   Wall tile.

1886. Beaver Falls, Pa.   Beaver Falls Art Tile Company., Ltd.   Wall and mantle tile.

1887. Covington, Ky.   Cambridge Art Tile Works.   Wall tile.

1888. Menlo Park, N. J.   Menlo Park Ceramic Company.   Glazed tile.

1890. Morrisville, Pa.   Robertson Art Tile Company.   Glazed tile.

1890. Anderson, Ind.   Columbia Encaustic Tile Company.   Floor and glazed tile.

1890. Perth Amboy, N. J.   C. Pardee works.   Glazed tile.

1891. Hamilton, O.   Ohio Tile Company.   Wall tile.

1892. Bendersville, Pa.   Penn Tile Works.   Encaustic tiles.

1895. Zanesville, O.   Mosaic Tiling Company.   Floor tile.   Wall tile since 1900.

CHAPTER II.

SEWER PIPE.

THE sewer-pipe industry as compared with pottery and bricks is of recent introduction, ranking rather closely with architectural terra cotta in age, and it is said that those used in the early part of the nineteenth century were imported from Europe.[1] The earliest record found was in 1844 when it is said that several plants were running or about to start in West Virginia.

The first to manufacture sewer pipe in Ohio was the late D. E. Hill of Akron, Ohio, whose firm of Hill, Foster & Co. in 1849 engaged in the manufacture of hexagonal water pipe. These were made in a mold, the opening being bored out by a machine made especially for that purpose.

Mr. McClave writes that " Mr. Hill in his travels became acquainted with the use and the need of sewer pipe and its great possibilities, so he started out to find a cheap material from which to make it. Late in the summer of 1850 while walking across the field to the north of what is now East Exchange Street, Akron, Ohio, he observed the clay-like appearance of the soil, and took a lump of this clay to his factory. Tests showed it to be what he wanted, the farm was purchased, and the first Akron shale pipe was made in the spring of 1851."

In 1853 George Carlyle and John McFadden, two Scotch potters who were making chimney tops at Anderson, W. Va., crossed the Ohio River to Newburgh (now Toronto, Ohio) and fitted up a small factory for making sewer pipe from the fire clay which had been used by the Freemans, Porters and others since 1830 for fire brick. Their pipe were made on a potters wheel. About the same time a party in New York had imported a sewer-pipe machine from England, but was not able to make it work. Mr. Hill hearing of the machine made a trip to New York, and by bribing the watch-

[1] For many of the data relating to the history of sewer pipe we are indebted to Mr. J. M. McClave of Toronto, O.

31

man succeeded in getting into the factory to examine the press. With the knowledge thus gained and the assistance of C. J. Merrill he produced the first successful machine for the manufacture of pipe. This press made only a ring or band pipe, the sockets or bowls being made by hand and stuck on. Two or three years after the Ohio River factory was started, James Edwards of Charlestown, Mass., was making sewer pipe on the potters wheel, and a little later on, in 1859, sewer pipe were said to have been manufactured at Michigan Bar in California, but the industry was probably only of a temporary character.

In the early '60's the Salamander works and Bowman and Sackett of New Jersey began making some pipe, and about the same time H. M. Thompson & Co., and the Evens & Howard Fire Brick Company of St. Louis started in the business.

The Indiana clays do not appear to have been used much until 1862 when the under clays of the top coal at Cannelton were mined for pipe making. The original factory remained for 30 years, the only sewer-pipe works in the State, and even after this the expansion of the pipe industry was not as great as other branches, because by 1904 there were only five factories in the State. Pipe manufacture was started in the vicinity of Baltimore by Lincoln & Rittenhouse in 1865, by Henry Gibson in 1866, and by the Baltimore Retort and Fire Brick Company in 1868. Only the first of these continued the manufacture of pipe to recent years. Jackson, Mich., began about the same time, or in 1867.

The Freeman Fire Clay Company began to make pipe at Freeman, Ohio, in 1869, and the following year D. E. Hill and O. Barber invented the first steam press for making sewer pipe. One can easily understand that this must have greatly cheapened the cost of making pipe and given a great impulse to the industry, for it resulted in the springing up of factories all over the country. About this time factories were started at Freemans, Elliottsville, Columbus and Wellsville, Ohio, but all are now abandoned for reasons to be mentioned later.

The Portland Stoneware Company of Portland, Me., also began making pipe about this time, but has discontinued. George Goodrich fitted up a factory in 1874, but this is no longer running.

Blackmer and Post of St. Louis, also started in the early 70's with a small plant, but subsequently built a much larger one. In 1875, Gladding, McBean & Co., of San Francisco, with works at Lincoln, introduced the sewer-pipe manufacture in the far west, and have continued their production up to the present time. The St. Louis factories get a large share of the Southern trade. A factory at Rochester, N. Y., was started in 1897, followed later by one at Black Rock, near Buffalo and Angola south of the same city, while other factories were running at Akron and Toronto, Ohio.

By 1884 there were three important sewer-pipe producing districts as well as scattered plants in Ohio. At that time and up to the present Ohio has led in the manufacture of sewer pipe, being followed by the States of Missouri, New Jersey, Illinois, Pennsylvania, and Indiana.

There are several States not previously mentioned in which the sewer-pipe industry has been developed. These include a plant started at Macomb, Ill., in 1884, at Beatrice, Nebr., in 1888, Stevens Pottery, Ga., several localities in Pennsylvania, Pittsburg, Kans., in 1901, and Saspamco, Tex., about the same year. Important additions were also made to the Missouri industry around St. Louis and Kansas City in the late 80's.

The incorporation in 1900 of the American Sewer Pipe Company was an important event. This corporation took over some twenty or thirty factories in Ohio, New York, and Pennsylvania, closing down some and strengthening others. The list of the plants, together with their date of establishment, is given below.

Name of Company.	Location.	Approximate date of establishment.[1]
Pittsburg Clay Manufacturing Company..	New Brighton, Pa.......	1887
Knowles, Taylor and Anderson Company..	East Liverpool, Ohio....	1886
N. U. Walker Clay Manufacturing Company..............................	Walkers, Ohio..........	1856
John Lyth and Sons....................	Wellsville, Ohio.........	1865
Empire Fire Clay Company.............	Empire, Ohio...........	1885
Freeman Fire Clay Company...........	Freemans, Ohio.........	1865
P. Connor...........................	Toronto, Ohio..........	1880
Calumet Fire Clay Company...........	Freemans, Ohio.........	1865
Ohio Valley Fire Clay Company........	Elliottsville, Ohio.......	1888

[1] The dates of establishment supplied by the American Sewer Pipe Company do not in every case agree with those given by Mr. McClave.

Name of Company.	Location.	Approximate date of establishment [1]
Great Western Fire Clay Company	Toronto, Ohio	1880
John Francy's Sons Company	......do......	1875
Toronto Fire Clay Company	......do......	1870
Kennedy, Kling and Company	......do......	1887
Diamond Fire Clay Company	Uhrichsville, Ohio	1888
Uhrichsville Fire Clay Company	......do......	1887
J. J. Mazurie	......do......	1890
Myers-Hartford Clay Company	Malvern, Ohio	1890
McElfresh Clay Manufacturing Company	Penrith, W. Va.	1875
McMahon, Porter and Company	New Cumberland, W. Va.	1875
Pennsylvania Sewer Pipe Company	Huntingdon, Pa.	1888
National Sewer Pipe Company	Barberton, Ohio	1887
Hill Sewer Pipe Company	Akron, Ohio	1855
Akron Sewer Pipe Company	......do......	1855
Camp & Thompson	Cuyahoga Falls, Ohio	1887
Sharon Clay Manufacturing Company	Sharon, Pa.	1888
Columbus Sewer Pipe Company	Columbus, Ohio	1874
Goucher, McAdoo and Company	Brazil, Ind.	1892
Grand Ledge Sewer Pipe Company	Grand Ledge, Mich.	1895
Jackson Fire Clay, Sewer Pipe and Tile Company	Jackson, Mich.	1867
Bennett Sewer Pipe Company	......do......	1883
United States Clay Manufacturing Company	Lisbon, Ohio	1884

[1] The dates of establishment supplied by the American Sewer Pipe Company do not in every case agree with those given by Mr. McClave.

The earlier established sewer-pipe plants in the United States used mostly impure fire clays but at the present time great quantities of shale are employed.

The growth of the industry responding to the increased demand for such products has been encouraged through the invention of the steam-pipe press accompanied by improvements in the other stages of the process of manufacture which have enabled the producer to meet this demand. Some of the present sewer-pipe factories contain all the latest improvements that the mechanical engineer can devise. A good idea of the advances made in the making of pipe may be gained from the statement that fifty years ago the largest pipe made was 15 inches with a shell one and one-eighth inches thick; to-day we have 30- and 36-inch pipe with a shell from two to three inches thick.

The production of sewer pipe in the United States since 1890 is given in the accompanying table.

VALUE OF SEWER PIPE PRODUCED IN THE UNITED STATES FROM
1890 TO 1907.

Year.	Value.	Year.	Value.
1890...........	$5,107,212	1901............	$6,736,969
1894...........	5,989,923	1902............	7,174,892
1895...........	4,482,577	1903............	8,525,369
1896...........	4,588,503	1904............	9,187,423
1897...........	4,069,534	1905............	10,097,089
1898...........	3,791,057	1906............	11,114,967
1899...........	4,560,334	1907............	11,482,845
1900...........	5,842,562		

CONDUITS.

These form a line of clay products the use of which has greatly
increased in the last few years. They may be defined as hollow
blocks of varying length, having sometimes several cross parti-
tions and rounded edges, and are used as pipes for electrical
cables and wires below ground. On this account they have to
be hard-burned with a dense body and are salt glazed. Their use
came about through a desire on the part of telephone and telegraph
companies to find some form of duct more durable than the iron
and wooden ones formerly in use.

The first underground conduits are said to have been manufactured by the late H. B. Camp at Cuyahoga Falls, Ohio, in
the year 1888.[1] Mr. Camp at first experimented with a form of
multiple conduit, which was in reality a square 8-inch hollow tile
with a partition through the center. Not finding it practical he
abandoned it at the time and started manufacturing the single
conduits, which to this day are known as the "Camp-Duct."

The manufacture of conduits was begun at Aultman, Ohio, by
Mr. Camp, about 1893[2] or 1894, and this is one of the two most
important localities of production at the present day, the other
being Brazil, Ind., where they have been regularly made by the
McRoy Clay Works, since 1896. Those made at the latter
factory were the first multiple-clay conduits to be used commercially for underground work. The first six- and four-duct con-

[1] C. C. Baird, McRoy Clay Works, private correspondence.
[2] J. A. Rossi, Perth Amboy, N. J., private correspondence.

duits were made 6 feet long, and the two- and three-duct, 3 feet long. They contained dowel pin holes and were scarified and beveled on the ends as now. This plant had previously been manufacturing salt-glazed hollow building blocks and drain tile. The same clay and same machines were used in making the conduits, although many new appliances were necessary to handle them successfully. Large quantities of conduits are now produced in the Perth Amboy district of New Jersey, the industry there dating back to about 1898. In addition they are also made at scattered works where fireproofing and sewer pipe are manufactured.

It is not possible to give any statistics of production, as the United States Geological Survey does not give them separately.

PAVING BRICK.

The beginning of the paving-brick industry is usually given as 1872, when some of the streets in Charleston, W. Va., were paved with brick. These were simply hard-burned building brick, and not regular pavers, but they nevertheless gave great satisfaction, and were moreover shipped to Ohio for a considerable period. They are not now made, the production having steadily declined after the making of the real pavers began.

In Missouri the industry is said to have begun about 1873, and was the result of attempts to find some use for the more impure layers which were found in the fire-clay mines. These early attempts were not wholly successful.

Bloomington, Ill., put down a brick pavement in 1875 which was made of a poor glacial clay, but lasted well for twenty years. Five years later, in 1880, brick pavements were tried in St. Louis without success, and while another trial, made in 1881, was better, it was found that the manufacturer was unable to supply a uniform and reliable product. Two years after this, in 1883, an impure fire-clay paver was tried with excellent results at Wheeling, W. Va., and about this same time a pavement of vitrified brick made of glacial clay (Ref. 142, p. 9) was laid at Decatur, Ill.

In 1884 Galesburg, Ill., which at the present time is, and for some years has been, an important producer of vitrified shale brick, laid a pavement of these which showed a high durability. It was about this time that the industry seemed to show abundant signs of life, for in 1885 brick pavements were laid in Columbus, Zanesville and Steubenville, Ohio (Ref. 142, p. 9), Peoria, Ill., and Chicago, Ill. At Canton, Ohio, paving-brick making was started in 1887, and since then the Ohio paving-brick industry has grown steadily. In the same year (1887) the coal-measures shales were first used in Kansas. They are now employed at several points in that State.

Many of the earlier plants of the Central States used impure fire clays, the use of shales for paving-brick manufacture having really developed slowly. Moreover the great growth of this industry has been in the Central and West Central States, few paving-brick plants being located in the east except in Pennsylvania. The reason for this is the lack of suitable raw materials. A second may be the smaller demand in the Eastern than in the Central States. Of the scattered Eastern plants, one of the first to be started was at Cumberland, Md., in 1888, the Devonian shales being used. This plant is still in operation.

In the early '90's several plants were built in New York State, all using the Devonian shale, except one at Syracuse, which employed alluvial clays. About the same time (1889) the industry started at Fort Smith, Ark., and is still in operation there.

A marked expansion in this branch of clay working occurred in the closing decade of the century, for it was about this time that clay workers in Indiana were beginning to appreciate the value of the coal measure clays and of the Knobstone shales. Paving-brick making by 1890 had also taken a firm hold in Missouri, and the first paving-brick works in Indiana was started at Brazil in 1891, with others following in 1892 and 1893. At this date there were in Ohio not less than 37 firms in operation, the materials used being mainly fire clays, and to a smaller extent shales and alluvial clays. E. Orton, Jr., in the Ohio Geological Survey Report of that year stated that the great shale deposits were just beginning to be understood, and *"might possibly be of value for pavers."*

The paving-brick industry of southeastern Pennsylvania began about 1892 with the use of Triassic shales at Montello. Owing, however, to better and more extensive deposits of shale in the western half of the State, more plants have become established there than in the east. In Michigan the use of Carboniferous shale for paving purposes began in 1895 with further developments about 1905 at Saginaw. At the present time (1907) the seven leading States named in the order of their rank are Ohio, Illinois, Pennsylvania, Kansas, West Virginia, Missouri and Indiana, the first three producing over $1,000,000 worth each, and the others, except Missouri, over $500,000 worth each.

The production of paving brick since 1890 is given below.

VALUE OF VITRIFIED PAVING BRICK PRODUCED IN THE UNITED STATES FROM 1890 TO 1907.

Year.	Value.	Quantity (thousands).	Average price per thousand.
1890	$ 982,000		
1894	3,711,173	457,021	$8.12
1895	3,130,472	381,591	8.20
1896	2,794,585	320,407	8.72
1897	3,582,037	435,851	8.22
1898	4,016,822	474,419	8.47
1899	4,750,424	580,751	8.18
1900	4,764,124	546,079	8.71
1901	5,484,134	605,077	9.06
1902	5,744,530	617,192	9.31
1903	6,453,849	654,499	9.86
1904	7,557,425	735,489	10.28
1905	6,703,710	665,879	10.07
1906	7,857,768	751,974	10.45
1907	9,654,282	876,245	11.02

FIRE BRICK.

The growth of the fire-brick industry depends largely on other lines of manufacturing in which the conversion of the raw material into the finished product has to be accomplished by great heat, this being done in furnaces or other receptacles which have to be lined with some refractory material. Large quantities of fire brick are therefore required in smelting operations, and these constitute the principal consumers. The clay industry, with its brick and pottery kilns, requires a large number, as also the portland-cement industry, the coking industry and many others. Some of these, like iron smelting, were in operation before fire brick were available, and sandstone blocks were used as furnace linings.

New Jersey seems to hold the honor of being the first producer of fire brick in the United States, for they are said to have been made there in 1812, although just where the plant was located is not known. It is definitely known, however, that in 1825 the Salamander Works of Woodbridge, N. J. (no longer standing), was in operation. This was followed by the erection of a factory by John Watson in 1833, which remained in operation for a number of years.

It is also stated that fire brick were made in Florida and shipped to New Orleans in 1827, and that stove linings were made in Connecticut about 1835.

According to Mr. McClave refractory brick were being produced in Toronto, Ohio, in 1830, but the industry was probably only temporary, for later the Ohio furnacemen appear to have been shipping in most of their refractory wares from New Jersey and Maryland, until in 1869 they were supplanted by those made at Sciotoville.

A permanent development did occur in Clinton County, Pa., for a fire-brick works began at Queens Run in 1836, according to Professor Rogers. This subsequently became the firm of Fredericks Monroe & Co.

It was in 1837 that the famous Mt. Savage, Md., fire clay was discovered, and two years later the Union Mining Company began operations which have continued up to the present. In some publications this is incorrectly stated to be the oldest fire-brick works in the United States. About this time the Lower Kittanning plastic clay and the Clarion County flint clay of Pennsylvania were being worked by S. Barnes & Co. of Rochester, Pa., who appear to have started one of the earliest fire-brick works in that State. They were followed in 1842 by James Glover, who discovered the Bolivar fire clay at the place of that name and ran a small fire-brick factory. He took his bricks to Pittsburg by boat and after some difficulty succeeded in disposing of them. So well were they liked that the bricks soon won a reputation, and Bolivar to this day is one of the important fire-brick producing localities. The industry continued to develop rapidly and we find factories starting operations in different States, especially if there was a chance of marketing the product, which in those days commanded a much higher price than now.

In the year 1845 another yard was established in the Wood-bridge district of New Jersey, viz. that of Berry & Son, with others following it later, among these being Sayre & Fisher, Sayreville, 1868; H. Maurer & Son, Maurer, 1856; M. D. Valentine & Bro., Woodbridge, 1865; and others. Kier Brothers of Salina, Pennsylvania, began in 1845.

The fire-brick industry was, however, slow in moving westward in its development, for in 1846 it began in St. Louis with a small factory located on Gravois road. This is no longer in operation, the oldest of the present plants being that of Evens & Howard and the Laclede Fire Brick Company which were established in 1855. St. Louis with its great deposits of Carboniferous fire clays and markets in the Central and Southern States was destined to become an important center of fire-brick making and other factories were opened later, among these being the Christy Fire Clay Company in 1857, the Parker Russell Company in 1866. The Christy and Laclede companies have since been consolidated. Another refractory asset which has helped to make St. Louis famous was its deposits of clay for glass-pot and zinc-retort manufacture.

In New York the making of gas retorts commenced in 1854, and spread to other States, but the production of these is not as great as formerly.

Fire brick were being made at Steubenville, Ohio, by 1857 to 1858, and the industry was started in Illinois not later than this. In 1859 Soisson & Co. of Connellsville, Pa., established their works at that locality, and three years later, in 1862, fire-brick manufacture began at Bath, S. C., but has never become of importance. At Pittsburg the Star Fire-Brick Works commenced operations in 1865, and three years later the industry was started at Canal Dover, Ohio.

The fire clays of the far west developed at a comparatively early date, those around Golden, Colo., being discovered in 1866, but those which have made the district rank foremost among the western producers were not opened up until later. The fire bricks which were made and are still being produced at Denver, those whose manufacture began later at Pueblo, and still later at Cañon City, are now much used throughout the Western States and have earned a good reputation, although they have to compete somewhat, of course, with those produced in the Mississippi Valley district.

The fire clays of Lewis County, Kentucky, were mined as early as 1871 for making fire brick in Cincinnati, and in the same decade we note the building of works at East Portsmouth, Ohio, in 1870, at Woodland, Pa., in 1871, and Retort and Manorville, Pa., in 1872.

West Virginia was a late comer in the line of fire-brick producers, the Kittanning clays of Hammond, Marion County, being one of the earliest deposits worked in the State. This was in 1876. Subsequent to that period, however, the industry progressed favorably.

By the year 1880 the fire-clay manufacturing industry had assumed wide and strong importance in many States, notably Ohio, Pennsylvania, New York, New Jersey, Indiana and Missouri. Several important additions occurred in the eighties as at Canal Dover, Ohio (1880); South Webster, Ohio (1883); Queens Run, Pa. (1883); Portsmouth, Ohio (1888); Wallaceton, Pa. (1888); Strasburg, Ohio (1889); there were still, however, several important but not necessarily large districts to be heard from. In 1882 the Tertiary clay around Holly Springs, Miss., was attracting attention and two years later, 1884, the Kentucky fire clays were worked at Amanda Furnace, and Bellport Furnace, followed by the Ashland Fire Brick Company, at Ashland, in 1886. The Texas Tertiary clays were being used around Athens in 1890, and those at Socorro, New Mexico, in 1894. The former are still worked, but not the latter. In 1895 the Olive Hill Fire Brick Company of Olive Hill, Ky., began using the Carboniferous flint clays, but it is not known how long previous to this these had been developed.

Developments continued in Pennsylvania and Ohio, and new works were still springing up. They included those at Phillipsburg, Pa. (1893); Clearfield, Pa. (1894); Beech Creek, Pa. (1900); and still later at Figart, Pa. (1901); and Strasburg, Ohio (1904).

The Dakota clays of Colorado, previously mentioned as occurring at Golden, were further developed at Cañon City in 1900, and since then at other localities. Later developments took place also in Utah, Montana and South Dakota, but no definite data are available regarding them.

After reviewing what has just preceded, one cannot help but be impressed by the great and steady development of the fire-brick industry in the Carboniferous areas of Ohio, Pennsylvania, and to a lesser extent Kentucky, Maryland and West Virginia. The product not only finds a ready market in the districts of production, but is shipped to many States in which high grade refractories are manufactured sparingly or not at all.

There are a number of small works making fire brick and stove linings, which are located at points some distance removed from the fire-clay districts, and ship in their raw clay. Not a few are located in New England.

It is needless to say the growth of the fire-brick industry has been attended by improvements in the methods of manufacture, not so much perhaps in the machinery used, although the production of machine-molded brick has increased because of lower selling cost, as in the compounding of proper mixtures, which will best individually withstand the conditions of use to which they are subjected. With the same object in view the manufacturers have also developed a great variety of shapes for special purposes. Some firms have likewise succeeded in making a product of astonishingly high refractoriness, while others have in recent years introduced the manufacture of bauxite bricks.

Mention should be made of the incorporation in 1902 of the Harbison-Walker Refractories Company with headquarters at Pittsburg, Pa. This corporation, which controls a large number of works in Pennsylvania as well as some in Ohio and Kentucky, produces a large percentage of all the fire brick produced in the eastern United States. All of the works make a fire-clay brick with the exception of the Chester, Pa., plant which makes nothing but magnesia and chrome brick, from imported materials. The Mount Union, East Chicago, and the Layton, Pa., plants, produce silica brick, while some silica brick are also made at the Hays Station, Pa., plant.

Refractories for Glass Melting.[1]

Glass-pot manufacture represents a special branch of the fire-brick business in which great skill is called for, and scrupulous care exercised in the selection of the raw materials.

It is probable that the manufacture of glass pots in this country was begun with the installation of the first glass factory, but in those days, and, in fact, until 1860, it was the custom for glass manufacturers to make their own glass-melting pots, the clays being imported from England and known as Stourbridge clays.

The making of tank blocks began actively about 1883. These are large blocks used for lining the large iron tanks in which glass is melted. These special shaped blocks, weighing sometimes ten hundred pounds, have to fit together accurately, and their manufacture calls for the finest grades of glass-pot clay, and plenty of time for making. Most firms make both the tanks and pots.

The Stourbridge clay continued to be used to some extent in this country until the early sixties. The German clay has also been used for a number of years, but it is not known just when its importation began. About the year 1858 or 1859, Missouri plastic clays were introduced. These clays are found in the neighborhood of St. Louis in what is known as the Cheltenham district, and were called "Cheltenham clays" in those days. This clay was introduced by a man named Christy, who induced James B. Lyon of the O'Hara Glass Company of Pittsburg, Pa., to try it for the manufacture of glass pots. It proved to be an excellent clay for that purpose and has largely supplanted the foreign clays.

The manufacture of glass-house pots, as a business for the purpose of supplying the wants of the glass manufacturers in that line, was first started by Thomas Coffin in Pittsburg in 1860, and

---

[1] The authors are indebted to Mr. H. L. Dixon of Pittsburg, Pa., for much valuable information.

until 1879 this remained the only pot-making plant. In that year the Pittsburg Clay-Pot Company was organized and is still in operation.

Shortly after the Pittsburg Clay-Pot Company started, came others, and among these may be mentioned the Phoenix Clay-Pot Company, New Kensington, Pa. (organized in 1880), making pots since 1880 and tank blocks since 1902. Ohio Valley Clay Company, Steubenville, Ohio, producing pots since 1882 and tank blocks since 1896. Gill Clay-Pot Company, established by J. S. Gill, at Bellaire, Ohio, in 1882, but now the Gill Clay-Pot Company, of Muncie, Indiana, and manufacturing tank blocks since 1896. Dixon-Woods Company, producing tank blocks in 1887. The Findlay Clay-Pot Company, Findlay, Ohio, organized for glass-pot manufacture in 1888, but producing tank blocks also since 1895.

As the business in melting furnaces progressed in the United States it was found that both the Stourbridge and German clays lacked the refractory qualities to stand the temperatures employed, but that while the Missouri clay supplied this defect, it was not able to resist the corrosive action of the molten glass as well as the German clay. The Stourbridge clay is no longer used. Clay from Mineral City, Ohio, is employed by some, as well as Pennsylvania clays, but not in those parts that come in contact with the molten glass. The manufacturers have therefore had to use different mixtures for different parts, according as they had to resist corrosion, heat, changes of temperature, etc.

As an example, one firm uses for its pots a mixture consisting of:

Missouri Raw Washed Clay.............. 2469 lbs.
Missouri Burned Washed Clay .... 2250 lbs.
German Washed Clay................... 1481 lbs.
Old pot fragments .... 3800 lbs.

The proportions used by the different manufacturers however vary, some using more Missouri and others less.

No separate statistics can be given, as they are not published, but the total value of the product forms a small percentage of the total for refractory wares.

The production of fire brick and refractory wares in the United States since 1894 is given below.

VALUE OF FIRE BRICK PRODUCED IN THE UNITED STATES FROM 1870 TO 1907.

Year.	Value.	Year.	Value.
1870	$ 493,400	1900	$ 9,830,517
1890	5,652,564	1901	9,870,421
1894	4,762,820	1902	11,970,511
1895	5,279,004	1903	14,062,369[1]
1896	4,944,723	1904	11,167,972
1897	4,094,704	1905	12,735,404
1898	6,093,071	1906	14,206,868
1899	8,641,882	1907	14,946,045

[1] Includes stove lining.

POTTERY.

It is somewhat difficult to follow the development of the pottery industry without going into a number of details, but in tracing out its growth, several interesting features present themselves.[1] The first is that pottery was made by the early colonists in this country almost as soon as common brick. A second is that few of the early establishments mark even the site of existing potteries, the important potting centers having been established at a much later date. Thirdly, the industry does not show a gradual progression from the lowest to the highest kinds of ware, many grades of pottery ranging from common flowerpots up to white earthen-ware having been produced at the same period.

The earliest reference found is of a pottery on Long Island in 1601, and another in Massachusetts in 1641. The latter was probably the first in the New England States and is no longer in operation. Virginia may have had potteries as early as this, for it is known that small earthen-ware factories were in operation in the seventeenth century.

New Jersey followed in 1685 with the production of white ware at Burlington, and Pennsylvania in 1690, at which date its first

[1] The artistic side of the development of pottery in the United States has been most admirably treated by E. A. Barber of the Pennsylvania Museum in his work on the History of Pottery and Porcelain in the United States.

established factory was making tobacco pipes. Maryland came next in 1764 with a pottery in Baltimore, and five years later a second works began making china in Philadelphia, Pa.

As early as 1776 there are said to have been scattered stoneware works in South Carolina, and a pottery had begun operations at Norwalk, Conn., in 1780. The establishment of a terra-cotta-ware pottery in West Virginia in 1785 is said to have been the first one west of the Allegheny Mountains, and this one was in operation until 1890. Among the early established works, still running, or at least in operation until recently, was an earthernware factory which began at Hartford, Conn., in 1790, and the next few years witnessed the establishment of many others in that State. In 1793 a pottery was started in Vermont, and by 1800 stoneware was being made there.

There is doubt as to the source of the raw materials used by these early potters, but in the majority of cases it was probably purely local.

Curiously enough, California was one of the early producers of pottery, earthen-ware being made in San Francisco from 1791 to 1800. In the latter year (1800) stoneware was being made by Van Wickle in Old Bridge, N. J., and other factories were running at South Amboy and Sayreville so that we can perhaps regard this as the beginning of the development of the stoneware industry of this State, which, however, has never become large, being unable to complete successfully with the great factories making this ware in Ohio. This same year (1800) also witnessed the commencement of a sturdy stoneware industry at Troy and Albany, N. Y., which continued for a number of years. In 1805 Fulper of Flemington, N. J., began the manufacture of stoneware, and this establishment still exists.

Whether Ohio should be included among the list of pottery producers prior to this is not known, but in 1812 an earthenware factory was in operation in Steubenville, and by 1837 the industry had attained such importance that the ware was being sent to other States.

Another works of interest was one in Jaffray, N. H., established in 1817, which brought its clay from Moncton, Vt. This represents one of the earliest records of the shipment of clay from one State to another.

In 1827 we find the first record of a stoneware factory in Calloway County, Missouri, which was still running in 1891. Pottery was being made in the same year (1827) at Pittsburg, Pa. Two years later (in 1829) the industry began at Louisville, Ky., and while potteries have been in operation there more or less continuously up to the present time, they have undergone frequent changes in ownership and management.

Up to 1830 the development of the pottery industry had been sporadic, and not of permanent character. In that year an appeal for aid was made to the Government, in the form of greater protection, but the bill passed by Congress in 1833, lowered the tariff instead of raising it. While this was discouraging to the whiteware manufacturers, at the same time it did not seriously affect the industry as a whole.

The year 1834 marked the beginning of the Beaver Valley, Pa., industry, with the establishment of Jackson's pottery at New Brighton, which, however, only ran for three years. The same year also saw the foundation of the pottery industry of Indiana, the first works being established at Troy, but it soon ended in failure, because of a misguided attempt to make whiteware. Illinois was producing stoneware by 1836, but it may have been manufactured there even earlier.

Three years after this, or in 1837, Bennett established a yellow and Rockingham works at East Liverpool, Ohio. This was the beginning of the pottery manufacturing industry at that place, and by the next year the stoneware industry of the Zanesville district had started. It was at least as early as 1837 that the Albany slip clay came into use for glazing stoneware, and has ever since then been employed in all parts of the United States. Other slip clays have been tried, but none have found the same favor as this one. It was also in this year (1838) that pottery works were established at Sargeants Bluff, Ia., which are said to have been the first in the State. If this is true the industry must have expanded rapidly, as by 1841 there were potteries in operation at many points in the State.

In 1840 the mining of pottery clay from the Coal-measure beds of Indiana began, and has continued actively up to the present time to supply numerous stoneware works.

The exact date of the establishment of potting in Cincinnati, Ohio, is not known, but by the early forties both stoneware and Rockingham ware were being turned out there.

Dallas County, Ark., had a pottery as early as 1843, but the business has not developed to any great extent and there are few plants in the State at the present time. The Portland Stoneware Company, at Portland, Me., was inaugurated in 1846, and the same year saw the establishment of Bennett's yellow and Rockingham ware factory in Baltimore, Md. He later added white ware.

The Greenpoint, L. I., porcelain works began in 1848, and about three years after that came the start of the Trenton, N. J., industry. Although beginning some years later than East Liverpool, Ohio, the Trenton industry has expanded at a more rapid rate and now outranks that of East Liverpool. While there may have been potteries in operation in Mississippi prior to 1848, the first definite record appears in that year, when it is said stoneware factories were running at several localities and some of these still exist.

In 1856 Whitmore, Robinson & Co., began the manufacture of Rockingham and yellow queensware at Akron, Ohio. This plant, considerably enlarged, is still in operation.

Three years later, in 1859, a plant for the manufacture of stoneware was running at Michigan Bar, Cal., and the first white ware was made at Peoria, Ill., evidently of clay shipped in from other States.

By 1860, the first year in which a census was taken, the industry seems to have been pretty well established, for there were potteries established in different States as follows: Alabama, 11; California, 4; Connecticut, 5; Delaware, 4; Georgia, 2; Illinois, 34; Iowa, 15; Kansas, 1; Kentucky, 6; Maine, 16; Maryland, 17; Massachusetts, 13; Michigan, 7; Minnesota, 1; Mississippi, 2; Missouri, 17; New Hampshire, 3; New Jersey, 24; New York, 45; North Carolina, 4; Ohio, 130; Pennsylvania, 108; South Carolina, 6; Tennessee, 5; Texas, 6; Vermont, 6; Virginia, 15; Wisconsin, 13; District Columbia, 2; Nebraska, 1; Utah, 2.

In 1862 the making of yellow and Rockingham ware was begun again at New Brighton, Pa., and has continued up to the present, while additional stoneware factories were starting up in Indiana.

Fig. 2.— Original plant of Knowles, Taylor and Knowles, East Liverpool, O.

The Onondaga Pottery of Syracuse, one of the important vitreous china factories of the United States began in 1871, and is still running.

Although white ware was made by William Bloor at East Liverpool, Ohio, prior to 1861, the permanent establishment of the whiteware industry at that place dates back only to 1873, and was begun by the Knowles, Taylor & Knowles Company, a firm which had begun operations in 1854.

Minnesota has never been an important pottery-producing State and it was not until 1877 that the stoneware industry, supported by the Cretaceous clays at Redwing, was started.

Two years after this, in 1879, the Wheeling Pottery Company of Wheeling, W. Va., started. This company made the first white ware produced in that State, but did not use any local clays.

In 1880, Remey & Son of Philadelphia began the manufacture of chemical stoneware made from New Jersey clays, and were followed later by the Graham Works of Brooklyn, N. Y. The following year the white ware industry at Beaver Falls, Pa., was begun by Mayer Bros. In the same year, the manufacture of C. C. ware was tried in Missouri from local kaolins, but was a failure, and has never again been attempted in that State. This year also saw the establishment of the majolica industry at Baltimore, but it gave way later to white earthenware.

By 1884 Hamilton and Columbiana Counties, Ohio, had developed into important centers of yellow and Rockingham ware, there being nine factories at East Liverpool and ten in Cincinnati. There were also several important stoneware districts whose wares had a wide sale. Kentucky was at this time also developing a number of stoneware factories but none were of any size.

The year 1888 was important as marking the establishment of the first art pottery in Ohio, now most widely known in this country, the Rookwood Pottery, of Cincinnati. Other Ohio potteries have since then turned their attention to art wares, notably the Weller Pottery of Zanesville, and the Roseville Pottery of Roseville.

It is not known when potteries were first worked in Kansas, but as late as 1893 there were only a few in operation.

By 1893 the Ohio pottery industry occupied the same limits as in 1884, but the output has greatly increased. Akron was the leading stoneware district, and an important feature was the growth of the cooking utensil industry. Since then the industry has grown, especially around East Liverpool, Zanesville and Akron.

There has been a remarkable development of American pottery in its more artistic forms since 1893, at which time, as pointed out by several writers, the fictile art of this country had literally a new birth.

The Rookwood factory, mentioned under Ohio, and started before 1893, is to be regarded, perhaps, as the pioneer, and certainly as the most important of American art potteries. But there are many others, all worthy of mention, and while few of them are large, they are without exception receiving deserved recognition, on account of the originality, beauty, and often high artistic merit of their wares.

PLATE IV.—Present plant of Knowles Taylor and Knowles, East Liverpool, O.

In addition to the Rookwood, we may mention among the older ones The American Terra Cotta Company of Chicago, well known for its Teco ware, the Grueby Faience Company of Boston, and the Hartford Faience Company of Hartford, Conn. The Chelsea Keramic Art Company of Dedham, Mass., might also be ranked here, as well as the Weller Pottery of Zanesville, Ohio, and the Roseville Pottery Company of the same State.

The Robineau Pottery of Syracuse, N. Y., deserves special mention since it is the first works in this country to produce decorative hard porcelain (Binns).

Equally meritorious, and of distinctly American type, is the Newcomb Art Pottery of New Orleans. Nor should the list be closed without mention of the Van Briggle Pottery of Colorado Springs, Colo., the Marblehead, Mass., ware, and the product of the works of Charles Volckmar, Metuchen, N. J.

All of these serve to show that the production of pottery in the United States is not confined to the more common types of ware such as white granite and semi-porcelain, dinner and toilet sets, as some people imagine.

It should also indicate that it is not necessary to depend upon imported materials, when decorative ware of burned clay is desired.

Only slight reference to Trenton has been made in this résumé since the establishment of the industry in 1852. It was, nevertheless, growing at a steady and rapid rate as the chronologic data given under New Jersey will show. Indeed many details are given there which need not be repeated here. Suffice it to call attention once more to the fact that this is the largest potting center in the United States, if not in the world, the products including C. C. ware, white granite ware, sanitary ware, belleek, and electrical porcelain.

The manufacture of electrical porcelain is a comparatively young branch of the pottery industry, which began first with the production of various pieces for low-voltage work, but subsequently developed switch blocks, insulators, etc., for the high-tension currents. The clays used are largely of the higher grades. Works are in operation in Ohio, New York, Indiana, New Jersey, etc. The first factory appears to have been that of

R. Thomas & Sons of East Liverpool, established in 1884. Others were as follows:

1890. Pass & Seymour, Syracuse, N. Y.
1890. Union Porcelain Works, Brooklyn, N. Y.
1891. Imperial Porcelain Works, Trenton, N. J.
1891. G. F. Brunt Porcelain Company, East Liverpool, Ohio.
1895. Lock Insulator Company, Victor, N. Y.
1896. Akron Smoking Pipe Company, Mogadore, Ohio.
1899. Star Porcelain Company, Trenton, N. J.
1902. Anderson Porcelain Company, East Liverpool, Ohio.
1902. Hartford Faience Company, Hartford, Conn.
1902. New Lexington High Voltage Porcelain Company, New Lexington, Ohio.
1903. Electrical Porcelain Company, Trenton, N. J.
1904. Adamant Porcelain Company, Ltd., Broadway, Va.
1905. Adamant Porcelain Company, Ltd., Harrisonburg, Va.
1906. United States Electric Porcelain Company, Findlay, Ohio.
    General Electric Company, Schenectady, N. Y.
    Colonial Sign and Insulator Company, Akron, Ohio.

In spite of the tremendous growth of the pottery industry in the United States there is very little high-grade porcelain made, most of that bought being of foreign make.

Much semi-porcelain is produced, but this is mostly of somewhat heavy character to meet the demands of hotel and restaurant trade, which consumes most of the output, and it is to be regretted that in order to get light weight ware for daily private use one is practically forced to purchase foreign goods.

Whether the hard porcelain of Europe will become naturalized here remains to be seen. The permanent introduction of bone-china is another possibility, and some writers (Binns) have pointed out that since it is the lightest and whitest of all our wares, its development should be strenuously pushed by American manufacturers.

While the pottery industry has assumed large proportions, the development of certain lines has been due no doubt to a high protective tariff, its influence being described by Mr. John Moses as follows:[1] "It was not, indeed, until the first real protection by the tariff ever accorded the potteries was enacted, as a war measure, that the American maker found himself able to enter the field against the English potter, especially in the two staple lines of *white granite* and *C. C. ware*. The premium on gold,

[1] One hundred years of American commerce.

doubling, as it did, the increased duty, gave the potters the long-needed opportunity, and new establishments sprang up in Trenton during the decade succeeding the war."

It must also be conceded, although it may not be universally admitted, that we always have been, and are still, dependent to a large extent upon foreign countries for some of our raw materials. This is particularly true of residual kaolin, the deposits of which thus far developed in this country have not been sufficient to supply the demand.

The period during which the pottery industry has grown in this country has witnessed important changes in the methods of manufacture, which not only produce a better ware from the same clay, but also greatly increase the capacity of the plant.

In the early days of potting the clay was simply thrown into a tank, manipulated with a spade, removed in large lumps, and cut through and through with a wire, rewelding the mass after each cutting. Now the clay or mixture of clays is carefully washed, mixed wet, and screened, before use.

The early potters knew no other tool than the potters wheel on which they formed their ware, and this machine is still seen in many small potteries, but in the larger works it has been largely forced out by the jolly or jig, by pressing in plaster molds, or by casting, all these methods producing a piece of ware much more rapidly and sometimes of greater structural perfection.

The production of pottery in the United States, for the census years 1850, 1860, 1870, 1880, and annually since 1896 is given below:

VALUE OF POTTERY PRODUCED IN UNITED STATES FROM 1850 TO 1907.

Year.	Value.	Year.	Value.
1850	$ 1,466,063	1900	$19,798,570
1860	2,706,681	1901	22,463,860
1870	6,045,536	1902	24,127,453
1880	7,942,729	1903	25,436,052
1896	7,455,627	1904	25,158,270
1897	10,309,209	1905	27,918,894
1898	14,589,224	1906	31,440,884
1899	17,250,250	1907	30,143,474

The value of imports into the United States since 1867 is given below.

VALUE OF EARTHENWARE, CHINA, BRICK, AND TILE IMPORTED AND ENTERED FOR CONSUMPTION IN THE UNITED STATES, 1867 TO 1907.[1]

Year ending.	Total.	Brown earthen and common stone ware.	China and porcelain, not decorated.	China and porcelain, decorated.	Other earthen, stone, or crockery ware, glazed, etc.	Brick, fire brick, and tile.
June 30:						
1867...	$5,187,859	$48,618	$418,493	$439,824	$4,280,924	....
1868...	4,005,681	47,208	309,960	403,555	3,244,958	....
1869...	4,459,549	34,260	400,894	555,425	3,468,970	....
1870...	4,460,228	47,457	420,442	530,805	3,461,524	....
1871...	4,632,355	96,695	391,374	571,032	3,573,254	....
1872...	5,308,893	127,346	470,749	814,134	3,896,664	....
1873...	5,751,944	115,253	479,617	867,206	4,289,868	....
1874...	4,831,724	70,544	397,730	676,656	3,686,794	....
1875...	4,441,216	68,501	436,883	654,965	3,280,867	....
1876...	4,112,956	36,744	409,539	718,156	2,948,517	....
1877...	3,772,059	30,403	326,956	668,514	2,746,186	....
1878...	4,096,725	18,714	389,133	657,485	3,031,393	....
1879...	4,044,876	19,868	296,591	813,850	2,914,567	....
1880...	5,500,388	31,504	334,371	1,188,847	3,945,666	....
1881...	6,383,326	27,586	321,259	1,621,112	4,413,369	....
1882...	6,866,779	36,023	316,811	2,075,708	4,438,237	....
1883...	8,686,061	43,864	368,943	2,587,545	5,685,709	....
1884...	4,363,497	50,172	982,499	2,664,231	(²)	$666,595
1885...	4,666,175	44,701	823,334	2,834,718	....	963,422
Dec. 31:						
1886...	5,204,704	37,820	865,446	3,350,145	....	$951,293
1887...	5,907,642	43,079	967,694	3,888,509	....	1,008,360
1888...	6,204,324	55,558	1,054,854	4,207,598	....	886,314
1889...	6,565,562	48,824	1,148,026	4,580,321	....	788,391
1890...	5,157,776	56,730	974,627	3,562,851	....	563,568
1891...	8,663,450	99,983	1,921,643	6,288,088	....	353,736
1892...	9,021,509	63,003	2,022,814	6,555,172	....	380,520
1893...	8,375,896	57,017	1,732,481	6,248,255	....	338,143
1894...	7,180,343	47,114	1,550,950	5,392,648	....	189,631
1895...	10,445,795	61,424	2,117,425	8,055,473	....	211,473
1896...	9,530,524	41,585	1,511,542	7,729,942	....	247,455
1897...	8,642,175	³32,227	1,406,019	7,057,261	....	146,668
1898...	7,079,934	³54,672	1,002,729	5,905,209	....	117,324
1899...	8,041,631	³40,164	1,125,892	6,740,884	....	134,691
1900...	8,912,073	³65,214	1,059,152	7,617,756	....	169,951
1901...	9,681,411	³51,551	1,094,078	8,385,514	....	150,268
1902...	9,806,271	³58,926	1,016,010	8,495,598	....	235,737
1903...	11,456,290	³95,890	1,234,223	9,897,588	....	228,589
1904...	11,488,411	³81,951	1,329,146	9,859,144	....	218,170
1905...	³12,148,141	100,618	1,157,573	10,717,871	....	172,079
1906...	³13,406,899	96,400	1,312,326	11,822,376	....	175,797
1907...	³13,810,932	113,477	1,315,591	12,156,544	....	225,320

[1] United States Geological Survey, "Mineral Resources of the United States," 1904, page 898, and 1907, Part II, p. 527.
[2] Not separately classified after 1883.　　　[3] Including Rockingham ware.

The following table gives the exports from the United States from 1895 to 1907:

EXPORTS OF CLAY WARES OF DOMESTIC MANUFACTURE FROM THE UNITED STATES, 1895 TO 1907.[1]

| Year.[2] | Aggregate value. | Brick. | | | | Pottery. | | |
| | | Total value. | Building. | | Fire (value). | Total value. | Earthen and stone ware (value). | China (value). |
			Quantity by thousands.	Value.				
1895	$262,758	$123,461	4,757	$34,732	$88,729	$139,297	$114,425	$24,872
1896	304,738	135,395	5,258	32,759	102,636	169,343	144,641	24,702
1897	348,612	141,009	4,606	30,383	110,626	207,003	177,320	30,283
1898	430,770	178,949	4,708	32,317	146,632	251,821	212,769	39,052
1899	803,890	292,158	9,872	77,783	214,375	511,732	467,925	43,807
1900	1,281,831	723,037	12,526	128,800	594,237	558,794	489,942	68,852
1901	1,068,409	541,589	9,072	74,210	467,379	526,820	476,957	49,863
1902	1,106,080	501,434	3,995	31,304	470,130	604,646	555,340	49,306
1903	1,028,278	439,277	8,783	63,774	375,503	589,001	527,689	61,312
1904	1,379,124	587,385	25,012	179,866	407,519	791,739	697,381	94,358
1905	1,783,432	799,878	34,242	263,876	536,002	983,554	882,069	101,485
1906	2,003,516	885,066	27,758	247,625	637,441	1,118,450	1,003,969	114,481
1907	1,948,612	816,971	22,340	185,192	631,779	1,131,641	1,022,730	108,911

[1] United States Geological Survey, "Mineral Resources of the United States," 1904, page 899, and 1907, Part II, page 528.
[2] Years ending December 31.

CLAY MINING INDUSTRIES.

As a usual thing manufacturers of clay products in the United States mine their own clay, and moreover obtain it not far from the works, as most grades of clay will not bear the cost of transportation for any great distance. There are not a few factories however which are not located near the source of their raw materials partly because these have to be obtained from several different localities, and it is more important to be placed where labor conditions, shipping facilities, and fuel supplies are advantageous. These factories which include many producers of the higher grades of pottery, wall tile, and some refractory wares, often bring their raw materials from a considerable distance. They can afford to do this because the selling prices of their wares are high as compared with those of other kinds and the amount of raw clay required is sometimes comparatively small.

We thus find that an important clay mining industry has grown up to develop the deposits of high-grade clays and to ship the product to the manufacturers. At the present day New Jersey, North Carolina, Georgia, Florida, South Carolina, Kentucky, Tennessee, and Missouri are the most important States in which the clay mining industry exists.

The Florida white clays seem to have been known as early as 1766, for it is said that in that year, Josiah Wedgewood was using them for his pottery in England, and in the same year he was also experimenting with Georgia clays. This was not the beginning of their permanent development, which did not come until many years later. Three years after this, in 1769, clay was being mined at White Clay Creek, Del., and shipped for a time to Bonnin's china factory in Philadelphia, and in 1800 white clay was mined near New Castle, Del., for making glass pots, fire brick, etc.

The kaolin deposits of Vermont had been discovered by 1810, and were not only used in that State but a little later were shipped to New Hampshire.

What may be said to be the beginning of one of our greatest clay-mining industries, occurred in 1816, when the first shipment of clay from the Woodbridge, N. J., district is recorded. This clay was sent to Boston for fire-brick making. It was followed by the development of many deposits in this district yielding fire clays, stoneware clays, ball clays, sagger clays, and paper clays. These are shipped by water to many factories along the New England coast for stoneware, fire brick, stove linings and pressed brick. They are also sent to Ohio, Pennsylvania, New York, Maryland, and other States.

In 1820 I. Hoppe discovered kaolin while digging a post hole on his property at New Garden, Chester County, Pa. He worked this deposit in a small way, using it for making fire brick until 1852, at which time he commenced shipping a little crude clay to a potter in Trenton, N. J., having to cart it some 12 miles to Newport, Del., for shipment.

The property changed hands from time to time, increasing in value with every change, until 1856, when it was sold to Howard Spencer who started a washing plant on a large scale, selling the clay to the paper men and to potters in Trenton, N. J., and East Liverpool, Ohio. It was owned and operated in 1905 by the American Kaolin Company. A continuation of this vein has been worked for a number of years by the Graham Kaolin Company. The Brandywine Summit Kaolin deposits were also developed about 1870(?) and worked for a number of years, until the kaolin gave out, after which the mine was worked for feldspar from which the overlying kaolin had originated by weathering.

The Delaware deposits were discovered in 1854 by Abner Marshall on his farm in Hockessin, Newcastle County, while plowing, and while the product at first was manufactured on the spot, the washing and shipping of the clay did not begin until 1861 when it was sent to a potter in Trenton. It was also sold to the paper trade. Marshall sold out to Trux & Parker in 1866 who built a fine plant for washing and preparing clay for the potteries and established a lively trade. This was carried on until 1875 when the deposit was exhausted. A continuation of this vein on the next farm was purchased by H. Graham in 1863, and worked in the same way as the other plant until sold in 1874 to Golding & Sons Company, who have operated it up to the present time.

Israel Lacey owned the adjoining farm to this, and worked the kaolin from 1861 to 1881 at which time he sold out to J. W. Burgess, who continued it up to recent date. The selling price of the clay has dropped from $20.00 per ton in 1874 to about $6.00 per ton in 1907.

There are probably few clays that have been more widely used than the Albany slip clay of New York, which is of value for glazing stoneware, and the mining of this began at least as early as 1846 or possibly earlier. The clay is used all over the United States from New York to Texas and California, and as a small quantity of it goes a long way the freight is not a very important item.

China clay was discovered in Washington County, Missouri, as early as 1848 and used for cream-colored ware, but the mining of it was abandoned when the war broke out. Eight years after these deposits were discovered, or in 1856, the white clays of South Carolina seem to have attracted attention, when Farar of Bennington, Vt., attempted their use for making porcelain insulators, but there is no evidence that the mining of the South Carolina white clays, which is now an important industry, began at that time, and numerous inquiries on the part of the authors have failed to determine the date of their permanent development.

The mining of Missouri kaolins began again in 1857 in Bollinger County. The clay was shipped to Cincinnati for about five years, and then discontinued. Some time after that, or in 1872, the south-eastern kaolin district of Missouri took a fresh start, but the output was irregular and unsatisfactory because of poor sorting.

In 1874, the well-known Indianaite which occurs in pockets at the horizon of a Subcarboniferous limestone in Lawrence, Martin and Owens counties in Ind.ana was discovered in digging a foundation. It has been tried in the manufacture of alum, encaustic tile, etc., but has proven unsatisfactory, and has not been worked since 1891. Two other important events in the year 1874 were the development of the Jackson-Cape Girardeau County pits in Missouri, and the discovery of the white residual clays of the South Mountain district of Pennsylvania. The latter were found in connection with the mining of residual limonites, and have since then been somewhat extensively developed around Mt. Holly Springs for use in the manufacture of paper, tile and pressed brick. Most of the clay, except that used for pressed brick, is washed before shipment.

Up to this time (1875) little ball clay had been found in the United States, nearly all of the supply for American potters having come from the Devonshire district of England, but in 1880, I. Mandle opened a pit of ball clay at Regina, Jefferson County, Mo., which has been an important source of material for the East Liverpool and other potting centers.

In 1888 the kaolin deposits of North Carolina were discovered in connection with mica mining operations, and these have continued up to the present day as the most important domestic source of supply. Two years after the development of these the ball clays of Florida were discovered through the explorations for phosphate, and C. S. Edgar, who had made an unsuccessful search for them in 1875, at once undertook their development. He, together with other companies since established, is still mining them. The beds of this clay are very extensive, but owing to certain physical qualities most potters hestiate to use a large quantity of it in the body of their wares.

The next important event was the development of the Cretaceous white clays of central Georgia, which were probably mined in the early 90's and are now much used by potteries, wall-tile factories, and paper makers. They are often spoken of as kaolins, although of sedimentary character, but in their physical properties they may perhaps be regarded as occupying an intermediate position between the kaolins like those of North Carolina, and the ball clays of Tennessee and Florida.

Among the most recent developments have been the opening up of the ball-clay deposits of Tennessee, and those of Mayfield, Ky. These had been worked by small potteries for some years previous to this.

The kaolin of West Cornwall, Conn., was also permanently developed in the year 1895, although it had been worked from time to time on a small scale for fire mortar for many years before that.

An interesting question often asked is whether the discovery of ball clays and china clays in the United States, has replaced the imported English ones to any extent. This is a somewhat difficult query to answer.

The strong demand for white-burning clays to be used in the manufacture of C. C. and other white ware did not begin probably until the early seventies. The china clay in use at this time and for some years later came chiefly from Delaware and eastern Pennsylvania, while the ball clay was obtained from New Jersey. This Jersey material was not regarded by many potters as a true ball clay. It is very plastic, although not as good in color or vitrifying as easily as the English ball clay. Later in the decade ball clay from Missouri was put on the market, and largely used by East Liverpool potters for several years. The Missouri material was said by some to be an ideal material in all its properties except color. Still it is possibly the most plastic ball clay known, and burns to a very dense body at whiteware heats, but its poor color prevents its use to any extent in any line demanding a whiteware body. The English ball clay came into general use, at least in the Central States, early in the 80's, and for several years was practically the only ball clay used by American potters. When the Tennessee ball clay appeared on the market it was quickly taken up by some potters, who found it a satisfactory substitute for the English ball clay and gave up using the latter, although others still thought the English article superior.

The washed china clay from the Delaware-Pennsylvania belt has been widely used by many potteries, and much of that mined in the 70's or early 80's is thought by some to have equalled any china clay ever put on the market, but as time went on the quality seemed to fall off, and at the present time the North Carolina kaolin is pronounced by many to be the whitest mined in this country, and to equal the imported English clay.

Many potters still use the imported clays almost exclusively, others use them in part, while still others find that the domestic article is entirely adapted to their needs. Had the pottery industry not been growing, the statistics of imported clays would, no doubt, show a falling off due to their partial displacement by the domestic product, but since the reverse has been true, there is a strong demand for both. If some of the domestic producers gave more care to the mining and washing of their clay there would be an increasing demand for the American materials among the makers of the higher grades of ware. This statement represents the views of a number of American potters who have been questioned on the subject.

The following table gives the statistics of production of the raw clay mined in the United States since 1894. These figures are taken from the Mineral Resources published by the United States Geological Survey, as are also the statistics of importation which follow. It should be stated that clay is mined in several States which have not been mentioned in the foregoing résumé, because only the most important occurrences could be considered.

VALUE OF CLAY MINED AND SOLD IN THE UNITED STATES, 1897–1907.

Year.	Kaolin.	Paper clay.	Slip clay.	Ball clay.
1897	$367,080	. . . .	. . . .	$213,566
1898	496,979	. . . .	. . . .	154,743
1899	471,282	. . . .	. . . .	109,369
1900	397,286	. . . .	. . . .	91,983
1901	584,523	. . . .	. . . .	68,907
1902	646,777	. . . .	. . . .	171,086
1903	357,785	(2)	(1)	217,344
1904	304,582	$267,381	$11,942	142,028
1905	326,835	307,238	33,384	167,212
1906	369,452	342,708	31,546	199,073
1907	340,311	293,943	37,925	195,515

Year.	Fire clay.	Stoneware clay.	Miscellaneous.	Total value.
1897	$397,802	. . . .	not given	$978,448
1898	672,362	. . . .	$60,682	1,384,766
1899	826,919	. . . .	237,758	1,645,328
1900	947,993	$94,705	308,410[1]	1,840,377
1901	1,514,508	114,613	294,381[1]	2,576,932
1902	891,185	113,842	238,182	2,061,072
1903	1,474,260	114,759	429,894	2,594,042
1904	1,306,053	83,904	204,272	2,320,162
1905	1,529,468	219,767	184,102	2,768,006
1906	1,878,011	150,774	273,692	3,245,256
1907	2,054,698	136,576	389,580[1]	3,448,548

[1] Includes brick clay.
[2] Included under Miscellaneous.

CLASSIFIED IMPORTS OF CLAY, 1885–1907.

Year.	Kaolin or China clay.		All other clays.						Total.	
			Unwrought.		Wrought.		Common blue.			
	Quantity.	Value.	Quantity.	Value.	Quantity.	Value.	Quantity.	Value.	Quantity.	Value.
	Long tons.		Long tons.		Long tons.		Long tons.		Long tons.	
1885	10,626	$83,722	9,736	$76,899	3,554	$29,839	....	....	23,916	$190,460
1886	16,590	123,093	13,740	113,875	1,654	20,730	....	....	31,984	257,698
1887	23,486	141,360	17,645	139,405	2,187	22,287	....	....	43,318	303,052
1888	18,150	102,050	20,604	152,694	6,832	53,245	....	....	45,586	307,989
1889	19,843	113,538	19,237	145,983	8,142	64,971	....	....	47,222	324,492
1890	29,923	270,141	21,049	155,486	2,978	29,143	....	....	53,950	454,770
1891	39,901	294,458	16,094	118,689	6,297	56,482	....	....	62,292	469,629
1892	49,468	375,175	20,132	155,047	4,551	64,818	5,172	$59,971	79,323	655,011
1893	49,713	374,460	14,949	113,029	6,090	67,280	4,304	51,889	75,056	606,658
1894	62,715	465,501	13,146	98,776	4,768	60,786	2,528	28,886	83,157	653,949
1895	75,447	531,714	18,419	125,417	5,160	60,775	3,869	40,578	102,895	758,484
1896	76,718	536,081	13,319	88,029	4,514	56,701	4,983	54,695	99,534	735,506
1897	71,938	493,431	9,405	56,264	7,839	52,232	4,562	50,954	93,744	652,881
1898	85,586	573,595	16,130	98,434	1,412	24,959	5,312	58,280	108,440	755,268
1899	92,521	615,717	19,614	118,679	1,716	31,948	9,223	106,618	123,074	872,962
1900	111,959	698,720	21,626	126,203	3,195	45,431	7,327	92,013	144,107	962,367
1901	117,756	663,379	27,597	156,838	5,707	75,721	6,136	73,839	157,196	969,777
1902	149,029	883,092	28,931	138,032	3,002	47,093	7,815	86,588	188,777	1,154,805
1903	157,088	898,573	32,661	152,018	2,725	36,211	10,165	110,794	202,669	1,198,418
1904	160,046	891,708	25,402	123,241	1,363	25,026	5,263	50,364	192,074	1,090,339
1905	187,863	1,019,650	30,661	151,583	1,560	38,036	5,909	54,390	225,933	1,263,659
1906	223,404	1,208,189	33,267	166,366	1,889	37,549	9,220	84,578	267,780	1,496,682
1907	239,023	1,582,803	31,196	145,698	2,520	81,155	12,378	110,686	286,017	1,920,432

PART II.

HISTORY OF THE CLAY-WORKING INDUSTRY BY STATES.

CHAPTER III.

ALABAMA.

As early as 1780 to 1813 Isabella Narbome was engaged in the manufacture of brick and tile at the "Bluffs" in Mobile (Ref. 143, p. 322). During the same period pottery was made near Rock Creek, Mobile. There were probably other brick yards in operation at this time, for in 1810 Forbes & Co. were conducting a lawsuit in Mobile over certain brick lands and certain brick-yard buildings (Ref. 143, p. 301).

One of the pioneers in the pottery industry of the State was Daniel Cribbs of Tuscaloosa County, who began utilizing the clays of the Tuscaloosa formation for pottery manufacture in 1829 (Ref. 144, p. 92). At the same time or perhaps earlier, W. D. Preston was running a pottery in Autauga County (Ref. 144), and later, in 1856, C. K. Oliver also started a pottery in Tuscaloosa County.

The Cribbs family had potteries in other counties as well, for Peter Cribbs, a brother of Daniel Cribbs, and later his widow, operated a pottery near Bedford, Lamar County, from 1865 to 1886. Whether all of the above were making earthenware or stoneware is not known.

The mining of the residual clays found in the Fort Payne cherts and the Knox dolomite began some time previous to 1897 and occurred chiefly in DeKalb and Tuscaloosa counties. These clays, which were said to make good porcelain, were mined by the Franklin County pottery and the Montague clay works in DeKalb County, and shipped to Trenton, N. J., where they brought $10

64

per ton, while the halloysite mined at the same locality sold for $20 per ton. Some of this white clay was also shipped to Chattanooga for fire brick. The shipments to Trenton were, however, discontinued some time ago.

Previous to 1887 but little fire clay had been shipped from the Alabama deposits as the materials could find no market (Ref. 145, p. 85), but for some years prior to 1900 the fire clays at Bibbville had been used in a small way for making fire brick. The works have been discontinued and the clay has been shipped to Bessemer for fire-brick manufacture at that point, as have been also the clays from Woodstock and Vance's Station. Still, so far as we know, the fire brick manufactured within the State have never supplied the entire demand of the furnaces at Birmingham and many have to be brought in from other States.

There are no records of the under clays of the Coal Measures having been utilized at an early date, but they have been used since 1900 for pottery manufacture at Jugtown near Sterrit, St. Clair County; at Fort Payne and Rodentown in DeKalb County; Vance's Station, Tuscaloosa County; Summit, Blount County, and Arab in Marshall County (Ref. 144, p. 80). Cretaceous clay had been used for pottery at Edgewood in addition to localities mentioned earlier. However the pottery industry has never assumed large proportions although there are many good deposits of pottery clay in both the Cretaceous and Carboniferous formations.

The Coal-measure shales in addition to being used for pottery have also been employed for at least ten years for making vitrified brick at Coaldale (Ref. 144, p. 80), and for several years they have been worked for the same purpose at Birmingham.

The most important developments then have been in the Cretaceous and Carboniferous areas, and it is in these that any important developments in the future will have to occur, as the southern half of the State with its younger formations contains clays of less importance so far as is known.

Attempts have been made to develop the kaolins of Randolph County but they have thus far been unsuccessful.

The statistics of production in Alabama since 1894 are given below, and indicate that common brick has been the most important clay product manufactured within the State. The production of fire brick has never been sufficiently large to supply the smelting industry around Birmingham. There has been a variable output of sewer pipe, hollow brick, fire proofing, drain tile, etc., but the number of firms producing any one of these during a given year is usually too small to permit their being listed separately.

VALUE OF CLAY PRODUCTS OF ALABAMA FROM 1894 TO 1907.

Year	Common brick.	Vitrified paving brick.	Front brick.	Fire brick.	Miscellaneous.	Pottery.[b]	Grand total.
1894	$205,531	$1,500	....	$57,514	$1,500	....	$266,045
1895	190,157	23,500	$3,325	900	83,459	$9,480	301,341
1896	263,708	22,252	22,300	56,300	1,200	6,425	372,185
1897	289,253	(a)	13,175	67,000	41,600	32,350	443,378
1898	280,567	56,450	15,880	87,200	650	13,650	456,597
1899	611,844	100,600	28,360	114,050	13,618	29,338	897,810
1900	500,313	30,250	9,560	148,665	3,643	20,046	712,727
1901	742,691	(a)	6,990	132,783	45,965	18,312	946,791
1902	730,907	(a)	500	222,660	35,798	26,499	1,016,364
1903	913,911	(a)	6,155	297,985	86,546	23,320	1,327,927
1904	840,236	(a)	4,450	140,678	298,651	32,533	1,289,548
1905	930,568	(a)	(a)	125,244	302,814	34,245	1,392,871
1906	1,046,986	(a)	(a)	157,147	446,770	37,996	1,688,899
1907	1,004,644	183,895	(a)	170,711	367,414	27,745	1,754,409

(a) Included under miscellaneous.
(b) Mainly red earthen-ware and stoneware.

ARIZONA.

There are few records showing the progress of the clay-working industry in Arizona, partly, no doubt, because there is little to record.

Clays and shales occur, but they are little utilized owing to the small demand for them. Small brick yards are scattered over the Territory and the brick clays have been worked for some time, for published statistics show (Ref. 116) that one yard was in operation in 1880.

The smelters in operation in the Territory obtain their refractory-clay products from other States and even the clay used for converter linings is brought in part at least from New Mexico.

The adobe clays which abound in many parts of the territory

have been worked for years by Americans, Mexicans, and Indians; the last named have also used the finer textured alluvial clays for a long period in pottery making.

The value of clay products produced in Arizona since 1894 is given in the following table, and indicates well the limited development of the industry.

VALUE OF CLAY PRODUCTS OF ARIZONA, FROM 1894 TO 1907.

Year.	Value.	Year.	Value.
1894............	$18,081	1901............	$92,986
1895............	6,855	1902............	114,608
1896............	55,663	1903............	109,755
1897............	54,143	1904............	68,885
1898............	81,509	1905............	90,436
1899............	101,954	1906............	93,694
1900............	112,737	1907............	101,462

ARKANSAS.

Clay working has never been an important industry in the State and very few data have been published relating to it, so that any statements must be regarded as of fragmentary character. It is known however that a pottery industry was established in Dallas County by Bird Brothers in 1843 (Ref. 96, p. 317). Another brother started a pottery near the Grant line. These potteries went through many changes in ownership and continued in operation until 1881 (Ref. 96, p. 317). The census for 1860 gives Arkansas credit for but six brick yards and no potteries (Ref. 25), so that it is evidently incomplete.

In 1889 paving-brick manufacture began at Fort Smith using a shale located for such work by Prof. J. C. Branner, while in 1891 a brick yard was in operation at Rogers and was employing a decomposed chert (Ref. 96, p. 63).

The United States Geological Survey has recently issued a report on the clays of Arkansas (Ref. 153) prepared originally for the Arkansas Geological Survey by Prof. J. C. Branner. This report sets forth in clear detail the fictile resources of the State, but naturally gives little attention to the historic side. The operation of a number of plants making a variety of products (mainly common and pressed brick, earthenware, stoneware and fire brick) is referred to in some detail, without in most cases giving the date of establishment. The following data have however been gleaned from the bulletin.

A small pottery was operated at Spring Hill, Hempstead County, before the Civil War; another one has been started there since 1906 using the Tertiary clays.

Two other potteries were in existence at this early date, one of them located southeast of Eldorado, Union County, and the other four miles below Wilmington Landing in the same county. Both ceased operations before the War.

In 1884 a small plant was started at Magnolia, Columbia County, employing surface clays. Five years later, as already noted, the manufacture of paving brick began at Fort Smith.

A common-brick yard was established at Marianna, Lee County, in 1890, and another at Pine Bluff, Jefferson County, in 1892, followed by a second one at the same place in 1898.

The Arkansas Brick and Manufacturing Company began at Little Rock, in 1897, making stiff-mud and dry-pressed brick from common surface clay. Four years later, or in 1901, the Carboniferous shales were worked for common brick at Mansfield, Sebastian County. The same year witnessed the establishment of the Leali Pressed and Fire-Brick Company at Kingsland for the manufacture of building and fire brick from the clays and shales at that point. This firm has moved its plant to Little Rock.

In 1902 the Texarkana Brick Company, making dry-pressed brick from shale, was started at Texarkana, and there is also a pottery in operation at this point.

One of the largest common-brick plants in the State, that at Hope, Hempstead County, was not started until 1904, while two years later a pottery was founded on the Tertiary clays at Spring Hill, as already mentioned.

Although these data are fragmentary, and therefore by no means represent the complete development of the industry, still Arkansas has never ranked as an important clay-producing State. This is owing partly to lack of raw materials, but more especially to remoteness from important markets. Most of the plants established therefore are for the purpose of supplying local demand.

The production in Arkansas since 1894 is given below, the miscellaneous column including mainly vitrified brick, fire brick and drain tile. The pottery product is common earthenware and stoneware.

VALUE OF CLAY PRODUCTS OF ARKANSAS FROM 1894 TO 1907.

Year.	Common brick.	Front brick.	Miscellaneous.	Pottery.	Total.
1894.....	$162,041	....	$50,055	....	$212,096
1895.....	185,009	$5,840	16,710	$38,400	243,959
1896.....	161,872	25,260	6,700	22,500	216,332
1897.....	133,555	8,656	25,228	16,660	184,099
1898.....	206,804	7,298	13,164	17,100	245,766
1899.....	279,997	8,690	30,384	20,071	339,142
1900.....	274,390	67,170	13,172	26,280	381,012
1901.....	368,359	11,570	15,829	11,405	407,263
1902.....	456,170	29,760	24,798	9,450	520,178
1903.....	553,716	11,020	13,610	11,600	589,946
1904.....	661,657	(a)	13,675	21,250	696,582
1905.....	606,671	2,650	14,550	20,088	643,959
1906.....	489,633	6,046	17,015	19,500	532,194
1907.....	468,706	11,940	38,690	16,950	536,286

(a) Included under miscellaneous.

CALIFORNIA.

Prior to 1784 the early settlers had used adobe brick for walls, but in that year roofing tile were made at Santa Barbara, the first ones being manufactured by Mexicans (Ref. 104, p. 643). Coarse earthenware was made in San Francisco (Ibid, p. 618) from 1791 to 1800. A man named Zins operating a brick yard at Sutterville, made 40,000 brick in 1847, and 100,000 in the following year (Ref. 105, p. 97). The industry evidently expanded rapidly, for by the year 1852 there were many "long established" yards supplying San Francisco with brick (Ref. 106, p. 416). That pottery also was being manufactured in these early California days is seen by statements in various Sacramento, San Francisco, and Alta newspapers telling of potteries in those towns in 1854–

1856 (Ref. 105, p. 99). In 1859 J. W. Orr started the Michigan Bar Pottery at Michigan Bar, making stoneware and sewer pipe (Ref. 107, p. 210), and in 1862 moved three miles out on the Ione Road where he continued his pottery until 1896. This probably represents the early exploitation of the Ione (Tertiary) clays, which are now much used.

Terra Cotta was first manufactured in San Francisco in 1874 (Ref. 105, p. 99) and porcelain making was commenced in Los Angeles one year later, or in 1875 (Ref. 105, p. 99), but nothing is stated regarding the source of the raw materials; indeed one may question whether the product was really porcelain, as no china clays from whch it could have been made have been reported from this State. None is made there now. Gladding, McBean & Co., in San Francisco, were making sewer pipe in 1875, mining some of their clay in Lincoln, and the works now located there has expanded so as to include pressed brick, terra cotta and roofing tile. In 1876 the California Pottery & Terra Cotta Company was established in Oakland, obtaining its clay from Carbondale (Ref. 107, p. 202), whose deposits of Tertiary clay have become one of the main sources of supply in the State, and the following year a pottery was in operation at May Post Office, near Carbondale itself (Ref. 107, p. 208), using, probably, the same clays. The Sacramento Transportation Company, at present owning the only brick yard in the county, has made common brick since 1884 (Ref. 107, p. 253).

Los Angeles has for some years been an important brick manufacturing center, the product being made in large part from Tertiary clays. Other grades of ware have, however, also been developed. Thus, the Simons Brick Company, started in 1887, began the manufacture of pressed brick in 1903, of fireproofing building blocks and roofing tile in 1906, and of bituminized paving blocks in 1908.

The Los Angeles Pressed-Brick Company of the same city started pressed-brick operations in 1887, added architectural terra cotta and hollow-tile fireproofing in 1888, fire-clay goods in 1898, roofing tile, mantel and hearth tile in 1904 and enameled brick and terra cotta in 1907. This firm, which appears to have been the pioneer in these lines around Los Angeles, obtains its clays from Riverside, Orange, and Los Angeles counties.

Another plant of varied products is the Steiger Terra Cotta and Pottery Works, at San Francisco, which, starting in 1895, has produced stoneware, hollow goods, and brick and terra cotta, the raw materials being mined in Amador County.

This great diversity in the character of the wares produced by one works is common to many of the plants along the Pacific Coast.

The first firm to make salt-glazed sewer pipe south of San Francisco was the Pacific Coast Clay Manufacturing Company, established at South Riverside in 1887 (Ref. 4, XXIII, p. 367), and the following year the California Sewer Pipe Company began operations in Los Angeles (Ref. 4, XXIII, p. 487). The Clarke Potteries were established in Alameda in 1899 (Ref. 4, XXIII, p. 496). Since 1891 clay for the Los Angeles pottery has been mined four miles north-west of Rosamond (Ref. 107, p. 212). But there are many common-brick yards around Los Angeles, which use the Tertiary clays and clay shales, some of which are also adopted for flowerpot manufacture.

All of the early firms mentioned above have not continued to the present time, but those referred to represent in general the development of the industry, which is quite successful at the present day. Lincoln continues to be an important center, but Los Angeles is no less important, and a number of works are in operation around San Francisco Bay.

The statistics of production in California since 1894 are given below, and indicate clearly the steady increase.

The miscellaneous column includes ornamental brick, stove linings, vitrified paving brick, earthenware and stoneware.

VALUE OF CLAY PRODUCTS OF CALIFORNIA FROM 1894 TO 1907.

Year.	Common brick.	Front brick.	Drain tile.	Sewer pipe.	Architectural terra cotta.
1894	$627,235	. . . .	$15,850	$102,950	$23,085
1895	922,712	$71,286	8,980	261,536	48,300
1896	391,567	34,424	4,528	208,000	2,000
1897	509,955	31,950	5,300	90,430	(a)
1898	598,823	42,700	6,660	305,833	19,300
1899	800,210	59,918	9,298	479,537	76,000
1900	698,583	32,584	8,141	357,867	74,800
1901	943,250	86,425	50,156	285,599	141,380
1902	1,291,941	119,302	10,459	381,076	173,194
1903	1,600,882	229,537	17,994	411,380	180,488
1904	1,843,936	291,813	29,440	568,626	221,000
1905	1,961,909	302,872	27,852	663,044	215,160
1906	1,962,866	501,746	30,545	827,477	254,932
1907	2,483,062	283,375	53,997	1,086,916	528,623

Year.	Fireproof-ing.	Fire brick.	Miscellan-eous.	Total pottery.	Grand total.
1894	. . . .	$2,575	$69,800	. . . .	$841,495
1895	. . . .	10,836	97,505	. . . .	1,421,154
1896	$2,700	11,875	8,091	$17,022	680,207
1897	(a)	7,720	13,847	44,208	703,410
1898	(a)	19,505	11,635	36,347	1,263,734
1899	7,100	28,798	93,794	32,863	1,587,518
1900	15,500	48,461	115,675	24,387	1,375,998
1901	12,825	87,665	128,221	27,534	1,769,155
1902	18,645	96,491	110,381	51,607	2,253,096
1903	61,649	200,332	90,803	49,478	2,831,543
1904	51,125	285,718	261,358	71,718	3,624,734
1905	45,551	290,878	262,668	95,213	3,865,147
1906	98,968	347,806	241,293	98,587	4,364,230
1907	149,959	374,378	682,389	97,838	5,740,537

(a) Included under Miscellaneous.

COLORADO.

The extensive use of wood as a building material in the West, has somewhat retarded the development of burned-clay products.

Golden, Clear Creek County, has always been the most important clay-working district, and the Dakota fire clays were mined here as early as 1864 or 1865, but their full development came later. A year or so later, in 1866, Henry Bell in prospecting for coal found a bed of fire clay and used it in making fire brick. Whether this was Dakota is uncertain, because the Laramie coals have associated fire clays, but these are inferior to the Dakota clays and are not much used. Since 1866, as stated, Golden has been the center of Colorado's clay-mining industry. All of the clays mined have not been used on the spot, for as the industry developed at other points along the eastern foothills, Golden clays were shipped to them. Knowledge of the fact that the Dakota formation with its enclosed fire clays was abundantly developed along the eastern border of the Rocky Mountains, led to development of these materials at other points. They had been exploited at Platte Cañon, Colorado City, and Morrison as early as 1896, and probably even before that. Those near Parkdale were worked at least as early as 1896 by the Standard Fire Brick Company of Pueblo, and four years later, or in 1900, fire-brick manufacture based on Dakota clays was begun at Cañon City, while about 1905 their development began at Graneros south of Pueblo. The clay from this last-named locality is shipped to Pueblo.

In 1882 the Golden Pressed Brick Company [1] was making fire brick and pressed brick, and in 1887 Golden clay was being mined and shipped to Denver and Pueblo potteries and brick yards. By 1893 brick yards were in operation in Denver, Golden, and Boulder; fire brick were made in Golden, Pueblo and Denver and three potteries were in operation in Denver (Ref. 4, xix, p. 264).

The Durango Pressed Brick Company began operations in 1898 using a Boyd dry press and making red-building brick from Cretaceous shales and a small amount of semi-refractory brick for boiler settings. In 1902 two plants were in operation, but at present there is but this one (Ref. 114, p. 297).

[1] Some roofing tile were made here in 1893, but the production has not continued.

The Geijsbeek Pottery Company began making dinner ware at Golden in 1899 (Ref. 6, p. 241), but has discontinued.

In other parts of the State but little has been done except to utilize surface clays for the manufacture of common brick, as there is but slight local demand, and good markets are too far off. The value of the several classes of clay products in Colorado since 1894 are given in the following table. The importance of the fire-brick industry is there brought out, as is also the fluctuation in annual production. Common brick are naturally the most important item. The miscellaneous column contains a variable production of paving brick, ornamental brick, drain tile, sewer pipe, fireproofing, hollow brick and terra cotta.

VALUE OF CLAY PRODUCTS OF COLORADO FROM 1894 TO 1907.

Year.	Common brick.	Front brick.	Fire brick.	Miscellaneous.	Pottery.	Total.
1894	$228,344	....	$113,393	$136,340	....	$478,077
1895	252,018	$113,105	42,264	145,996	....	553,383
1896	153,627	80,700	46,323	48,030	.. ..	328,680
1897	134,920	101,494	38,465	114,475	$17,509	406,863
1898	196,499	101,608	48,145	420,515	....	766,767
1899	422,524	136,613	162,633	333,568	16,050	1,071,388
1900	471,235	143,470	207,475	363,139	15,200	1,200,519
1901	760,867	196,147	292,269	318,884	26,700	1,594,867
1902	986,882	334,332	609,495	248,989	21,285	2,200,983
1903	893,566	281,929	631,074	204,872	56,869	2,068,310
1904	544,661	214,498	110,053	295,209	24,870	1,189,291
1905	638,376	253,277	274,095	418,488	48,995	1,633,231
1906	787,084	256,770	278,407	297,824	47,083	1,831,088
1907	803,701	254,522	430,897	508,211	44,144	2,041,475

CONNECTICUT.

The first mention we have of the use of clays in Connecticut is that in 1780 stoneware was made in Norwalk (Ref. 8). About 1790 a man of the name of Souter built a pottery at Hartford and made earthenware (Ref. 8, pp. 435-7). This factory passed through various hands and is now the property of Seymour and Bosworth (Ref. 8, pp. 435-7). Bean pots and children's banks made of clay, were made at Bean Hill near Norwich and dated 1794-1812 (Ref 4, XXXIV, pp. 352-3), but were probably not the only product then made. From 1796 to 1800 mere mention is made of Norwich, Stonington, and Norwalk, the Stonington factory making a gray, soft-paste ware with salt glaze and the Norwalk firm making red ware with lead glaze, (Ref. 12, pp. 400–401). The Stonington pottery is mentioned again by Barber as the property of Adam States in 1800 (Ref. 8, p. 435). "Porcelain clay" was discovered near New Milford in 1807 by a goldsmith who used it for making crucibles (Ref. 24, p. 73), and in the Connecticut Geological Survey report for 1837 it was stated that Mr. L. Hine had utilized this deposit at New Milford for eight years, employed six hands, and with Anna Hine, who began in 1835, they turned out annually $6000 worth of furnace linings and firebrick (Ref. 24, pp. 73–74.) The fire brick were sold at two-thirds the price of Stourbridge (English) brick and were considered nearly equal in quality (Ref. 24, pp. 73–74). A clay in South Kent derived from graphic granite was tried at the Jersey City potteries previous to 1837 and found to be of good quality, but transportation charges prohibited its shipment with any profit (Ref. 24, p. 74). Door knobs were being manufactured in South Norwalk in 1853 by a Mr. Wheeler who previously had made pottery buttons of wet-pressed clay, obtained probably from New Jersey. In 1860 two concerns in Connecticut were making fire brick, and there were also seven common brick yards in operation as well as five potteries (Ref. 25).

Since that time the main developments have been in the line of common brick, the Pleistocene clays having been worked at scattered points. At the present day the Connecticut River valley is the most important district. Several fire-brick and stove-lining factories also continue in operation, but bring their clays by boat from New Jersey. Another important but not extensive industry is the manufacture of architectural faience at Hartford which was begun by the Hartford Faience Company in 1894. This same firm also produces art pottery with a stoneware body, and added electrical porcelain to its product in 1902. It depends on other States for its raw materials.

The only deposit of high-grade clay which the State contains is the kaolin, worked at West Cornwall, since about 1895. This

material, which in its washed form is used mainly by paper manufacturers, is said to have been utilized from time to time during the
preceding fifty years to supply fire mortar for the small blast furnaces which were in operation in the western part of the State.

The statistics of production for Connecticut cannot be given
separately, as the United States Geological Survey combines them
with those of Rhode Island. Connecticut is never likely to become
an important clay-working State, largely because the raw materials
are lacking. The miscellaneous column of the following table
includes small quantities of paving, front and ornamental brick,
drain tile, fireproofing, and hollow brick produced from time to
time. It also includes a steady but not large production of
stove linings.

VALUE OF CLAY PRODUCTS OF CONNECTICUT AND RHODE
ISLAND FROM 1894 TO 1907.

Year.	Common brick.	Miscellaneous.	Pottery.	Total.
1894.....	$789,650	$221,950	....	$1,011,600
1895.....	670,462	458,463	....	1,128,925
1896.....	1,141,738	258,160	$48,700	1,448,598
1897.....	1,017,250	247,920	71,500	1,336,670
1898.....	670,880	204,700	72,600	958,180
1899.....	751,251	241,201	81,750	1,074,202
1900.....	862,334	176,388	36,250	1,099,972
1901.....	822,079	217,630	43,700	1,130,909
1902.....	896,171	204,610	66,547	1,217,678
1903.....	890,989	202,630	77,250	1,206,069
1904.....	1,039,204	106,830	69,575	1,215,609
1905.....	1,329,220	174,258	105,100	1,608,578
1906.....	1,503,929	109,832	133,444	1,747,205
1907.....	1,240,575	120,903	123,116	1,484,592

DELAWARE.

The use of clay in Delaware is first noted in 1769, when one
Bonnin, of Philadelphia, used White Clay Creek clay from near
Wilmington at his pottery (Ref. 8, p. 99). About 1800 white clay
from below New Castle was being mined and used for glass pots,
fire brick, etc. (Ref. 49, p. 35). Bricks were being made in New
Castle, Kent, and Sussex Counties in 1841 (Ref. 50, p. 177). More
important, however, was the discovery in 1854 of kaolin, by A.
Marshall on his farm in Hockessin. He used it for making fire

brick and common brick until 1859 when he began manufacturing yellow and Rockingham ware. He introduced the washing of kaolin in 1861 and found a market for the washed clay in Trenton at $42 [1] a ton, for use in paper manufacture. In 1866 he sold out to Trux and Parker who built a large washery and continued until the deposit was exhausted in 1875. The adjoining farm was exploited by Mr. Graham in 1863, and in 1874 sold to Golding & Sons, of Trenton, N. J., who worked it for a period. A near by farm was worked from 1861–1881 and then sold to a Mr. Burgess (private communication).

The only other reference found in regard to the brick industry of Delaware is the fact that in 1860 (Ref. 25) there were in operation in the State four brick yards, one drain tile plant, one fire brick firm and four potteries. The State has never become prominent in the clay-working industry, and probably never will. Statistics of production are given below.

VALUE OF CLAY PRODUCTS OF DELAWARE FROM 1894 TO 1907.

Year.	Common brick.	Miscellaneous.	Total.
1894	$43,528	$2,500	$46,028
1895	48,915	10,700	58,615
1896	57,433	3,570	61,003
1897	64,111	4,347	68,458
1898	81,435	9,120	90,555
1899	138,319	30,166	168,485
1900	144,860	11,414	156,274
1901	126,092	5,072	131,164
1902	115,684	29,250	144,934
1903	188,058	24,850	203,908
1904	152,470	6,500	158,970
1905	210,182	16,882	227,064
1906	222,628	15,140	237,768
1907	175,410	15,030	190,440

DISTRICT OF COLUMBIA.

Though of small size, and not possessed of abundant or rich clay resources, the District of Columbia nevertheless maintains a somewhat active clay-working industry, which has been running for a considerable period. Unfortunately we have no data bear-

[1] The present price of about $7 per ton for domestic kaolin affords an interesting comparison with these figures.

ing on its development in the past, and can simply give the statistics of production since 1894. The miscellaneous column includes a scattered production of vitrified paving brick, front brick, ornamental brick, drain tile, fireproofing, and earthenware.

VALUE OF CLAY PRODUCTS OF DISTRICT OF COLUMBIA
FROM 1894 TO 1907.

Year.	Common brick.	Sewer pipe.	Miscellaneous.	Total.
1894.....	$317,565	$61,100	$12,007	$390,672
1895.....	277,750	64,631	30,923	373,304
1896.....	220,762	39,558	93,245	353,565
1897.....	209,110	66,360	13,511	288,981
1898.....	257,932	34,000	28,388	320,320
1899.....	358,232	69,495	53,418	481,145
1900.....	168,127	69,374	51,432	288,933
1901.....	179,184	95,000	49,824	324,008
1902.....	185,480	37,820	44,327	267,627
1903.....	236,833	54,500	39,178	330,511
1904.....	194,695	44,000	67,765	306,460
1905.....	220,680	37,657	58,684	317,021
1906.....	242,085	30,004	63,050	335,139
1907.....	219,110	(a)	102,974	322,084

(a) Under miscellaneous.

FLORIDA.

Josiah Wedgewood was experimenting with Florida clay from Pensacola in his pottery in England in 1766 (Ref. 57, I, p. 471). In 1827 brick were being made in West Florida and especially were fire brick in demand for shipment to New Orleans (Ref. 69, p. 69), while in 1837 brick were still being shipped from Pensacola to New Orleans, most of them being fire brick (Ref. 68, p. 114). From 1856 to 1860 Mr. Crary made both mud and dry-pressed brick in Escambia Bay near Pensacola, these being the brick used in the construction of Fort Jefferson (Ref. 67, pp. 13–14).

Some years later, in 1875, Mr. C. S. Edgar having heard rumors of kaolin deposits in Florida went there from the North, but was unable to find any. However, in 1890, in mining phosphates in Florida the kaolin was found and sent to the Trenton, N. J., potters who referred it to Mr. Edgar. He returned to Florida and began mining the white clay in 1892 under the name of the Edgar Plastic Kaolin Company, and since that time has shipped great quantities of the clay to white-ware factories throughout the

United States. (Private communications.) Another firm, the International Kaolin Company, began mining clay in 1900, at Oakahumpka. In 1907 four plants were engaged in the mining of ball clay. Two of these, operated by the Edgar Plastic Kaolin Company, are located at Edgar, Putnam County. The other two are the Richmond Kaolin Company of Richmond and the Florida Clay Company of Yalaha, both in Lake County (Ref. 146, p. 33).

These Florida white clays are classed by some potters as ball clays. They are of sedimentary character, and of intermediate plasticity between the residual kaolins of North Carolina and the white sedimentary kaolins of Georgia.

In 1895 there were a number of small yards scattered over the State, and engaged in the manufacture of common brick. The largest of these was at Jacksonville (Ref. 125, p. 871), but even in 1907 Florida ranked but thirty-seventh in the list of clay-working States, her production being only.23 per cent of the country's output.

The only important clay resource of Florida is the white clay, which is shipped to white-ware and wall-tile potteries all over the United States. Good brick clays are not abundant, and even if they were the local demand is limited, so there is little prospect of the development of an important clay working in the State.

VALUE OF CLAY PRODUCTS OF FLORIDA FROM 1894 TO 1907.

Year.	Common brick.	Miscellaneous.	Grand total.
1894............	$82,387	$1,200	$83,587
1895............	108,775	5,240	114,015
1896............	89,219	32,925	122,144
1897............	87,335	2,100	89,435
1898............	112,587	18,400	130,987
1899............	132,123	5,685	138,808
1900............	136,779	3,825	140,604
1901............	185,759	4,915	190,674
1902............	170,852	4,590	175,442
1903............	218,086	3,209	221,295
1904............	248,579	4,285	252,864
1905............	326,929	2,809	329,738
1906............	285,224	4,420	289,644
1907............	343,704	10,871	354,575

GEORGIA.

The Georgia clays were known in England as early as 1766, and used by Wedgewood in his pottery (Ref. 57, 1, p. 471), but aside from this few early records have been found.

The Stevens Pottery was established in Baldwin County about 1860 and about the same time one was in operation in Milledgeville. In 1870 one of the first terra-cotta works in the South was established in Atlanta (Ref. 66, p. 382), and in 1883 the Chattahoochee Brick Company of Atlanta was organized (Ref. 66, p. 382). Brick yards were, however, in operation there before that date.

The residual clays derived from the Paleozoic shales and limestones, have been used since 1892, for brick manufacture at Cartersville (Ref. 123, p. 283), but most of the bricks of northwestern Georgia were at that time made from alluvial clays, as at Cartersville, Rome, etc. (Ref. 123, p. 287).

Among the most important clay resources at the present day are the Cretaceous clays of central Georgia (Ref. 124, p. 303), which have been mined at a number of points for some years. The product is a white refractory clay which is shipped to fire-brick and terra-cotta manufacturers, to Ohio and New Jersey potteries, and to northern paper mills, about 25,000 tons being mined and shipped annually.[1]

In the following table the miscellaneous column includes paving brick, ornamental brick, drain tile, sewer pipe, architectural terra cotta, roofing tile, fire brick, hollow brick and stove linings.

VALUE OF CLAY PRODUCTS OF GEORGIA FROM 1894 TO 1897.

Year.	Common brick.	Front brick.	Fire brick.	Miscellaneous.	Pottery.	Grand total.
1894.....	$585,693	....	$17,650	$96,544	....	$699,887
1895.....	655,275	$46,265	29,950	129,865	6,000	867,355
1896.....	615,771	21,678	25,297	235,907	7,160	905,813
1897.....	599,158	35,381	12,904	300,870	14,200	962,513
1898.....	530,346	26,250	25,650	252,662	22,350	857,258
1899.....	968,310	78,175	24,400	170,842	22,268	1,263,995
1900.....	982,083	49,800	35,502	104,801	21,033	1,193,218
1901.....	1,182,553	55,700	35,000	254,600	17,230	1,545,083
1902.·....	1,114,527	46,560	(a)	330,743	16,839	1,508,669.
1903.....	1,305,896	25,748	73,600	303,636	22,142	1,731,022
1904.....	1,374,318	42,064	28,100	454,397	22,057	1,920,936
1905.....	1,444,479	28,676	73,050	551,151	22,390	2,119,746
1906.....	1,783,988	20,747	51,310	524,322	20,257	2,400,624
1907.....	1,807,148	16,450	82,391	550,363	33,885	2,490,237

[1] These are discussed in great detail from an economic but not historic standpoint in Bulletin 18, issued by the Georgia Geological Survey.

ILLINOIS.

Although Illinois is one of the leading States in the manufacture of clay products, but few facts relating to the history of
these appear to have been published. Moreover the gathering
of data through various channels has met with little success,
many of the inquiries sent to manufacturers having remained
unanswered.

Brick. According to the statement of one correspondent,
brick were made in Cook County as early as 1812, but another
authority (Ref. 4, XVII, p. 130) sets 1833 as the initial date, and
Mr. D. V. Purington informs us that at that time a brick yard
was in operation on the North branch of the Chicago River, on
the site of the present Chicago and Northwestern Railroad Station. From this small beginning the local industry has expanded,
as records published from time to time show. So by the year
1851 there were a number of yards at which brick were made, all
of hand-molded character, while the burning was done in clamps
(Ref. 4, XVII, p. 130). Indeed up to 1880 nearly all of the brick
made in Chicago were molded either by hand or in horsepower
soft-mud machines. About this date, however, the use of stiff-
mud machines and artificial dryers was introduced, and this
change can be truthfully said to have revolutionized the industry
of that district. In 1900 the Illinois Brick Company was organized and took in thirty-six different firms in the Chicago district.

While Chicago has for many years been the main brick-manufacturing center of Illinois, the industry has also developed at
other points, perhaps in some cases as early as it did at Chicago,
but definite data are lacking on this point.

By 1870 brick clays were being worked all over the State, and
the Illinois Geological Survey (Ref. 91) records the manufacture
of common brick at Dundee, Quincy, Woodstock, and Morris,
the surface clays being presumably the raw materials used. The
industry had also started at Gilbert and McHenry.[1] About the
same time a man named Gregg started a yard at Gregg's Station
near Hinsdale, for the purpose of making dry-pressed brick, but

[1] W. D. Gates, private correspondence.

as the product was crumbly the venture failed.[1]   The making of dry-pressed brick was also attempted near Rockford in 1873, and some writers have referred to this as one of the earlier experiments with this process.   The press has been described as a "powerful compressing machine called the 'Little Giant' and operated by steam, pressing dry dust into bricks" (Ref. 92, p. 91).

Another attempt at dry-pressed brick manufacture is said to have been made in 1880 by the Anderson Pressed-Brick Company, which had an extensive plant on the North Branch of the Chicago River, producing brick of many colors.   This attempt also appears to have been a failure. Four years later, or in 1884, the production of pressed brick was begun at Momemce, but the plant was altered into an enameled brick works in 1893.   Still later in 1887 the La Salle Pressed-Brick Company of La Salle started the production of dry-pressed brick from Carboniferous shales, employing the same clays formerly used by the Anderson Pressed-Brick Company mentioned above.[2]

Dry-pressed brick from under-coal clay are also made at Collinsville.   Since that time the pressed-brick business has developed at several points within the State.

Important centers of brick production at the present day outside of Chicago are Danville, Springfield, Peoria, Bloomington, etc.

Terra Cotta.   A terra-cotta company known as the Chicago Terra-Cotta Company was established as early as 1868 although one reference (Ref. 8, p. 386) gives it as 1857.   It is no longer in operation and we are in doubt as to the exact character of its wares. The Northwestern Terra-Cotta Company of Chicago, now one of the foremost establishments in the United States, was started early in the seventies by an architect named Loring, but changed to the present firm name in 1876.   The main sources of the raw materials are the Carboniferous formations of Indiana and Illinois.

The American Terra-Cotta Company of Terra Cotta, referred to especially under pottery, is likewise a producer of architectural terra cotta.

Paving Brick.   According to Prof. I. O. Baker, the first brick

---

[1] W. D. Gates, private correspondence.
[2] Private correspondence.

used for paving in Illinois were made by a Mr. Hoefer of Bloomington about 1875. These were also shipped to some of the smaller cities in the middle eighties.

In 1885 the first brick pavement was laid in Chicago and the brick for it were made in Ottawa, Ill. (Ref. xxxi, p. 436), from Carboniferous clays. Between 1885 and 1890, pavers were also made at Decatur by a Mr. Shey, and about the same time, at Lincoln, Carboniferous clays being used. Two years later, or in 1892, paving brick were also made at Danville, and since 1893 they have been manufactured at Alton.

The great paving-brick manufacturing center however is at Galesburg. Here a small brick and tile plant, the Galesburg Brick and Tile Company, was started in 1892, and followed soon after by the Galesburg Brick and Terra-Cotta Company. For several years the brick business was moderate, the brick attracting attention by reason of their strength and toughness. In 1890 the Purington Paving-Brick Company began operations and has continued up to the present time. Its product is made from the Carboniferous shales occurring at that locality, and it represents probably the largest paving-brick plant in the United States. According to Mr. D. V. Purington the use of shale for paving brick was first developed at Galesburg by a man named Joseph Stafford.

At Streator, Ill., the use of shale for paving brick was begun in 1898, by the Streator Paving-Brick Company, and in the southwestern part of the State in the region around Glen Carbon the Carboniferous shales have been utilized for the same purpose, since about the same date.

Fire Brick. Fire clays are abundant in the coal measures of Illinois, and fire brick have been manufactured at a number of points for some years. Just how early the refractory ware industry began cannot be stated with exactness, but Mr. Lines informs us that it probably had its birth at Utica, about 1859, and this locality has remained an important center of production up to the present day. Fire brick were made at Ottawa a few years later than at Utica and the industry is still important there also. The fire-brick industry is mentioned at Salina as early as 1875 (Ref. 93).

Other important centers of production at the present day are Carbon Cliff, Rock Island County, and Golden Eagle, Calhoun County. At the last-named locality fire brick have been made for about eight years (since 1901). About 20 per cent of the clay for fire brick is obtained from drift mines.

Pottery. While the manufacture of brick has been noted as having been carried on in the first half of the nineteenth century, no records have been found of pottery manufacture in that period, although small plants must have existed.

It is definitely known that stoneware [1] was being made at Ripley in the year 1836, but we are not able to state that this was the first pottery made in Illinois. This locality was at one time an important potting center, but has since declined to a great degree, although some potting is still done there.

A white-ware pottery is reported to have been erected by Fenton & Clark at Peoria, in 1859, but after three unsuccessful years they ceased operations, and the factory was taken over by others for stoneware manufacture. No further mention of the pottery industry was noted until 1873, when the Peoria pottery was established for making stoneware, but this was changed to white ware in 1889. These two works are interesting since they indicate the probable shipment of white clays into the State at an early date, unless they possibly used some of the white Cretaceous-Tertiary clays found in the southern part of Illinois.

The earliest mention of the pottery industry in the Illinois Geological Survey Reports appears to be in the one for 1866 (Ref. 89, pp. 323 and 425) which refers to the potteries at Upper Alton and Mound City. Two years later important potteries were stated to be in operation at Anna and Fieldon (Ref. 90), but there were also numerous small ones running at other localities. In the same year the fire clays from LaSalle County were utilized at the Lowell pottery (Ref. 90, p. 284).

By 1870 the pottery industry was known to be in active operation at a large number of points, but few have received specific mention, only Ripley and Jugtown being listed in the Fourth Report of the Illinois Geological Survey (Ref. 91). Three years later or in 1873

[1] Private communication, E. F. Lines.

the industry is also mentioned at a point four miles south of Eliza-bethtown (Ref. 92, p. 40). Stoneware was produced at Saline in 1875 (Ref. 93).

It was about this time that potting was begun in McDonough County and following it in Green County.[1]

Between 1883 and 1888 the Pauline Pottery was in operation in Chicago (Ref. 8, p. 332) making decorated art wares with earthen-ware body and lead glaze, but this factory was later moved to Wisconsin.

Previous to 1883 the Carboniferous clays near Macomb were used for stoneware by the Eagle Pottery Company and the Macomb Pottery Company, but the former has been discontinued while the latter was taken over in 1906 by the Western Stoneware Company, which also assumed control of two plants at Monmouth and one at Whitehall.

The Cretaceous-Tertiary clays of southern Illinois have attracted attention from time to time, but they have never reached an im-portant stage of development. Small potteries have used those near Round Knob for some years, and, since 1886 at least, clays from this point have been shipped to Paducah, Ky., for pottery manufacture.[2]

A most important development in the pottery industry of Illi-nois was the establishment in 1886 of the American Terra Cotta and Ceramic Company, for the manufacture of art wares, of which the Teco Pottery has won a wide and enviable reputation. This industry is based in part on the local calcareous clays, others being obtained from Brazil, Ind.

At the present day, the stoneware industry of Illinois is of some importance, and practically all the clay which is used for that pur-pose is taken from the vicinity of Colchester in McDonough County and from Whitehall and Drake in Green County. It is confined to a single horizon, immediately beneath a limestone that lies a short distance below what is at present termed Coal No. 2. (Upper Pottsville.) Mr. E. F. Lines of the Illinois Geological Survey, who has supplied the above information, estimates that approximately seventy per cent of the clay being manufactured into

[1] Private communication, E. F. Lines.　　[2] Private correspondence.

stoneware in Illinois is taken from drift mines, and that in practically every case the clay is mined independently of the associated coal, the latter where associated with the stoneware clay being of secondary importance.

Miscellaneous. The clay used in the manufacture of sewer pipe and fireproofing is in the majority of cases the same as that used in the manufacture of stoneware. Sewer pipe, however, are also made from the Pennsylvanian and Mississippian shales.

Sewer pipe, drain tile and flue linings were made from the Carboniferous clays around Macomb as early as 1884, the clays previous to that date having been used only for stoneware. A second sewer-pipe plant sprang into existence at this locality in 1899, but has since been absorbed by the Macomb Sewer-Pipe Company, and is now turning out clay conduits in addition to sewer pipe.

Important sewer-pipe plants are also located at (1) Columbia, (2) Monmouth, (3) Griffin, (4) East Alton, (5) Streator and (6) Whitehall. Nos. 1, 3 and 5 use shale, while Nos. 3, 4 and 6 use fire clay. The Columbia plant has been running since 1907, and the East Alton plant but a few years.

The foundation of a works in 1884 by the Illinois Terra-Cotta Lumber Company, represents perhaps the first attempt to manufacture terra-cotta lumber in Illinois, the clay used at present being dredged from the bottom of Lake Calumet. Since its establishment the industry has expanded and has been started at a number of points.

Among the later developments in this line is that of the Monmouth Brick and Tile Company which took over a common brick plant and is making hollow bricks and blocks from Carboniferous clays.

Another important development in the vicinity of Chicago was the establishment about 1892 of a roofing-tile plant. This works used the local clay of that vicinity for the manufacture of interlocking tile according to the Ludovici patterns. They were of non-vitrified character, and are still being produced.[1]

---

[1] Some were made by the American Ceramic Works at Eola about 1893, and at Ottawa for several years prior to 1902.

Illinois in 1907 ranked fourth among the producing States, and contributed 8.32 per cent of the country's total. The production since 1894 is given in the following table.

VALUE OF CLAY PRODUCTS OF ILLINOIS FROM 1894 TO 1907.

Year.	Common brick.	Vitrified paving brick.	Front brick.	Ornamental brick.	Drain tile.	Sewer pipe.
1894	$4,495,613	$843,217	....	$72,920	$1,418,572	$308,963
1895	3,786,747	643,997	$330,318	19,500	1,028,581	389,680
1896	2,831,752	486,519	196,658	52,624	517,684	187,350
1897	2,376,498	719,371	218,788	61,067	531,993	165,071
1898	3,123,202	639,153	246,416	30,453	797,579	200,312
1899	3,231,332	700,524	252,244	27,868	1,026,192	229,040
1900	3,981,577	720,089	240,989	15,705	734,249	271,035
1901	5,188,654	899,454	204,980	13,105	694,588	348,716
1902	5,131,621	839,784	240,466	11,893	693,783	360,149
1903	5,388,589	1,015,710	274,723	12,927	892,807	532,858
1904	5,167,165	1,234,703	251,762	11,733	1,002,463	550,344
1905	6,259,232	973,247	348,354	13,567	1,051,852	580,538
1906	5,719,906	1,306,476	341,298	11,635	1,052,588	587,805
1907	6,499,777	1,405,821	266,270	(a)	1,031,192	662,487

Year.	Fire-proofing.	Fire brick.	Miscellaneous.	Earthenware.	Stoneware.	Other pottery.	Grand total.
1894	$81,288	$116,904	$1,136,883	....	....	....	$8,474,360
1895	71,685	117,040	976,796	....	$255,540	....	7,619,884
1896	213,315	125,408	830,455	$2,050	399,432	$20,000	5,938,247
1897	177,782	106,377	522,727	498,900		120,000	5,498,574
1898	202,374	109,465	673,884	5,725	431,812	200,000	6,866,715
1899	198,360	132,759	677,949	52,600	572,327	138,630	7,259,825
1900	76,347	175,259	716,836	57,068	578,405	72,800	7,708,859
1901	263,276	212,510	1,069,882	6,600	585,649	83,900	9,642,490
1902	358,015	199,048	1,280,217	19,400	582,708	92,306	9,881,840
1903	308,561	233,106	1,513,678	27,685	662,363	208,685	11,190,797
1904	324,264	217,008	1,188,309	24,250	777,696	27,750	10,777,447
1905	323,550	176,692	1,691,747	25,350	864,507	253,150	12,361,786
1906	409,171	236,032	1,986,367	37,543	897,650	47,710	12,634,181
1907	404,265	241,008	1,705,503	37,045	898,267	68,854	13,220,489

(a) Included under miscellaneous.

INDIANA.

The first brick yard in Indianapolis furnished the brick for the first brick house in 1822 (Ref. 84, p. 21). The first pottery noted was established at Troy, Perry County, in 1834, by a man named Clews from Liverpool, Eng. Clews, after a visit to this locality, conceived the idea that he could make a fortune manufacturing white ware there. He accordingly brought over 600 people from England, but after several attempts found that his schemes were impracticable and turned his attention to making fire brick, common brick and yellow ware (Ref. 85, p. 123). In 1839 the company induced I. Vodrey to assume the management and it continued in operation until 1846 (Ref. 8, p. 161). The next year (1840) the mining of pottery clay began at Bloomingdale (Ref. 85, p. 47) and has continued to the present time.

This was followed in 1841 by the establishment of a pottery by H. R. Atcheson, at Annapolis, Parke County, Indiana, which W. S. Blatchley mentions as the oldest one in the State (Ref. 133). The plant, which is still running, obtained its clay from Coke-Oven Hollow, a locality long known for its variety of clays, which occur in the Coal Measures.

Another pottery established in 1842 at Loogootee, ran until 1892 (Ref. 85, p. 101), and in 1846, one was started at Clay City (Ref. 85, p. 81). B. Griffith, the present owner, is using an under clay of the Coal Measures which can be easily secured.

The record up to this point is manifestly incomplete, and with one exception makes reference only to potteries, while it is probable that brick yards must have been in operation in different parts of the State using the Pleistocene surface clays.

That this supposition is probably correct is shown by the fact that the census of 1860 (Ref. 25) reports for Indiana, 56 brick yards, and 32 potteries, with the specific mention that thriving potteries were found in Clay, Martin and Perry counties. No reference is made to the character of the raw materials used, but it is not unlikely that some of them at least made their product from the under clays of the Coal Measures.

The industry established at Troy evidently prospered, for, in

1863, a second pottery was established there and continued in operation until 1892 (Ref. 85, p. 123). The clays of this locality also seemed to have been adapted to the manufacture of yellow or Rockingham ware, which was formerly made here in large quantities, but is no longer produced anywhere in Indiana (Ref. 133).

The utilization of the Indiana clays for sewer pipe does not appear to have been undertaken until 1862, when the under clays of the top coal near Cannelton were used. This factory for 30 years remained the only sewer-pipe works in the State (Ref. 85, p. 124), and even after this the expansion of the sewer-pipe industry was not as great as that of other branches of the clay-working operations, because in 1904 there were only five sewer-pipe factories in the State.

There was continued growth in the pottery industry however, for the establishment of a new pottery is recorded near Bloomingdale in 1866 (Ref. 85, p. 49), and in 1869 the Carboniferous clays were already being extensively used around Brazil (Ref. 86, p. 80) for stoneware. In addition, however, they were found adapted to making fire brick and terra cotta.

The pottery clays at Shoals (Ref. 87) were developed, and in 1872 fire brick were being made at Montezuma (Ref. 85, p. 67). This plant which used the under clay of coal 10, is said by Blatchley (Ref. 133), to be the oldest fire-brick factory in the State.

The peculiar type of clay known as Indianaite was known at this time, and previous to 1874 the deposits of it at Huron were called "Taller beds." In 1874 they were exposed in digging out under a blast furnace, and the material sold to the Cincinnati porcelain manufacturers. Later it was used by the Pennsylvania Salt Company for making "alum cake," and also in paper manufacture, while in 1882 the deposits of this clay in Owen and Lawrence counties were worked to supply the United States Encaustic Tile Works with clay (Ref. 88, p. 24). The use of this material was finally abandoned and the deposits have not been worked since 1891 (Ref. 85, p. 104). It was about 1872 that the first use of clay for hollow brick was recorded (Ref. 133), the manufacture being established by the Weaver Clay and Coal Company of Brazil.

The United States Encaustic Tile Works were established in Indianapolis in 1876 although not under that name until 1886 (Ref. 41, p. 231). In 1882 A. M. Beck built a pottery in Evansville and made majolica, being succeeded in 1884 by Bennighof, Uhl and Company, and then in 1891 by the Crown Pottery Company (Ref. 6, p. 40). In 1884 the Indianapolis Terra-Cotta Company was established at Brightwood (Ref. 8, p. 397) the clay used being mainly the under clay of coal IV from Brazil, Clay County. The North Vernon Tile Company began at North Vernon (Ref. 8, XXIII, p. 375) in 1886.

The early nineties witnessed the recognition and development of the Coal Measure and Sub-Carboniferous (Knobstone) shales, whose value had hitherto been unknown and neglected.

On this point we may do well to quote from the 1904 report (Ref. 133) of W. S. Blatchley, who writes as follows: "A dozen years ago[1] the term 'shale' was unknown among the natural resources of the State. These materials, which covered great areas in the coal-bearing counties, were looked upon as a nuisance which had to be removed or tunneled through before the underlying veins of coal could be reached.

"These Carboniferous shales have since 1892 been developed into the most important clay resource of the State, being now used for the manufacture of sewer pipe, hollow block, conduits, paving brick, pressed, front and ordinary brick, drain tile, etc. Some of these deposits have been developed with the coal-seams, the two being raised through one shaft. Indeed, in many cases it might be economically impracticable to work the clay alone.

"Of more recent development than the Carboniferous are the Knobstone shales, of Lower Carboniferous age, and lying to the east of the Carboniferous ones. These are now worked in a belt extending from Jasper County to the Ohio River, and their employment for common, pressed and paving brick is steadily increasing."

Mr. Blatchley in referring to these undeveloped shales says that as late as 1890–96, twenty-seven towns and cities expended $884,667 for paving brick and blocks, most of these being brought from Ohio and West Virginia.

[1] This would be about 1891 or 1892.

As evidence of the above-mentioned expansion, it may be well to give a brief list, chronologically arranged, of the more important works, founded on these Carboniferous shales between 1890 and 1904 (Ref. 133).

1890. Evansville, Vanderburgh County. The Evansville Pressed Brick Company established here. The clays first used came from Spencer County, and later the shales near Evansville were found adapted to its uses.

1891. Brazil, Clay County. The plant of the Indiana Paving Brick and Block Company is the oldest paving-brick works in the State. The material used is Carboniferous shale.

1892. Veedersburg, Fountain County. Manufacture of vitrified blocks from Carboniferous shale.

1893. Clinton, Vermilion County. Manufacture of vitrified bricks from Carboniferous shale.

1893. Brazil, Clay County. Carboniferous shales and clays for sewer-pipe manufacture, by Chicago Sewer Pipe Company.

1893. Terra Haute, Vigo County. Carboniferous shales selected by Terra Haute Brick and Pipe Company, for making paving brick, hollow brick, and vitrified ware.

1894. Mecca, Park County. Carboniferous shales used by W. C. Dee Clay Manufacturing Company for sewer-pipe manufacture. This, together with a second factory erected in 1894, constitutes the largest clay-working plant of Indiana, and (in 1904 at least) the biggest sewer-pipe factory west of Akron, Ohio.

1895. Brazil, Clay County. Carboniferous shale used by Excelsior Clay Works for hollow blocks.

1895. East Montezuma, Parke County. Carboniferous shale used for common brick by one of the largest brick works in the State.

1895. Brazil, Clay County. McRoy Clay Works began manufacture of vitrified conduits, and now one of the largest producers in United States.

1901. Terra Haute, Vigo County. Hollow block manufacture from Carboniferous clay shale begun by Vigo Clay Company.

1901. Crawfordsville, Montgomery County. Utilization of Knobstone shales by Paston Paving Brick Company.

1902. Brazil, Clay County. Hollow block manufacture from Carboniferous clay-shale begun by Ayer-McCarel Clay Company.

1902. Montezuma, Parke County. Fire brick manufacture from Carboniferous under clay by Standard Fire Brick Company.

1903. New Albany, Floyd County. Use of Knobstone shales for dry pressed brick by Goetz Paving Brick Company.

1904. Evansville, Vanderburg County. Manufacture of dry-pressed brick from Carboniferous shale.

The use of surface clays for common brick has been referred to in passing, but it was stated that little mention is made of them in published accounts of the clay-working industry.

The most important development of these Pleistocene clays has been in Northwestern Indiana. It is not known just when the development of these clays began, but the surface clays have been worked around Hebron, Porter County, since before 1874 (Ref. 133, p. 457).

Around Hobart, Lake County, common brick had been made for a number of years, but in 1887 W. B. Owen began the manufacture of terra-cotta lumber and fireproofing from the Pleistocene clays, and this has developed into one of the most important industries of the State, the Hobart Terra-Cotta Lumber Company. Located within easy reach of Chicago, the products of this district find a ready market there.

Since 1890 hydraulic pressed brick have also been made from these Pleistocene clays at Porter, Porter County.

The Columbia Encaustic Tile Company began operations at Anderson in 1891 using gas for fuel (Ref. 41, p. 233), and a year later roofing tile were being made at Montezuma (Ref. 4, XVII, p. 241).

Although most of the clay-working plants of Indiana are supported by local clays, some raw materials, such as ball clays and kaolins, are shipped into the State for use in the white-ware potteries at Evansville, the electrical-ware factory at Pem, and the sanitary-ware works at Kokomo and Evansville.

Indiana is one of the leading states in the clay-working industry. It ranked seventh in 1907 and supplied 4.32 per cent of the country's output. The importance of the industry is well shown in the following table.

Mention should also be made of the fact that raw clay is produced and shipped from a number of points in the State, some of it being ground before shipment.

VALUE OF CLAY PRODUCTS OF INDIANA FROM 1894 TO 1907.

Year	Common brick	Vitrified paving brick	Front brick	Drain tile	Sewer pipe	Fire-proofing	Hollow brick	Grand total
1894	$1,720,017	$224,473	....	$954,264	$ 1,000	$ 50,000	....	$3,135,569
1895	1,488,370	204,000	$161,336	820,602	42,000	60,000	....	3,117,520
1896	1,207,247	175,670	99,954	475,919	125,839	136,461	....	2,674,325
1897	1,012,547	266,638	94,935	559,524	156,450	121,135	....	2,712,309
1898	1,359,596	264,796	101,935	622,198	134,980	74,629	....	3,331,997
1899	1,727,607	258,471	139,978	839,046	161,935	62,575	....	4,235,354
1900	1,391,873	331,276	172,752	674,602	279,719	116,581	....	3,858,350
1901	1,624,133	320,221	234,775	772,241	253,626	91,081	....	4,406,454
1902	1,710,385	441,495	215,202	807,516	311,223	342,854	$162,172	5,283,733
1903	1,697,190	482,907	232,487	1,014,706	363,212	(a)	219,476	5,694,625
1904	1,630,072	513,209	197,890	1,205,717	294,000	210,800	150,607	5,902,589
1905	1,778,270	474,600	231,353	1,267,691	430,680	393,985	99,404	6,499,573
1906	....	502,509	395,368	1,373,441	486,897	323,015	110,192	7,158,234
1907	1,509,415	548,448	437,796	1,437,135	487,537	304,151	....	6,858,124

Year	Tile not drain	Fire brick	Miscellaneous	Total brick and tile	Red earthen-ware	Stone-ware	Total pottery
1894	$101,855	$22,720	$161,240	$3,135,569	....	....	....
1895	139,463	12,510	177,839	3,106,120	....	$11,400	$ 11,400
1896	175,390	23,350	126,250	2,545,980	$5,400	45,945	128,345
1897	223,750	24,245	55,360	2,514,584	29,725		197,725
1898	247,990	29,766	108,320	2,944,220	6,210	36,532	266,742
1899	328,041	72,350	298,087	3,888,180	4,818	49,788	347,174
1900	343,985	40,976	180,682	3,553,450	4,337	44,207	278,374
1901	478,130	51,526	109,350	3,935,083	6,650	47,121	467,371
1902	579,896	66,725	153,153	4,628,449	4,650	24,130	583,741
1903	463,082	115,526	562,314	5,113,056	9,700	63,400	510,658
1904	(a)	130,216	549,876	5,198,898	4,300	61,090	703,691
1905	(a)	163,728	824,710	5,567,426	5,397	69,065	932,147
1906	(a)	149,354	1,116,293	6,224,541	6,550	66,774	933,693
1907	(a)	160,373	1,003,923	5,988,970	5,075	45,579	869,154

(a) Included under "Miscellaneous."

CHAPTER IV.

IOWA.

THE Iowa brick clays were worked by LeRoy Jackson in Dubuque in the summer of 1837, he having constructed the first brick house in Dubuque in the fall of that year. Mr. Sylvanus Johnson established a brick yard in Iowa City, in 1840, and furnished the brick for the State Capitol there. This building is now in use by the State University. Brick were no doubt made in the river cities by that date also. (Private correspondence.) The Sargeants Bluff Pottery at Sargeants Bluff started in 1838 (Ref. 97, v, p. 225). The Iowa Geological Survey report for 1903 states that potteries have been in operation there from time to time, some of them evidently using the Cretaceous clays, but there were none running in that year. Three years after the Sargeants Bluff Pottery was started, or in 1841, another pottery was in operation at Vernon (Ref. 97, IV, p. 246), and soon after that we read of a number of potteries beginning operations, but nothing is known regarding the character of the clays that they were using. In 1858 there were two in operation at Danville (Ref. 98, p. 207), one at Red Oak in 1864 (Ref. 97, IV, p. 441), and one in West Boone in 1865 (Ref. 97, v, p. 225). The firm of C. Holman & Bros. Brick & Tile Works was established at Sargeants Bluff in 1867, and molded bricks by hand and horse-power until 1879. In that year a "Soft-mud" machine was introduced, and since 1886 stiff-mud machines have been used (Ref. 4, XXVI, p. 117).

In the Iowa Geological Survey for 1870 (Ref. 97, II), potteries were mentioned in operation at Woodbury, Eldora, Fairport and Boonsboro, as well as in the places already mentioned. At the same time cream-colored brick were made at Clermont (Ref. 97, II, p. 326).

Brick yards were started in Wilton, Keosauqua, Cantril and Douds between the years 1890 and 1894 (Ref. 97, IV, pp. 246–7),

94

while in 1892 paving brick were being made at Sargeants Bluff by Holman and by a North Riverside firm which was also making vitrified sewer pipe (Ref. 97, 1, pp. 152–5), all from Cretaceous shales.

By 1902 the clay-working industry had expanded to considerable size, Iowa ranking eighth in the list of producing States. The product included common, pressed and paving brick, fire brick, drain tile, sewer pipe, red earthenware and stoneware.

Burned clay for railroad ballast has been used by some of the Iowa railroads for a number of years, the practice having been followed at least as early as 1892.

The foregoing data are somewhat fragmentary, and evidently do not chronicle all the important events which led up to the present development of the Iowa industry, for at this time a wide range of materials is used obtained from many different geologic formations ranging from the Ordovician to the Pleistocene.

As can be seen from the statistics given below, a variety of clay products is now made in the state, with one important exception, viz., white ware. The miscellaneous column includes ornamental brick, sewer pipe, fireproofing, fire brick and terra cotta, while the pottery production consists mainly of red earthenware and stoneware.

VALUE OF CLAY PRODUCTS OF IOWA FROM 1894 TO 1907.

Year.	Common brick.	Vitrified paving brick.	Front brick.	Drain tile.
1894.	$1,317,473	$376,951	....	$557,312
1895.	1,095,074	243,928	$87,130	290,515
1896.	1,003,624	112,985	47,386	648,906
1897.	850,834	426,056	57,230	372,070
1898.	1,164,247	289,963	54,752	343,265
1899.	1,328,050	225,044	160,890	359,568
1900.	1,386,641	151,286	79,632	377,586
1901.	1,611,040	241,108	88,164	534,935
1902.	1,575,959	232,056	80,711	672,212
1903.	1,355,129	232,510	135,849	1,028,383
1904.	1,440,758	199,528	91,269	1,294,134
1905.	1,366,653	134,802	60,669	1,509,226
1906.	1,118,709	185,990	101,795	1,721,614
1907.	1,085,383	223,193	96,316	2,011,793

VALUE OF CLAY PRODUCTS OF IOWA — *Continued.*

Year.	Hollow brick.	Miscellaneous.	Pottery.	Grand total.
1894...............	....	$27,770	......	$2,379,506
1895...............	....	128,045	$25,600	1,870,292
1896...............	....	88,722	43,035	1,694,402
1897...............	....	76,041	39,016	1,821,247
1898...............	....	264,170	34,425	2,183,022
1899...............	....	130,176	30,080	2,233,808
1900...............	....	259,517	36,489	2,291,251
1901...............	....	236,058	23,290	2,737,825
1902...............	....	237,011	45,387	2,843,336
1903...............	$131,191	154,579	55,762	3,093,403
1904...............	161,658	205,372	68,134	3,460,853
1905...............	137,554	112,859	70,359	3,392,122
1906...............	162,664	120,255	58,000	3,469,027
1907...............	176,854	146,364	18,882	3,728,785

KANSAS.

The earliest record of a clay-working plant in Kansas is the establishment in 1887 of the first "glazed" (probably vitrified) paving-brick plant in the State.[1] This was started at Atchison by T. Beattie. The brick were made of the Coal Measures shale, and have been used on pavements in various cities in Kansas and surrounding States (Ref. 109, p. 55). It is highly probable that both brick and pottery were made before this, but we have no record of them. The clay industry by 1893 had grown to be of great importance in the State, and plants were making paving brick in Leavenworth, Atchison, Topeka, Osage City, Pittsburg and Kansas City (formerly Wyandot). In the same year (1893) common brick were being manufactured practically all over the State, particularly in the eastern part, although this product antedated the paving brick. Pressed brick were being made in 1893 at Fort Scott, Leavenworth, Junction City, Wichita, and Kansas City (Ref. 109, p. 55). Clays for pottery manufacture are not widely distributed, as far as known, and the competition of established potteries in other States has hindered the development of the industry in Kansas. In 1893 the most important potteries were at Fort Scott and Geneseo, both making brown ware (Ref.

---

[1] The first street-paving brick used in the United States were made at Charleston, W. Va., in 1872.

109, p. 57). By the year 1898 Kansas City industries were very prosperous especially in the line of paving brick, the plants at Pittsburg, Coffeyville and Columbus doing a large business, and also manufacturing some drain tile (Ref. 110, p. 61). In 1899 new plants were erected at Cherryvale, Iola and Lawrence (Ref. 111).

One item of interest in 1900 was the burning of clay for railroad ballast, and along the Union Pacific Railroad this became an important material. In 1901 a sewer-pipe plant was established at Pittsburg, and brick plants started at Chanute and Neodesha (Ref. 112, pp. 60 and 61), and the production of roofing tile from Carboniferous shales was started at Coffeyville, in 1903. The manufacture of terra cotta from Missouri and Kansas clays was begun in Kansas City as late as 1906 by the Western Terra Cotta Company, thus adding another kind of clay product to those already made here, and which include common and pressed brick, paving brick, sewer pipe and hollow tile. The value of the different classes of products since 1894 is given below. It is not possible to give the production of each kind of product separately, partly because the output has not been continuous, and partly to prevent disclosing individual statistics. The miscellaneous column, therefore, includes sewer pipe since 1900; fire brick since 1894; fireproofing, hollow brick and roofing tile in occasional years, and stoneware in nearly all years.

VALUE OF CLAY PRODUCTS OF KANSAS FROM 1894 TO 1907.

Year.	Common brick.	Vitrified paving brick.	Front brick.	Drain tile.	Miscellaneous.	Total.
1894	$141,042	$57,310	....	$8,048	$12,175	$218,575
1895	121,892	62,190	$25,775	4,090	32,700	246,647
1896	110,254	125,293	9,440	4,400	10,700	260,087
1897	103,081	127,600	14,887	5,450	5,500	256,518
1898	221,481	200,022	13,209	4,172	6,091	444,975
1899	408,196	278,164	106,353	6,550	40,504	839,767
1900	482,952	417,924	57,764	6,950	51,160	1,016,750
1901	555,928	312,994	50,340	3,330	58,428	981,020
1902	606,726	285,156	229,990	6,625	93,091	1,221,588
1903	706,010	430,744	118,561	24,265	207,424	1,487,004
1904	890,474	621,424	129,576	10,883	191,273	1,843,630
1905	917,084	580,695	180,201	13,212	215,168	1,906,360
1906	1,376,552	658,392	187,577	19,694	190,156	2,432,371
1907	1,189,263	727,979	236,876	15,320	200,620	2,370,058

KENTUCKY.

Very little has been written concerning Kentucky's clay-working industries, even the State histories giving little attention to the subject. The first establishment noted is that of the Lewis Pottery Company, which was started in Louisville in 1829. It, however, only continued until 1836 [1] when Mr. Clews induced the owners to move to Troy, Ind. (Ref. 8, p. 157). Again in 1840, another pottery was established, by a Mr. Hancock, in Louisville (Ref. 8, p. 156). In the Survey Report for 1856 a Calloway County clay is said to have been used by Captain Bonner in the county for making stoneware (Ref. 61, p. 124). This material was possibly one of the Tertiary clays of the Jackson Purchase area, some of which have since become important for use in pottery and tile manufacture. Of the fire clays in the eastern part of the State, those in Lewis County are said to have been worked as early as 1871, for fire-brick manufacture in Cincinnati. One of Kentucky's oldest important yards is the Hydraulic-Press Brick Company's plant at Louisville. This was established in 1875 (Ref. 4, XVIII, p. 541), and in the same year a third pottery was established in Louisville. It is not known just when the development of the Carboniferous clays began, although attention must have been attracted to them for making fire brick to be used in the early iron furnaces of that district. In 1884, however, mention is made of a fire clay at Amanda, used at Bellefont Furnace (Ref. 62, p. 141), while in 1886 the Ashland Fire Brick Company was in operation at Ashland using local clay. (Private communication.) Pottery works were started at Paducah in 1886, but the clays employed came from Grand Chain, Ill.; Boaz, Ky.; and Round Knob, Ill., and for the past several years the entire supply of raw material has been shipped from the last-named point. In 1887 the Cambridge Tile Manufacturing Company began the manufacture of wall tile in Covington, the only plant of the kind in the State (Ref. 41, p. 232). The clays in the last six or seven years have been obtained in part from Kentucky, although some were shipped in from Whitlock, Tenn., South Carolina, and Florida. By the year 1888, potteries making brown

---

[1] From another source mentioned under Indiana the date is given as 1834.

jars and jugs were in operation at Pottertown, Bell City, Lynn-
ville, Paducah, Columbus, and Hickman, but they were small
plants, built to supply a local trade (Ref. 63, p. 96), all located in
the Jackson Purchase region, and probably established on Tertiary and Cretaceous clays.

The most important fire clay area which has been opened up in
Kentucky is the flint clay district of northeastern Kentucky extending through Greenup, Carter, Rowan, and Elliott counties. The
clay which occurs in the Pottsville formation is regarded as the
equivalent of the famous Sciotoville clay of Ohio. Olive Hill is
the most important locality in this region which deserves more than
passing mention.

It was some time prior to 1883 that a large tract of land in this
district was purchased by the Tygart Valley Iron Company[1] who
proposed to erect furnaces and make pig iron from the local deposits of ore. This project was abandoned and the land divided into
three parts, each of the three members of the iron company taking
one portion. That portion taken by Sebastian Eifort is now owned
and operated by the Olive Hill Fire Brick Company, the pioneer
manufacturers in this district. The fire clay was discovered by
Mr. Eifort, who in 1883 began shipping it to Portsmouth and
Ironton, Ohio; Ashland, Ky.; and Pittsburg, Pa., where it was
used for making fire brick.

Mr. Eifort finally sold the land to the Olive Hill Fire-Brick
Company which in 1895 erected its plant at Olive Hill. The
company was originally formed by Messrs A. E. and O. Hitchins,
G. H. Parks, and J. J. Hoblitzell, and it is at present controlled
by descendants of these first owners. The clay is of high refractoriness and some of the flinty phase shows an extraordinarily high
alumina content. In 1897 the company made its first blast-furnace
lining for the Illinois Steel Company at Joliet, which lining was
in use for a period of more than six years. The factory has a
daily capacity of 60,000 brick, and has in use all over the United
States between 45 and 50 blast-furnace linings.

Some few years after the Olive Hill Fire-Brick Company started,

[1] The data on this district have been kindly supplied by E. S. Hitchins of the
Olive Hill Fire Brick Company.

a Mr. K. B. Grahn, who was one of the former owners of the Tygart Valley Iron Company, organized the Louisville Fire-Brick Company with its plant located at Louisville, Ky. The clay for this plant is mined a few miles east of Olive Hill.

The next operation to be started in Carter County was that of the Ironton Fire-Brick Company, which erected a factory at Enterprise, Ky., about eight miles west of Olive Hill. This company has since been absorbed by the Ashland Fire-Brick Company.

In 1901 the Harbison Walker Refractories Company erected a large plant at Olive Hill on property adjoining that of the Olive Hill Fire-Brick Company. This plant, with a daily capacity of 40,000 brick, has been in operation since the time it started. At about the same time, or possibly a little earlier, the plant of the Kentucky Fire-Brick Company was built at Soldier about nine miles west of Olive Hill, and this also is still running, with a capacity of about 15,000 brick per day.

Common-brick yards are scattered all over the State, but most of these are founded on the alluvial surface clays.

The more extensive formations, such as the Ordovician, Silurian, Devonian and Lower Carboniferous shales have been little developed, although they contain clays of promise (Ref. 121, p. 122). In central Kentucky, the Irvine formation (Tertiary) has, however, been utilized for some years (exact number not definitely known) for making pottery (Ref. 122).

In 1902 the Newport Pressed Brick and Stone Company began the use of shale at its works and made fire brick (private correspondence).

At the present time potteries are in operation in western Kentucky, at Paducah, Potterstown, Rock, Tompkinsville and Wickliffe (136), a continuation of the industry established for many years in the Jackson Purchase region.

The statistics of production since 1894 are given below, and from these it will be seen that common brick and fire brick are important products. The refractory industry is so well developed because of the presence of high grade fire clays. Under miscellaneous, the most important wares included are vitrified paving brick, sewer pipe, wall tile, and roofing tile (Cloverport, Ky.).

VALUE OF CLAY PRODUCTS OF KENTUCKY FROM 1894 TO 1907.

Year.	Common brick.	Front brick.	Drain tile.	Fire brick.	Miscellaneous.
1894	$418,886	....	$31,400	$87,800	$221,589
1895	455,927	$14,240	17,332	126,539	195,040
1896	317,749	15,550	24,750	168,210	208,800
1897	355,313	19,390	28,065	157,499	120,671
1898	422,458	27,004	19,533	202,077	227,632
1899	546,535	20,275	36,132	334,630	316,251
1900	608,334	21,098	26,727	393,220	300,498
1901	621,756	16,535	29,498	377,741	329,316
1902	659,612	47,027	26,039	605,448	397,874
1903	689,403	53,769	20,621	873,294	414,045
1904	796,074	20,571	26,564	680,084	506,371
1905	862,330	128,777	28,865	739,059	490,236
1906	881,879	109,771	27,359	898,527	507,678
1907	932,469	86,568	32,723	940,415	452,568

Year.	Total brick and tile.	Red earthenware.	Stoneware.	Total pottery.	Grand total.
1894	$759,675	....	....	....	$759,675
1895	809,078	....	$30,120	....	839,198
1896	735,059	$9,000	86,750	$95,750	829,684
1897	680,938	119,930		125,430	806,368
1898	898,704	13,165	76,521	89,686	1,000,940
1899	1,253,823	10,290	94,315	104,605	1,358,428
1900	1,349,827	21,202	110,295	131,497	1,481,324
1901	1,374,846	19,929	115,768	135,697	1,514,543
1902	1,736,000	16,221	120,822	137,043	1,873,043
1903	2,051,132	19,207	120,620	139,827	2,190,959
1904	1,929,664	20,171	137,442	157,613	2,087,277
1905	2,249,267	22,674	134,409	157,083	2,406,350
1906	2,425,214	26,637	140,572	167,209	2,592,423
1907	2,444,743	27,546	139,075	166,621	2,611,364

LOUISIANA.

The only items obtainable regarding this State were that at St. Tammany there are evidences of ante-bellum brick yards (Ref. 99, p. 209) and that in 1895 brick yards were in operation in the Florida parishes of eastern Louisiana.

As pointed out elsewhere, brick were made in large numbers outside the State, notably in Florida and Mississippi, and shipped into New Orleans about 1850–1860, and it is probable that before the war very little clay industry was carried on. Even now little is manufactured besides common brick and some earthenware.

No account of the history of clay working in Louisiana would be complete, however, without some mention of the Newcomb Pottery at New Orleans, an institution which was started as an experiment in the practical field of applied art in 1895. As Prof. Woodward, the director, states, "industrial conditions in the far South did not give much encouragement for the study of art as a profession, owing to the lack of manufacturers who might call for trained designers, etc. To give an object lesson in the value of art training, we introduced pottery manufacture " . . . "and we now have a business of some magnitude." The school is equipped with machinery, work rooms, and studios. The ware, which is a warm gray in color, is made from clay obtained from Biloxi, Miss., and Iuka, Miss., together with some kaolin from Georgia. So successful has this school been, that the ware is known throughout the country.

The statistics of production since 1894 are given below. The production consists mainly of common brick, while under " miscellaneous " there is included a scattering of front brick, vitrified paving brick, ornamental brick, drain tile, architectural terra cotta, stove lining, fire brick, tile other than drain, stoneware and red earthenware.

VALUE OF CLAY PRODUCTS OF LOUISIANA FROM 1894 TO 1907.

Year.	Common brick.	Miscellaneous.	Total.
1894............	$442,862	$74,400	$517,262
1895............	378,418	37,300	415,718
1896............	370,487	31,925	402,412
1897............	322,328	48,582	370,910
1898............	457,018	60,041	517,059
1899............	515,577	39,152	554,729
1900............	463,613	44,081	507,694
1901............	560,375	55,328	615,703
1902............	597,833	44,591	642,424
1903............	689,187	124,200	813,387
1904............	914,585	96,893	1,011,478
1905............	738,220	82,889	821,109
1906............	811,185	89,512	900,697
1907............	839,236	89,334	928,570

MAINE.

Maine was never an important clay-working State and even up
to the present time the chief clay products manufactured are
common brick, these being molded mainly from the marine clays
along the coast and the banks of the principal rivers. Owing to
this fact there are few published data relating to the history of its
clay-working industry.

The earliest information we have of the industry in the State
is for the year 1675 or previous to this date, when brick were made
on the Sabestacook River (Ref. 1, p. 221). The earlier settlers
noticed the clay banks bordering the rivers and probably soon after
locating began utilizing the material. In 1760 land was granted
in Portland to Augustine John for a brick yard (Ref. 2, 1, p. 244),
and in 1789 and 1790 brick were imported from Piscataqua, but
whether made in Maine or New Hampshire could not be ascertained
(Ref. 1, p. 222). In 1796 common brick were made by a Mr.
Gillet in Hallowell (Ref. 2, IV, p. 355), and several yards were
already in operation (Ref. 3, p. 57) in Castine by 1814. The first
mention of a yard in Brewer is that of a Mr. Holyoke, begun in
1830 (Ref. 4, 31, 1899, p. 16), but in 1838 there were in the same
place 8 yards making 3,000,000 brick per year of which 100,000
were made by machines (Ref. 5, 11, p. 26). In 1832 Mr. Bates
made brick at Leeds Junction (Ref. 4, 26, p. 106), and in 1838
brick making was going on in Bangor and Prospect (Ref. 5, 11,
26, 36).

Farnham and Hopkins established a yard in New Castle in 1845
(Ref. 4, 26, p. 106), and in 1846, the Portland Stoneware Company, now one of the largest clay-working establishments in Maine,
was started (Ref. 6, 464). This is the first stoneware plant noted
in the clay-working industry of Maine, but most, if not all, of its
clay is obtained from New Jersey and from Long Island, N. Y.
In the United States Census for 1860 there are reported 111 brick
yards in Maine and 16 potteries. In 1873 additional yards were
established in New Castle (Ref. 4, 26, p. 106) and in Wales. In
the latter place machines built of wood were used until 1877 when

iron machines were installed and the yard now has a number of good machines (Ref. 4, 26, pp. 106–7). In 1875 Mr. J. P. Norton erected a brick yard in Waterville and in 1883 built one in York (Ref. 4, 19, 1893, 491).

Sewer pipe were first manufactured in Maine by the Portland Stoneware Company in 1872 (?) but not from Maine clays. The production of these has been discontinued.

Since then there appear to have been few developments, except the starting of some new yards, while many of the old ones have ceased operations. From the statistics presented in the following table it appears that clay working in Maine is on the decline, the value of the products in 1907 being only about two-thirds of that of 1896. There has been a small but continuous production of fire brick, but these are not made from Maine clays, and there has been a scattering production of ornamental brick, drain tile, fire-proofing, hollow brick, and red earthenware.

VALUE OF CLAY PRODUCTS OF MAINE FROM 1894 TO 1907.

Year.	Common brick.	Miscellaneous.	Total.
1894	$401,982	$429,800	$831,782
1895	403,217	333,887	737,104
1896	375,353	619,378	994,731
1897	273,929	526,810	800,739
1898	309,488	290,541	600,029
1899	399,110	263,575	662,685
1900	353,731	371,203	724,934
1901	407,354	327,324	734,678
1902	377,059	279,589	656,648
1903	407,214	269,968	677,182
1904	326,240	232,121	558,361
1905	341,466	277,828	619,294
1906	383,011	297,359	680,370
1907	394,003	264,900	658,913

MARYLAND.

In a work entitled " A Relation of Maryland," published in
1635, we find the following quaint statement: " There is found
good loame whereof we have made as good brick as any in England
. . . also good clay for pots and tyles." (Ref. 47, p. 47.)
Brick making was undoubtedly an important industry throughout
this period, and much corroborative evidence has been found in the
early records regarding this subject.   In the Maryland archives
for 1637–8 it is reported that a brick maker sat in the Assembly,
and a letter from S. Cornwalleys (Calvert Papers I, p. 174) to Lord
Baltimore in 1638 states that he is building a house with cellar and
chimney of brick (Ref. 47, p. 48).

In the Provincial court records 1649–1657, we read of a brickmaker's agreement to make " 36,000 Good Sound well Burned
Bricks in consideration of 300 acres of land on the Patuxent River."
(Ref. 47, p. 48.) Dr. Wm. B. Clark, State Geologist (Ref. 47, p. 48),
says that the popular belief that large numbers of common brick
were imported from England in the early days seems unfounded,
that a careful search of ancient records and bills of lading has
failed to disclose a single authentic case of importation, and that
the use of the word " English " brick referred probably to the
prevailing shape of the brick rather than to the locality from
which it came (Ref. 47, p. 48).   There seems however to
be a difference of opinion on this point, as indicated by the
following:

Bishop relates (Ref. 1, 1, p. 229) that " Charles Carrol, an original proprietor
of lands now covered by the city, in 1754 erected, ' at the Mount,' buildings
of bricks imported for the purpose. Two years before it had but four brick
houses, and only twenty-five in all, the others very primitive in style. A
pottery was erected in the town ten years after, by John Brown, from New
Jersey, who had learned the business at Wilmington, Del. The town, at that
date, contained about fifty houses. Thirty-two years after, it contained one
thousand nine hundred, and was the fourth in the Union, having more than half
the number of New York. This unparalleled increase in building, the ele-
gance of the buildings at the capital, Annapolis, and of Fredericktown, which
was chiefly built of brick and stone, must have made brick making a considerable manufacture."

In 1829 it is said that good enough fire brick were made to stop importation (Ref. 1, II, p. 340), assuming that importations were going on at that period. Baltimore no doubt had its quota of brick yards, supported by the abundant deposits of brick loams existing there, and which at the present day, and indeed for a great many years, have formed the basis of an important industry.

The Mt. Savage fire clay, holding such a good reputation at the present time, was discovered in 1837 and used in lining blast furnaces in operation at Mt. Savage by the Maryland and New York Coal and Iron Company. Many of the brick were also shipped to Ohio in the fifties and sixties. In 1841 the Union Mining Company was organized and has been in continuous operation since then as one of the largest fire-brick concerns in the country (Ref. 48, p. 479), being followed at a later date by the Savage Mountain Fire-Brick Works at Frostburg. One of the early dry-press brick machines was in operation in Baltimore in 1846. It had a plunger exerting 200 tons pressure and turned out 30,000 brick in 12 hours (Ref. 45, II, p. 28). In the same year Mr. E. Bennett left his pottery in Pittsburg, Pa., and settled in Baltimore, erecting there what is said to have been the first pottery south of the Mason-Dixon line (Ref. 6, p. 43). Sewer pipe were being made near Baltimore in 1865 by Linton and Rittenhouse, from local clays, and in 1868 the Baltimore Retort and Fire Clay Company began the manufacture of sewer pipe at their works (McClave), also using the local Mesozoic clays in part. Only the former continued the production of these to recent date, and it is surprising to have seen such a small industry exist in a region unsuited to it.

In 1876 Mr. Bennett was making roofing tile at his Baltimore works (private communication). The large pottery of D. F. Haynes & Son was established in Baltimore in 1881 first making majolica ware, then Avalon, in 1885 Parian, and later white ware (Ref. 6, p. 280), but the materials used came almost entirely from other States.

Although small brick yards, scattered over the State and working surface clays, have been in operation for a considerable, but unknown period, the establishment of some of the larger ones is very recent, considering the early date of settlement of the State. Thus the Queen City Brick and Tile Company of Cumberland, using Devonian shales, did not begin operations until 1888, but this is not surprising as the use of shale was not feasible until sufficiently strong machinery for handling it had been made.

In 1896 one of the few enamelled brick plants in the country was established at Mt. Savage by A. Ramsay (Ref. 48, p. 481), the product being made from the Carboniferous fire clays. One item of interest was the consolidation in 1899 of fourteen common-brick yards around Baltimore under the name of the Baltimore Brick Company, which still continues.

A terra-cotta works, making also some roofing tile, was established at Baltimore before 1900, and at present terra-cotta clay is shipped from Maryland to Pennsylvania.

Since 1900 there have been practically no new developments in the State.

The detailed figures of production since 1894 are given below.

VALUE OF CLAY PRODUCTS OF MARYLAND FROM 1894 TO 1907.

Year.	Common brick.	Front brick.	Drain tile.	Stove lining.	Fire brick.	Miscellaneous.[1]	Total.
1894	$974,669	....	$3,050	....	$164,848	$1,142,567	$1,344,865
1895	743,023	$35,229	3,079	....	232,270	1,013,601	1,066,987
1896	987,706	97,426	1,945	....	150,655	1,237,723	1,450,055
1897	702,957	92,344	25,524	....	141,650	962,475	1,305,282
1898	716,674	87,304	1,649	....	77,672	883,299	1,542,853
1899	682,247	157,918	3,673	$32,457	325,812	1,202,107	1,679,641
1900	724,013	60,729	2,363	36,049	321,666	1,144,820	1,711,856
1901	676,708	76,792	2,402	40,237	342,055	1,138,194	1,605,655
1902	879,995	45,375	2,105	21,540	277,290	1,226,305	1,905,362
1903	976,969	40,479	1,355	....	272,295	1,291,098	1,908,821
1904	1,048,850	37,537	2,848	....	235,136	1,324,371	1,872,059
1905	1,423,663	24,118	4,703	32,890	224,667	1,710,041	2,249,367
1906	1,267,771	31,968	3,315	32,200	266,980	1,602,234	2,136,539
1907	1,026,922	19,854	3,190	31,048	242,312	1,333,326	1,886,362

[1] Includes vitrified brick, ornamental brick, and tile (not drain) for all years, as well as a scattered production of sewer pipe, architectural terra cotta, red earthenware, yellow ware, C. C. ware, white granite ware, china, and sanitary ware.

MASSACHUSETTS.

Previous to the year 1629 all of the brick used in Massachusetts and throughout New England were imported, but in 1629 importations ceased (Ref. 4, XXXIII, p. 266) and the first brick kiln in New England was started at Salem (Ref. 1, p. 217). The records show a grant of marsh land near Boston, in 1636, to a Mr. Mount for brickmaking, and the first brick house in Boston was erected in 1638 (Ref. 4, XXXIII, p. 266). That the industry continued is shown by the fact that in 1643 the watch house at Plymouth was built of brick (Ref. 4, XXXIII, p. 266). Land in Malden was sold in 1651 to a brickmaker named Johnson (Ref. 16, p. 433) whose operations were evidently extensive, because in 1669 laws were passed to keep the clay pits from encroaching on the highways (Ref. 16, p. 433).

In 1656 there was a yard at North Hampton (Ref. 17, p. 37), and in 1660 brick were made in Cambridge (Ref. 4, XXVI, p. 106).

Boston, about 1657, is described as having "large and spacious houses, some fairly set forth with brick, tile, slate and stone . . ." In 1667 the Massachusetts court appointed a committee to frame a law to regulate the size and manufacture of bricks (Ref. 1, I, p. 220).

Haverhill's brick industry began in 1700 when Hannah Dunston's husband was guarded by soldiers as he carried clay from the pit to the yard (Ref. 18).

Probably the first pottery established in New England was one at Salem which began operations in 1641 (Ref. 15, p. 133), and another pottery was established in 1760 at Germantown, now a suburb of Quincy (Ref. 8, p. 90), through the exertions of J. C. Palmer and R. Cranch, two progressive land owners, who were instrumental in establishing manufacturing enterprises of various kinds at that point.

Previous to 1765 A. Hews started the manufacture of terracotta utensils in Weston, bringing the clay first from Watertown and later from Cambridge (Ref. 8, p. 88), but in 1870 the plant was moved to North Cambridge, where it has continued to the present day, and is now operated under the name of A. H. Hews & Co. (Ref. 8, p. 89). *The Boston Evening Post* of 1769 had an advertisement of a Boston pottery (Ref. 8, p. 101), which indicated the establishment of a china works there, but it is doubtful if true porcelain was to be manufactured. Brick were being made at Andover in 1793 by Mr. Mann (Ref. 19, p. 31), and by 1811 there were three yards in Beverly (Ref. 20, p. 202). Berkshire County in 1829 had a large output of brick (Ref. 21, p. 197), and potteries had been in operation in Lee and Williamson for many years (Ref. 21, p. 587). One of the largest brickyards in the region was established in 1832 at Cambridge, and another began in 1845 (Ref. 4, XXVI, p. 106). The present brickyard at West Barnstable, the only yard on Cape Cod, was established about 1845 (Ref. 136, p. 441).

With the growth of the towns the brick industry naturally assumed prominence, so that in 1846 one yard in Boston was making 100,000 brick a day with 20 machines (Ref. 22, II, p. 359), and in 1847 a Charlestown yard was turning out 15 to 20 million brick a year (Ref. 22, III, p. 145). Frederick Hancock in the year 1858 started a pottery in Worcester (Ref. 8, p. 157), which he operated until 1877, when he sold his interest and returned to Bennington, where he had previously been in the same business.

The New England Pottery was established in Boston by F. Meagher in 1854 and made yellow and Rockingham ware, drawing its supply of clay from various parts of New England (Ref. 8, p. 245), but the product was later changed to white ware, necessitating the importation of clays from other states or countries.

In 1860 the Census figures show 70 brickyards and 13 potteries in Massachusetts. About this time several more yards were started around Cambridge, the Bay State Company in 1863, and in 1869 the New England Brick Company (Ref. 4, pp. 106–107). The latter after a few changes in 1884 set up the first dryer in Cambridge (Ref. 4, pp. 106–107).

In the year 1866 A. W. Robertson ran a small plant in Chelsea, Mass., for the manufacture of brown earthenware such as was common in Great Britain, and also lava ware like the German goods.

This was followed by the production of flower pots, filters, etc. Mr. Robertson took his brother into partnership in 1868, and his father in 1872, at which time the works was enlarged and named the Chelsea Keramic Art Works. A red bisque ware, in imitation of antique Grecian terra cotta and Pompeiian bronzes, was made quite extensively. In 1877 the Chelsea faience was developed. After considerable labor they were successful not only in producing the Chinese ox-blood color but also good imitations of Japanese and Chinese crackle ware, which has not been duplicated on a commercial scale by any others in this country. Owing to lack of funds the plant was closed in 1888, but it was reopened in 1891 under the name of the Chelsea (U. S.) Pottery Company, and the works moved to Dedham. The products of this works rank high among American Art Pottery (Refs. 8, pp. 260–261, Ref. 154, October, 1908, and Ref. 156, April, 1902).

Sewer pipe were made by Goodrich of Boston in 1877 (Ref. 7), and the Low Art Tile Works were established in Chelsea in 1879 (Ref. 6, p. 356), thus adding new products to the list of those already made in the State. The Low Company continued in business for a number of years. Porous terra cotta was manufactured in Boston by the New England Terra Cotta Company in 1885, but in 1893 the firm name was changed to the Boston Fireproofing Company (Ref. 4, XIX, p. 265).

Pressed and ornamental brick manufacture was begun at Boston in 1888 by the Philadelphia and Boston Face Brick Company, using red burning clays from Maine and Massachusetts, but bringing buff and cream burning clays from New Jersey.

In 1897 the Grueby Faience Company was organized in Boston (Ref. 6, p. 263), but is dependent upon clays obtained outside of New England. This is one of the well-known art potteries, and has devoted considerable attention to the development of matte

VALUE OF CLAY PRODUCTS OF MASSACHUSETTS FROM 1894 TO 1907.

Year.	Common brick.	Stove lining.	Fire brick.	Miscellaneous brick and tile.[1]	Red earthenware.	Stoneware.	Miscellaneous pottery.	Total pottery.	Grand total.
1894	$1,648,065		$93,825	$598,044					$2,339,934
1895	1,443,677		187,710	599,203		$1,800		$1,800	2,321,590
1896	1,601,537		131,950	323,144	$147,923	11,270	$47,150	206,343	2,264,974
1897	1,457,683		184,665	307,709	$186,515		42,829	229,344	2,179,396
1898	1,057,806		175,180	301,519	160,078	22,746	59,441	242,265	1,809,070
1899	1,256,767	$143,547	22,792	464,571	163,431	35,435	95,167	294,033	2,181,710
1900	1,123,586	144,044	69,400	742,653	154,704	22,198	61,672	238,574	1,833,101
1901	1,060,493	135,570	57,945	335,461	122,704	22,291	136,373	281,368	1,879,837
1902	1,529,671	133,752	54,342	357,447	123,115	26,902	75,197	225,304	2,375,667
1903	1,236,103		200,225	371,521	111,542	26,840	162,454	300,836	2,108,685
1904	1,012,226			428,517	133,594	21,386	133,335	288,315	1,729,058
1905	1,264,787	173,151	68,180	245,498	185,074	23,876	89,891	298,841	2,050,457
1906	1,415,864	186,815	57,940	234,580	171,160	18,210	88,164	277,534	2,172,733
1907	1,294,918	206,042	74,115	251,001	166,978	17,693	118,073	302,744	2,128,820

[1] Under miscellaneous brick and tile are included a steady production of front and ornamental brick, architectural terra cotta, and fireproofing, as well as occasional outputs of sewer pipe, and drain tile. The miscellaneous pottery includes a continuous output of C. C. ware and white granite, together with an occasional production of china, yellow ware, and electrical porcelain.

glazed wares of green and other colors.   It also produces architectural faience.

A more recent industry started in 1905 is that at Marblehead, Massachusetts, producing decorative faience thrown and glazed at low temperatures, but made only in part from Massachusetts clay.

In 1900 many of the brick plants of Massachusetts, as well as some in New Hampshire, New York, and Maine, were combined to form the New England Brick Company, which was reorganized in December, 1900.   In Massachusetts it includes yards located at Cambridge, Glenwood, Belmont, Bridgewater, Middleboro, Taunton, Still River, Brookfield, and Turner's Falls.   The clay in every case is surface material obtained near the yard.   The company's total capacity (including all plants) is about 180,000,000 brick per annum.

The table on page 111 shows the value of clay products produced annually in Massachusetts from 1894 to 1907.

MICHIGAN.

There seems little doubt that brick were employed as a structural material in this State at a very early date, for a man who came to Detroit in the year 1778 left a memoir in which he stated that there was a brick building in the village at that time.   It belonged to King George III and was used as an arsenal.[1]

A few years later, in 1805, a list of the losses sustained in the fire at Detroit in that year, includes 112,000 brick.   These were bought up by Judge James May and used for constructing a hotel, the Mansion House.

The year following this, or in 1806, brick were used for constructing the church of St. Anne, as shown by the following interesting copy of a contract, kindly supplied the authors by Mr. Burton.

---

[1] Private communication from Hon. C. M. Burton of the Michigan Pioneer and Historical Society.

Propositions de Jacques Lasselle pour la Bâtisse du Mur de L'église Ste Anne.

Pour un millier Briques employé

Pour chaque Millier de Briques livré sur la place de l'église............................ } 80/.

Pr Employer la ditte Brique per millier 32/
2 Jours de nourriture pour le maçon qui employera la ditte Brique .... } à 4/ p. Jour.

P^r chaque millier de Briques.................
3 quarts de chaud livré sur la place....... } à 10/ p. quart.

2 Voyages de Sable pour la d^{te} chaud .... à 4/ p. voyage.
2 Journées de manoeuvre................... à 8/ p. jour.
2 Ditto de Nourriture pour Ditto........... à 3/ p. jour.
façon du mortier d'avance 12/

Pour la charpente des voûtes de chacque ouvertures y compris les cadres de chacque ditte ouvertures .... } 60/ p. chacque ouverture.

Solage

Fournissant la chaud moime, les fondations creusées à mes frais; en un mot, le tout à mes frais, excepté le chavroyage de la Pierre........... } 88/ par chaque Toise de Pierre

Autrement

pour la façon seule dué autrement Solage, les fondations creusées aux frais de la fabrique & la chaud fournie par la ditte fabrique; en un mot tout aux frais de la fabrique; excepté les maçons les manoeuvres ainsi que leurs vivres....... } 58/ par Toise.

Pour les frais deséchafauds; des madriers et planches, cassés et peraus & tout autres frais necessaires à ce sujet.................... } £ 100.

Le tout Exclusivement du Credit en dedans
Detroit 20 Juin 1806.

Messieurs:
Tout est calculé au plus bas prix & supposant même qu'il ne m'arriva aucun accident dans le cours de ces travaux cy.

N.B. — Il est entendu que pour l'une ou l'autre proposition, la pierre sera fournie par la fabrique.

A brickyard on the Raisin River in Monroe County was established between 1840 and 1850 (Ref. 79, p. 423).

Previous to 1848 whatever brick were made in the State were hand-molded, but in that year the Hall soft-mud machine was introduced (Ref. 4, XXIII, p. 258), and in 1858 R. H. Hall began the manufacture of machine-made brick around Detroit.

The first hand-power press to be used at Detroit was introduced by the late Senator John Greusel, and in 1850 a power press known as the Verbalen Machine was introduced, and regarded by many as a great improvement over the Hall press, because it was capable of molding 10,000 brick in a half-day.   It was later used by all of the two or three plants then in existence at Detroit.   Four years later, or in 1854, the Sword press, a steam-power machine, was introduced.   Mr. John Greusel informs us that this was employed for many years, and that the brick made by it were eminently satisfactory to the old contractors, but owing to the flinty hardness as well as the smoothness of the product the machine was discarded when the present common type of soft-mud machine operated by steam power was put on the market.   Since 1850 the industry around Detroit has expanded steadily up to the present time, there being now a number of yards engaged in the making of brick from the Pleistocene clays.

The clay-working industry seems to have become pretty well established by 1860 (Ref. 25), for the Census report of that year states that there were fifty-six brickyards and seven potteries in operation throughout the State.   Sewer pipe were being made in Jackson in 1867 (McClave), and their production from Carboniferous shales has continued up to the present.

In the State Survey Report for 1876 note is made of a brickyard at Coldwater and one at Union City (Ref. 80, p. 88), but both of these have been discontinued.

The making of pottery probably began also at an early date, but accurate records are lacking.   Senator W. Palmer of Detroit writes that his father operated a pottery in that city about 1820, but he doubts if it was a very profitable operation, from the fact that wagons loaded with crocks and pots were taken to the country and the ware exchanged for apples and other farm produce.   Common earthenware has been produced from glacial clays at Ionia since at least 1898 (Ref. 127).   The Carboniferous shales have been quarried at Flushing south of Saginaw for paving-brick manufacture for about the same period of time, while the development of the Coal measures shale and clays began around Bay City about 1904.   Roofing tile are made at Detroit.

Michigan has, however, never assumed great prominence as a producer of clay products, partly because of lack of variety of raw materials, since most of the available clays are adapted only to the production of brick, tile, and common earthenware.

The following table gives the statistics of production since 1894, and indicates the predominating importance of common brick. The miscellaneous column includes a production of vitrified brick and sewer pipe for all years, and a scattered production of ornamental brick, terra-cotta, fireproofing, hollow brick, stove linings and fire brick. The last two are not made of Michigan clays.

VALUE OF CLAY PRODUCTS OF MICHIGAN FROM 1894 TO 1907.

Year.	Common brick.	Front brick.	Drain tile.	Miscellaneous.	Pottery.	Total.
1894	$924,872	....	$741,327	$588,130	....	$2,254,329
1895	267,203	$47,719	200,893	613,380	....	1,129,195
1896	590,095	13,827	225,293	156,040	$20,150	1,005,405
1897	546,638	10,515	165,564	46,853	22,300	791,870
1898	748,339	15,500	146,816	114,607	17,900	1,043,362
1899	933,176	58,920	140,171	121,629	29,741	1,283,997
1900	863,250	48,411	114,747	120,970	34,317	1,181,695
1901	1,095,254	64,031	98,972	238,912	44,865	1,542,034
1902	1,331,752	42,792	96,645	189,753	83,098	1,744,040
1903	1,251,572	19,000	129,028	262,814	48,007	1,710,421
1904	1,116,714	7,500	208,088	338,590	43,621	1,714,513
1905	1,152,505	5,995	205,445	355,801	45,961	1,765,707
1906	1,178,202	14,162	314,098	286,905	51,110	1,844,477
1907	1,181,015	32,116	289,868	283,191	61,574	1,847,764

MINNESOTA.

The clay-working industry seems to have begun in the State in 1844 when brick were being manufactured at Dodge City and drain tile at Kasson (Ref. 94, p. 375).

Common brick were made near Dayton in Wright County in 1855 (Ref. 95, p. 260), and in the following year, 1856, the manufacture of red brick was undertaken at Sunrise (Ref. 95, p. 424). That these represent practically all the firms in operation at that time is seen by the fact that the Census of 1860 gives returns from but two brickyards and one pottery.

In the sixties, several firms began the manufacture of brick, all using, so far as we know, surface clays. The localities and approximate dates of establishment are as follows: La Sueur, 1860; St. Cloud, Stearns County, 1861; Yellow Medicine, 1862; Oshawa, 1862 (using Minnesota River alluvium); Shakopee, 1864; Chaska, 1864; Baldwin, 1865; Blue Earth County, 1867; Shelby, 1867; and Carver County, 1869 (Refs. 94 and 95). Of these the Yellow Medicine yard was in operation only until the Indian outbreak of 1862; some of the others went out of existence later; but works at St. Cloud, Shakopee, and Chaska are still in operation, the industry at Chaska having developed so that by 1884 there were eight yards using machinery and shipping brick to St. Paul and Minneapolis and also into adjoining States (Ref. 95, p. 141).

The most important industry developed in the seventies was the establishment of a pottery at Red Wing. The original owner of the land was Joseph Pohl who manufactured pottery previous to 1870 (Ref. 95, p. 55). In all probability his pottery is the one mentioned in the Census of 1860. In the early seventies the clay (Cretaceous) was being worked by a Mr. Boynton and later by a Mr. Philles at Red Wing for pottery manufacture. From this beginning the Red Wing Stoneware Company was established in 1877. At this date a somewhat successful business of the same kind was being conducted by David Hallem, who sold out to the new company, making for them their first molds and kilns (Ref. 95, p. 55). Of Mr. Hallem, Col. Codvill writes: "Hallem was a very ingenious man, and an enthusiast. He had to learn kiln burning and making by his own experiments. He was really broken down by the Akron folks, who, after he had succeeded in making good ware, put the price of their ware down one half to our dealers who were fools enough to buy, thus destroying his market and their own local enterprise" (Ref. 95, p. 55). The Minnesota Survey Report (Ref. 95, p. 56) says, "The Red Wing Stoneware Company carry on the largest establishment of its kind in the United States, producing in 1885 the enormous amount of more than 1,500,000 gallons besides a large quantity of flower pots." Their glaze came from Albany, N.Y. (Ref. 95, p. 56). This pottery is still in operation, and the company is also starting a plant at Hopkins, which will be supplied by clay from Red Wing, Minn., and Fort Dodge, Ia. Two miles north of Minneapolis brickmaking began in 1871 (Ref. 95, p. 423), and the following year, 1872, yards were established at Fergus Falls in Otter Tail County, and at Henderson, the latter yard using Minnesota River alluvium (Ref. 95, p. 177 and p. 558).

During the next eight years brickmaking was begun in different places as follows: in Clay County, 1874; New London, 1875, using lake clay; Princeton, 1876; Glenwood, 1876; and Alexandria, 1877, using surface clays; Fish Lake, and in McLeod County, in 1878; and in 1879 at Litchfield, Kingston, DeGraff, Montevideo, Beaver Falls, Brainerd, and points in Waldema and Rood counties (Ref. 95). During the period 1875–80 potteries were established at Mankato and New Ulm (Ref. 94), and brickyards were established at Caledonia, Jonesville, Jackson, and New Ulm.

Red-pressed brick were made at Red Wing in 1882, and the Capitol at St. Paul is constructed from them (Refs. 94 and 95, p. 55). At the same time common brick were made extensively at Red Wing, there being five yards in operation (Ref. 95, p. 55).

The pottery at Mankato began the manufacture of drain tile in 1884, while a pottery at Owatonna in the same year was making pottery and fire brick, using, in part at least, a clay from Eldora, Iowa (Ref. 94, p. 402). The Mankato pottery discontinued a number of years ago, and the New Ulm works has been shut down for several years.

A review of the Minnesota geological reports of the early eighties shows that the brickmaking industries were firmly established, and mention is made of yards, in addition to those noted above, as established at Farmington, Dakota County, in Grant and Stevens counties, in Hennepin County, Detroit in Becker County, and at a number of localities in Wabasha County (Ref. 95). Mention is also made of a porcelain clay said to occur in the northern part of Chester and Guilford counties, but it is not worked (Ref. 95, p. 19). At the present time brickyards are in operation at a number of points in the State, but the most important markets being at St. Paul and Minneapolis, the industry is naturally stimulated in that region. These markets also attract bricks from northwestern Wisconsin, especially from the Menomonie district.

Hollow brick are produced in large quantities at Zumbota and Brickton, while the only important pottery is at Red Wing.[1]

The figures of production from 1894 to 1907 are given in the following table. Common brick, front brick, and drain tile are the only ones showing a steady annual production by three or more firms, and hence capable of being listed separately. The miscellaneous column, includes sewer pipe and fireproofing for all years between 1894 and 1907, and a scattered production of vitrified brick, ornamental brick, architectural terra cotta, hollow brick, fire brick, red earthenware and stoneware.

VALUE OF CLAY PRODUCTS OF MINNESOTA FROM 1894 TO 1907.

Year.	Common brick.	Front brick.	Drain tile.	Miscellaneous.	Total.
1894	$473,904	. . . .	$77,300	$703,105	$1,245,309
1895	578,329	$30,635	2,775	488,396	1,100,135
1896	398,872	21,368	5,240	271,221	696,701
1897	366,734	31,750	3,810	479,775	882,069
1898	611,357	22,370	5,170	492,687	1,132,584
1899	754,499	41,230	11,400	411,568	1,218,697
1900	811,457	46,830	2,745	535,665	1,396,697
1901	852,303	55,016	6,739	634,589	1,548,647
1902	1,103,515	75,850	2,219	720,147	1,901,731
1903	982,728	78,930	10,087	455,253	1,527,008
1904	970,247	113,260	11,100	225,400	1,319,907
1905	977,837	85,300	15,770	420,479	1,499,386
1906	986,982	98,170	41,779	476,348	1,603,279
1907	1,045,874	(a)	49,622	594,437	1,689,933

(a) Included under miscellaneous.

MISSISSIPPI.

The first we know of clay-working in Mississippi is the statement by a Mr. Crary (Ref. 67) that in 1850 he was manufacturing dry-pressed brick at Biloxi Bay and supplying them for a large custom-house building at New Orleans. Potteries were in operation at Natchez, Marshall, and Brandon in 1854 (Ref. 100, p. 226), and at Hartford and in Tippah County in 1857 (Ref. 100,

[1] F. F. Grout, private correspondence.

p. 244). No further developments are noted until 1880 when the Tanner Brick-Manufacturing Company was established at Vicksburg. The molding was done by hand, and this method was still employed in 1902 (Ref. 102, p. 240). In 1881 the Taylor yard was established at Jackson (Ref. 102, p. 191), and in 1882 fire brick were made at Holly Springs and used in the Pottery kilns (Ref. 102, p. 209). This industry was based on the white Tertiary clays, which at the present time represent the most important clay resource of the State. Their exploitation has been considerably developed, and they are now worked at a number of other points, for the manufacture of stoneware and fire brick. In 1893 a brickyard was begun at Durant (Ref. 102, p. 196), and one in Armory in 1894 (Ref. 102, p. 213).

A number of yards have been established since 1900, but at the present time brick, tile, and stoneware are the only products made in the State. The pottery of George Ohr at Biloxi produces a ware which has won not a little reputation because of its unique character.

VALUE OF CLAY PRODUCTS OF MISSISSIPPI FROM 1894 TO 1907.

Year.	Common brick.	Miscellaneous.	Total.
1894............	$134,930	$7,770	$142,700
1895............	174,800	19,950	194,750
1896............	208,109	16,700	224,809
1897............	236,650	38,950	275,600
1898............	277,953	43,830	321,783
1899............	510,600	36,141	546,741
1900............	552,061	21,307	573,368
1901............	443,939	12,534	456,473
1902............	496,735	19,469	516,209
1903............	658,491	18,541	677,032
1904............	710,878	64,616	775,494
1905............	782,549	36,348	818,897
1906............	801,420	49,660	851,080
1907............	783,789	62,740	846,529

MISSOURI.

The fire clays of St. Louis County, the potter's clay of Henry County, and the kaolins of the southeastern part of the State, make Missouri of especial interest in the clay-working industry, although, as compared with the eastern clay-working centers, its development has been recent, in fact the greater part of it since 1850. Little is known regarding any operations in the State prior to that time. A stoneware pottery was in operation in Caldwell, Callaway County, in 1827, and was still running in 1891 (Ref. 134, p. 356). In 1840 the Boonville pottery at Boonville, Cooper County, was established (Ref. 134, p. 356), and the *Scientific American* for 1847–8 (Ref. 45, III, p. 145) states that a Mr. Walford in Washington was making granite ware and china.

The source of the material or further history regarding this venture are not known. It seems probable, however, that this is the same occurrence as Barber mentions (Ref. 8, p. 453), namely, that kaolin was discovered in 1848, thirteen miles from Iron Mountain, in the present Washington County, and that Mr. E. H. Shepard built there a pottery in 1851 and made cream-colored ware till 1861 when the war broke out and the plant was abandoned. This is the earliest record of the kaolin industry in the State.

It is said that the fire-brick industry in St. Louis began about 1846 when a small plant was erected on the Gravois road near Meramec Street, but no data regarding this plant are obtainable (Ref. 134, p. 288). The oldest of the present plants in St. Louis is the Evens and Howard, which was established by Richard Howe in 1855. In the same year, 1855, a Mr. Hamilton started making fire brick. He was succeeded by James Green who organized and became president of the Laclede Fire Brick Company (Ref. 134, p. 289). These factories, as well as all other fire-brick concerns in operation in and around St. Louis, depend for their material on a fire clay of the Lower Coal measures known as the Cheltenham seam.

The Christy Fire Clay Mine of St. Louis, which is such an important producer of glass-pot clay at the present time, was opened in 1857. The deposit is said to have been discovered by an English laborer who, while boring a well near the lot now numbered 4373 Morganford Road, penetrated some clay which to him appeared to resemble the famous Stourbridge fire clay of England. It was brought to the attention of Mr. W. T. Christy, Sr., who had it tested in a glass-pot works of Philadelphia. The tests proved satisfactory, and he began shipping crude pot clay.[1] With this establishment of the fire-clay industry, there came simultaneously the mining of the first kaolin in Bollinger County in 1857, by Mr. Dallas who was running a pottery, later known as the Brockman works, at Cincinnati, Ohio. He mined this clay and shipped it to his pottery for five years (Ref. 134, p. 173). Another pit five miles east of Beesville was shipping kaolin to St. Louis potteries in 1862.

In 1863 the firm of Mathieson & Hegeler, who operate a large zinc smelter at La Salle, Ill., began mining the Cheltenham clay of St. Louis for making zinc retorts, and even to this day the clay is much used for that purpose. Probably the first roofing tile made in the State were produced by the Mitchell Clay Company of St. Louis in 1866. After five years' effort the management found the enterprise was ahead of the times, stopped the manufacture of roofing tile and began making fire brick instead. The Parker-Russell Mining and Manufacturing Company, at present one of the important manufacturers of refractory ware in St. Louis, began mining clay in 1866. As early as 1820 James Russell was mining coal on the property, and for many years his mine was one of the large coal mines of the district. Experiments were made on the clay in 1866, and in 1869 a plant was erected. In 1887 the mining of coal was discontinued entirely (private communication) (Ref. 134, pp. 254 and 292).

In the seventies development was being carried on along all lines. A number of new pits were opened up in the southeastern kaolin district. At Lutesville in Bollinger County several shafts were sunk into the kaolin beds in 1872 to test them, but were not reopened till 1886. The citizens of Glen Allen, Bollinger County, also began active prospecting in 1872, opening up fifty pits and shipping clay to Cincinnati, East Liverpool, and Eastern markets.

[1] L. Parker, private correspondence.

Proper care was, however, not exercised in the sorting of the kaolins, and the industry suffered accordingly. This was felt as early as 1874, and although in 1884, five hundred tons a year were sent out, the production has steadily diminished (Ref. 134, p. 174).

The kaolin pits near Jackson, Cape Girardeau County, were the next to be opened, being first worked in 1874, both at Jackson and at the English clay pits, two miles from Jackson. The latter pits were at that time leased by the Cincinnati Pottery Company (Ref. 134, p. 169). The Brown pit north of Jackson was opened in 1877, but is now exhausted (Ref. 134, p. 170).

The mining of flint clays in the State, so far as we know, began in 1871 at High Hill, Montgomery County, when the Big Miller pit was opened (Ref. 134, p. 218). In 1872, the Rolla, Phelps County, flint clay deposits were discovered while prospecting for iron, but these were not opened till 1883 when the Kelly pit was started (Ref. 134, p. 233). Extensive shipments have been made of flint clay from Crawford County since 1879, and in 1898 it was one of the largest producers in the State (Ref. 134, p. 227). The first pit was at Leasburg, leased by George McClintick, and some of the clay was shipped as far east as Pittsburg, Pa. (Ref. 134, p. 229).

But one new clay mine was opened during the seventies in St. Louis, that of George Jamieson in 1878, known as the Coffin Mine (Ref. 134, p. 261).

During this period the foundation for the paving-brick industry in the country was established. In the early seventies George Sattler was investigating various clay deposits in north St. Louis, and in 1873, while operating a coal seam near Chain of Rocks, found a good clay which he shipped to the St. Louis Zinc Works for testing. It proved unsatisfactory. Soon after a well dug near by disclosed a good fire clay with some beds of glass-pot clay. The less pure clay was a great hindrance in working the pot clay, and Mr. Sattler decided to utilize the impure clay in paving-brick manufacture, being inspired by the success of brick pavements in Holland (Ref. 134, p. 469). Owing to his inexperience and the quality of the clay, the brick made at first were of little value, but by 1878 he made some of which the tests were encouraging, and they were laid on the Eads bridge in 1880, with funds raised by citizens. Their softness, the poor foundation, and the heavy traffic to which they were subjected, caused this pavement to be short lived. Two other varieties of brick were tried the same year (1880) and met with little success. They were a Laclede Company brick, a salt-glazed mixture of shale and fire clay, and a common brick boiled in tar. In 1881 some of Mr. Sattler's brick were used throughout St. Louis with good success, and he established a regular plant. Working with such a refractory clay was unsatisfactory, and the percentage of good brick was low. He died in 1890, and no paving brick have been made from that clay since (Ref. 134, p. 470).

A number of common local stoneware plants were established during the seventies, some of which were Huggins and Company, Lakenan, Shelby County, 1870; Glassir and Son, Washington, Franklin County, 1872; Mrs. Robins & Son, Calhoun, Henry County, 1873; R. Winfell, Perry, Ralls County, 1876; the Washington Clay Company, Washington, Franklin County, 1877; and H. A. Smith, Gainesville, Ozark County, 1879 (Ref. 134, p. 356). It is not known how many of these are still in operation.

Between 1880 and 1890 the kaolin industry was probably at its height. In 1881 a young potter named James Post successfully made Rockingham ware of Cape Girardeau clays in' that town. The following year he induced local capital to form a company, and C. C. ware was made for several years, using local materials. After several failures the kilns were finally torn down and the plant converted into a grinding mill. This experiment so disgusted capitalists in Missouri that it has been a great setback to pottery manufacture ever since (Ref. 134, pp. 167–168).

In Morgan County twelve miles south of Versailles there is in the old Buffalo lead mines a pocket of kaolin which was worked from 1880 up to at least 1897 by George Clark, and the product shipped to the St. Louis Stamping Works for enameled-ware manufacture (Ref. 134, p. 186). Various other pits were in operation in Cape Girardeau and Bollinger counties in the eighties, some of which are still shipping clay, but many have become exhausted or have failed because of careless sorting of the material.

The first mention we find of ball clays or plastic china clays in

Missouri is in 1880 when the Mandel ball-clay pit was opened at Regina, Jefferson County. It is the largest and most important deposit of ball clay in the State, and met with a ready market at East Liverpool and other centers (Ref. 134, p. 189). These clays are now controlled by the Mandel-Sant Company.

The development of numerous deposits of flint clays also took place in the eighties. Of these the deposits at Truesdale in Warren County have been the most important.

The Big Kelly pit, as it was called, was discovered in 1886, leased in 1888, and has been in operation ever since, most of the clay being shipped to St. Louis (Ref. 134, p. 212). The Mexico Fire Brick Company of Mexico, Mo., began working the Truesdale flint clays in 1880 when they shipped 1500 tons to their Mexico plant for fire-brick manufacture (Ref. 134, p. 214). Numerous other pits were opened in Warren, Phelps, Crawford, Franklin counties and other portions of central Missouri, and the product was shipped to Chicago, Ill., St. Louis, Mo., and to the fire-brick works in Fulton and Mexico, Mo.

The progress of the fire-clay industry during this period was marked by the opening up of Tole and Thorp's mine in St. Louis in 1880, Jameson's mine at Bartholds, and other smaller ones throughout the district (Ref. 134). In 1881 the Missouri Fire-Brick Company began the manufacture of terra-cotta lumber, but went back to fire-brick manufacture very soon after (Ref. 139, p. 289). Coffin & Co., owners of a large glass-pot works in Pittsburg, established a plant in St. Louis in 1884, and made fire brick and glass pots (Ref. 134, p. 289). In 1896 this plant was owned by the Mississippi Glass Company. The clay used for the glass pots is obtained at the company's mine at Gratiot Station, St. Louis, and mixed with German pot clay. The Fulton Fire-Brick and Mining Company was established in 1885 in Fulton, and uses mainly local clay (Ref. 134, p. 295).

The present Salamander Fire Brick Company, Vandalia, Audrain County, was established as the Audrain Manufacturing and Coal Mining Company in 1883. It uses local clay (Ref. 134, p. 295), and in 1889 the Mexico Fire-Brick Company was put in operation at Mexico (Ref. 134, p. 295).

But few data are obtainable concerning the stoneware industry of Missouri. In the eighties this branch of the clay-working industry was augmented by the opening up of a number of coal-measure clay banks, especially in Henry County at Clinton and Calhoun which are the only extensive centers of stoneware industry in the State. The clay from the Jegglin Clay Pit near Calhoun was first used in 1884 by the Boonville and Calhoun potteries, while other banks were opened in 1889–1890. In 1887 a clay bank of Coal-Measure clay was opened up at Knobnoster in Johnson County and since then has supplied clay to the Kansas City Sewer Pipe Company, Kansas City (Ref. 134, p. 333). Potteries were established at numerous points in the State, and by 1891 there were nine in operation in Henry County alone, with forty-two in the State in the year 1892 (Ref. 134, p. 356).

One of the first successful terra-cotta manufacturers was the Winkle Terra Cotta Company established in St. Louis in 1883. This company employed shales, fire clays, and loess from Cheltenham, and a bluff clay from Glencoe (Ref. 134, p. 435). A second firm, the Kansas City Terra Cotta Lumber Company, was established at Kansas City, Missouri, in 1886, and for a while made terra-cotta lumber, but in 1896 were making simply brick (Ref. 134, p. 436).

The development of the sewer-pipe industry forms a most interesting chapter, of which many details have been supplied by Mr. L. R. Blackmer. According to Mr. Blackmer there were in 1867 three firms engaged in the making of sewer pipe, viz.: the St. Louis Stoneware Company, at 7th and Russell Avenue; H. M. Thompson & Co., at 18th St. and Missouri Pacific Railway; and the Evens and Howard Firebrick Company, at Cheltenham.

The first mentioned employed Cheltenham clay for their pipe, but the product was so rough that a large amount supplied to the city of Chicago in 1868 failed to pass inspection, and it was necessary to change the clay. This was subsequently brought from Alton, Ill., and mixed with loam from the bottoms of the Des Perces River below Carondelet. This likewise gave dissatisfaction, so clay was then tried from Washington, Mo. This last, mixed with a newly discovered local fire clay and loam, gave good results.

Mr. Blackmer left the St. Louis Stoneware Company in 1877, and two years later joined with Mr. Post to build a small factory at Ewing Avenue, in the Mill Creek Valley, and another on Papon Street. The entire plants were later concentrated at Reber Place station on the Oak Hill railroad in 1887. The factory was rebuilt in 1893. The product is now made of Coal Measures and surface clays (Ref. 134, p. 441).

Two other firms, the Kansas City Sewer-pipe works and the Dickey Sewer-pipe works of Deepwater were also established about the same time (Ref. 134, pp. 442–443). The latter firm has also made conduits since 1902. Then, of course, other plants, such as the Evens and Howard and the Laclede Works, made a quantity of sewer pipe as a side line. The former began in 1858 or 1859.

Before 1890 or 1891 brick as a paving material had taken a firm hold on the people, and Kansas City, St. Joseph, Springfield, Sedalia, and Hannibal as well as St. Louis had brick pavements. Plants for paving-brick manufacture were in operation at Montserrat, Johnson County, Billings, Christian County, St. Joseph, Kansas City, Tarkio, Atchison County, Moberly, Knobnoster, Deepwater, and other localities (Ref. 134, p. 477).

The use of burnt-clay ballast for railroad construction was introduced into this country in 1884 by William Davey, and was soon after taken up in Missouri, and by 1892 many extensive pits were opened in the counties bordering the Missouri and Mississippi rivers (Ref. 134, p. 545).

Mineral Resources of the United States for 1907 shows that Missouri then ranked sixth in the production of all clay ware, with a production valued at $6,898,871, ranking even higher in the production of sewer pipe and fire brick.

The production since 1894 is given below.

VALUE OF CLAY PRODUCTS OF MISSOURI FROM 1894 TO 1907.

Year.	Common brick.	Vitrified paving brick.	Front brick.	Orna-mental brick.	Drain tile.	Sewer pipe.	Fire brick.
1894	$1,541,553	$190,220	....	$47,933	$172,200	$150,000	$202,722
1895	1,251,200	54,640	$275,725	1,500	15,820	212,000	484,415
1896	1,317,916	61,500	293,193	136,964	23,383	171,652	328,148
1897	999,352	182,625	224,016	86,723	25,800	458,368	157,502
1898	1,046,669	264,092	258,786	65,581	85,748	403,075	268,173
1899	1,345,792	188,787	281,797	49,219	53,575	436,624	375,023
1900	1,057,497	252,783	228,070	42,096	57,900	624,932	510,166
1901	1,595,031	225,247	298,158	62,108	45,114	788,513	620,116
1902	1,832,118	194,250	358,089	49,411	35,887	903,279	739,385
1903	1,725,253	307,237	333,965	39,756	45,363	1,050,794	925,915
1904	1,690,460	480,671	322,445	32,967	80,479	1,176,679	925,520
1905	2,028,957	470,935	362,996	44,632	59,858	1,101,938	1,117,209
1906	1,810,304	539,700	394,563	30,689	64,063	1,208,236	1,324,895
1907	1,844,255	462,341	387,455	33,638	72,316	1,332,080	1,634,209

Year.	Miscella-neous.[1]	Total brick & tile.	Red earthen-ware.	Stone-ware.	Other pottery.	Total pottery.	Grand total.
1894	$310,950	$2,615,578	....	....	....	....	$2,615,578
1895	207,753	2,790,818	....	$8,400	....	$8,400	2,799,218
1896	296,556	2,629,312	$50,933	....	....	50,933	2,810,245
1897	349,683	2,484,069	52,459			52,459	2,536,528
1898	604,824	2,996,948	3,880	49,378	$5,000	58,258	3,112,716
1899	857,002	3,587,819	6,379	63,790	8,628	78,797	3,666,616
1900	891,549	3,665,093	10,865	58,509	2,100	71,474	3,736,567
1901	775,619	4,409,906	13,800	48,827	....	62,627	4,474,553
1902	990,482	5,112,901	6,401	39,419	3,600	49,420	5,166,414
1903	1,181,923	5,610,206	6,697	43,304	600	50,601	5,661,607
1904	791,465	5,410,686	7,749	61,578	1,491	70,818	5,481,504
1905	973,518	6,160,043	4,054	39,314	....	43,368	6,203,411
1906	1,254,325	6,626,775	4,429	65,071	....	69,500	6,696,275
1907	1,054,390	6,820,684	3,289	69,323	5,575	78,187	6,898,871

[1] Includes architectural terra cotta, hollow brick, fireproofing, tile (not drain), and stove linings.

The quantity and value of raw clays mined and sold during 1907 was as follows:

	Quantity, short tons.	Value.
Kaolin..	307	$2,194
Fire clay......................................	167,043	428,349
Stoneware clay................................	2,510	1,673
Miscellaneous.................................	425	10,625

MONTANA.

The Census for 1870 (Ref. 115) shows but two brickyards in operation in Montana producing 225,000 brick, and in 1880 there were five producing 3,650,000 common and 200,000 pressed brick. Mineral Resources of the United States for 1883 speaks of the industry around Helena, where fire brick and crucibles were being manufactured from a local clay for use in smelters at Helena and Butte.

While fire clays are known to exist in Montana they have never been developed to any extent, the large smelters obtaining most of their brick from other States. Small yards for supplying local demand for common brick are scattered over the State, their raw material consisting mainly of surface clays. In recent years the Cretaceous clays have been worked at Belt and Armington in Cascade County, for fire-brick manufacture. Much of this clay is used by the Anaconda Copper Mining Company at Butte.

J. P. Rowe (Ref. 171, p. 53) states that the clay-working industry is still in its infancy, and some of the best clay beds are yet totally undeveloped. He describes a number of plants, but gives few historic data. According to him the works of the Western Clay Manufacturing Company, at Helena, were started in the early seventies, and are still in operation, although in greatly improved form.

Silver Bow County has one of the best plants in the State, that of the Butte Sewer Pipe and Tile Company, located at Butte. When this company was organized, in 1889, only common brick were made, but about 1903 a fire-brick department was added and has since done a large business, the product being shipped as far west as Seattle and northward into Canada.

The Amalgamated Copper Company has for several years operated a common and fire brick plant at Anaconda, but draws its clays from near Armington.

The following table gives the statistics of production since 1894. The "Miscellaneous" column consists mainly of sewer pipe, front and ornamental brick.

VALUE OF CLAY PRODUCTS OF MONTANA FROM 1894 TO 1907.

Year.	Common brick.	Fire brick.	Miscellaneous.	Total.
1894................	$80,629	$545,700	$17,700	$644,029
1895................	112,083	69,035	23,075	204,193
1896................	204,366	54,520	17,425	276,311
1897................	122,494	79,486	29,669	231,649
1898................	178,728	65,164	29,734	273,626
1899................	188,339	(a)	125,051	313,390
1900................	219,465	117,566	13,458	350,489
1901................	357,210	152,650	29,361	539,221
1902................	130,339	113,112	35,276	278,727
1903................	197,604	101,700	30,013	329,317
1904................	145,642	102,611	31,178	279,431
1905................	157,575	115,431	40,000	313,006
1906................	203,365	45,034	48,900	297,299
1907................	188,819	35,553	48,500	272,872

(a) Included under "Miscellaneous."

NEBRASKA.

The brick and tile industry was well established in Nebraska in 1870, and the clays were no doubt worked before that time. In that year (1870) there were 17 yards producing over 6,000,000 brick (Ref. 115). It was a growing industry, and by 1880 there were 87 yards producing common, pressed, and fire brick (Ref. 116). The principal brickmaking centers in 1887 were Lincoln and Omaha, five new yards having been established in Omaha in that one year (Ref. 117). In 1888 more yards were established in Omaha, and brick were being made at Elkhorn and Grand Island (Ref. 118). In the same year the sewer-pipe works at Beatrice were in operation, and brick were being manufactured there for paving the Beatrice streets (Ref. 4, XXI, p. 156). Vitrified-brick production had begun in 1889. Most of the important plants are based on the Cretaceous clays.

The industry has increased slowly but steadily, but it has not assumed large proportions, since by 1907 Nebraska had only attained twenty-seventh rank among the clay-producing States.

The western part of Nebraska is sparsely settled, and most of the development, for some time at least, will be in the eastern part of the State, where the Dakota clays will serve as the basis of a flourishing clay industry, and indeed they have already been the means of forming a strong nucleus.

VALUE OF CLAY PRODUCTS OF NEBRASKA FROM 1894 TO 1907.

Year.	Common brick.	Vitrified paving brick.	Front brick.	Miscellaneous.	Total.
1894......	$411,409	$52,800	....	$55,575	$519,784
1895......	175,480	3,800	$29,659	5,602	214,541
1896......	124,746	800	9,512	9,315	144,373
1897......	288,980	26,169	31,706	4,530	351,385
1898......	446,126	26,315	29,921	11,203	513,565
1899......	781,246	15,090	23,653	21,836	841,825
1900......	553,905	28,055	95,528	6,470	683,958
1901......	668,863	28,150	85,260	24,200	806,473
1902......	638,901	25,150	87,415	6,202	757,668
1903......	710,399	35,700	111,403	10,526	868,028
1904......	904,750	45,063	106,572	11,022	1,067,387
1905......	874,695	(a)	(a)	132,048	1,006,743
1906......	835,702	(a)	(a)	155,006	990,708
1907......	789,170	24,600	100,654	39,008	953,432

(a) Included under "Miscellaneous."

NEVADA.

In 1870, Nevada, according to the Census, had but one yard producing 350,000 common brick (Ref. 115), and ten years later but two yards are recorded producing both common and fire brick (Ref. 115). Since then small yards have started up here and there to supply a local demand, but the industry is nowhere largely developed.

VALUE OF CLAY PRODUCTS OF IDAHO AND NEVADA.

Year.	Value.	Year.	Value.
1894[1]...........	$30,268	1901............	$85,953
1895[1]...........	18,390	1902............	138,648
1896[1]...........	16,000	1903............	264,012
1897[1]...........	15,914	1904............	199,417
1898[1]...........	27,365	1905............	230,780
1899............	52,470	1906............	282,889
1900............	58,962	1907............	327,078

[1] Idaho alone.　From 1900 on, Idaho and Nevada combined.

NEW HAMPSHIRE.

The earliest record in regard to brickmaking in New Hampshire is the statement (Ref. 1, 1, p. 231) that brick to the value of $129,000 were exported to the West Indies from the State in 1789. Pottery was being manufactured as early as 1817 in Jaffrey, the clay being obtained at Moncton, Vt. (Ref. 8, p. 438). We first hear of brick manufacture in Keene in 1840, when a Mr. Edwards began making "water-struck" brick (Ref. 4, XXVI, p. 106). In 1841 a potter's clay in Alstead was utilized for brick manufacture (Ref. 9, p. 65), and brick clay was said to be abundant in Bath, brick being manufactured at many yards. According to the United States Census for 1860, New Hampshire had at that time fifty-six brickyards and three potteries. Another yard was started in Keene in 1865 by a Mr. Ball, and in 1872 he began making "sand-struck" brick (Ref. 4, XXVI, p. 106). The first pottery in Keene was established in 1871 by Taft & Co., who began then the manufacture of red ware, later making stoneware and majolica (Ref. 8, p. 271), and at the present time are turning out semi-vitreous art pottery, most of it with a matte glaze. The ware is made largely from clays obtained outside of New Hampshire. In 1878 a firm in Hooksett turned out five million brick a year, and employed sixty hands, while throughout the State forty-one towns are mentioned as contributing to the brick industry (Ref. 10, p. 86). At present the New England Brick Company obtains raw materials from Exeter, East Kingston, Epping, Rochester, Gonic, Barrington, and Hooksett, and states that these have been worked for fifteen to twenty years.

It will be seen from the above record, even though it is somewhat imperfect, that New Hampshire is not an important producer of clay products, this fact being emphasized by the following statistics.

VALUE OF CLAY PRODUCTS OF NEW HAMPSHIRE FROM 1894 TO 1907.

Year.	Common brick.	Miscellaneous.	Total.
1894.............	$482,330	$21,175[1]	$503,505
1895.............	469,567	52,000	521,567
1896.............	550,789	30,380	581,169
1897.............	417,272	47,900	465,172
1898.............	365,511	46,478	401,989
1899.............	505,951	46,801	552,752
1900.............	423,713	61,300	485,013
1901.............	741,589	24,375	765,964
1902.............	861,975	25,149	887,124
1903.............	546,172	22,449	568,621
1904.............	446,603	33,382	479,985
1905.............	529,734	25,000	554,734
1906.............	716,051	10,000	726,051
1907.............	500,599	10,000	510,599

[1] Mostly front brick and fire brick.

CHAPTER V.

NEW JERSEY.

Brick.   Brick clays were no doubt worked at a very early period, but little mention was found of them.   According to Mr. George E. Fell (Ref. 129, p. 243), Trenton was but a small village at the time of the Revolution, and the few brick buildings then erected were constructed chiefly of brick brought from England.   About the time of the Revolution, however, a few bricks were made on the north bank of Assanpink Creek, between Broad and Montgomery streets, although it is very doubtful whether these were the first bricks made in the State.   Between 1780 and 1800, brick were also made between White Horse Tavern and Hamilton Square, and still a little later at Maiden Head, now Lawrenceville.   They were still being made in 1814 (Ref. 37, p. 244).

About 1826 a man named Embly came to Trenton from Connecticut and began making brick in the square bounded by Princeton and Brunswick avenues and Sandford and Bond streets. Later, in 1831, Joseph Himer and Peter Grim of Philadelphia established a yard on the Hedden Farm now (1904) owned by the S. K. Wilson estate, about half-way between the two city reservoirs, the brick used in the original part of the present State Prison being made by them.   This yard was abandoned by Grim in 1839, and another started on the present site of the Fell and Roberts yard, while a yard was established in 1845 by James Taylor on the site abandoned by Grim.   Between this year and 1856 a number of yards were started around Trenton and served as the nucleus of a thriving brick industry, which has continued up to the present.

All of these yards used the surface loams which form an extensive sheet immediately underlying the surface in the region about Trenton.

The pressed-brick business of Trenton commenced about 1865, and increased steadily up to 1894, since which time it has declined.

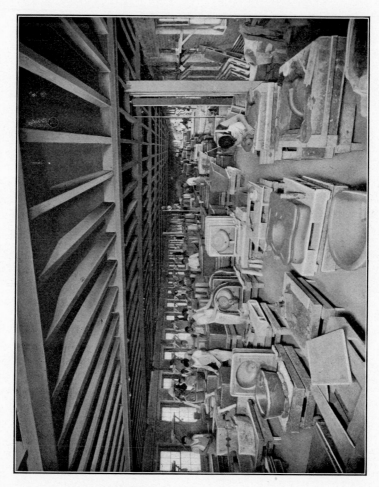

PLATE V. — Interior of large sanitary-ware plant, Trenton, N.J. (Photo loaned by E. C. Stover.)

The explanation of this decline is to be found chiefly in the fact that the demand for red pressed brick has greatly decreased in late years, owing to the introduction of buff, mottled, speckled, and other types of fancy front brick. Since the clay found at Trenton burns red, it cannot be utilized for these newer styles.

Outside of Trenton it is known that brick were first made in Middlesex County in 1851 at Roundabout (now Sayreville) by James Wood, and in the fall of that year Peter Fisher and James Sayre purchased a small property of twenty-three acres and commenced the manufacture of common brick, but gradually branched out into the manufacture of other grades. In 1887 this copartnership merged into a corporation known as the Sayre & Fisher Company, which is now by far the largest individual brickmaking concern in the State. The inexhaustible supplies of brick clays (of Cretaceous age) in this region early led to the establishment of other yards, so that now there are at least ten large brickyards at South River and Sayreville. Common brick made from red-burning clays were the first product, but with the growing demand for pressed brick, especially the buff ones, the fire clays were drawn upon for this purpose, and enameled brick were also manufactured.

Raw materials have not been the only factor responsible for the successful development of the brickmaking industry around Sayreville and South River, for proximity to water routes, and large cities have also contributed to the success.

In the Hackensack region, brick have also been made for many years, but although the New York market is only seven miles distant in a straight line, yet the water route via Newark Bay is thirty-one miles long. As the Hackensack River is obstructed by numerous low drawbridges, shipping is done almost entirely by barges, and as the cost of towage is high, the otherwise cheap facilities for shipping are minimized and the nearness to the New York market is more apparent than real.

Some of the smaller yards scattered over the State, and using local clays, have been in operation for a long time as indicated by the list below. Thus: Lambertville, 1816; Flemington, 1840; Yorktown, 1866; Millville, 1869; Rosenhayn, 1887; Petersburg and Marshallville, 1857 (no longer running). The hydraulic-press brick works at Winslow Junction were started in 1890.

Terra Cotta. The terra-cotta industry was, so far as known, first established at Perth Amboy in 1849 (Ref. 129, p. 274),[1] the first works being known as the Hall Terra-Cotta Works, which in 1879 changed to the Perth Amboy Terra-Cotta Company. It is also said that in 1855 a Mr. Davies made terra cotta in Trenton (Ref. 36, p. 246), but the works are no longer in operation. In 1888 the New Jersey Terra Cotta Works was established at Perth Amboy. The present Standard Terra-Cotta Works was organized in 1890, under the name of the Architectural Terra-Cotta Works. Other plants are located at Rocky Hill, South Amboy, and Moorestown.

In 1907, the Standard, Perth Amboy, Excelsior (Rocky Hill, N. J.) and Atlantic Terra-Cotta Company (Tottenville, Staten Island, N. Y.) were consolidated under the name of the Atlantic Terra-Cotta Company.

All of these industries are based on the Cretaceous clays, mostly of semi-refractory character, and improvements in the character of the wares or new designs are due, not to the discovery of new deposits of clay, but improvements in the technology of the manufacture.

Fireproofing. One of the most interesting statements to be found in the New Jersey Clay Report of 1878, and one which serves well by comparison to show the great strides that have been made in the clay industry of New Jersey, is the following: "They (the hollow brick) have not been much used in this country. Henry Maurer of Perth Amboy has begun their manufacture, and there is now an opportunity to make a trial of this promising improvement in building materials."

According to Mr. Pfeiffer, of Henry Maurer & Son (private communication), they were first made in 1875. In 1902 there were nine factories in New Jersey whose product consisted *largely* or *entirely* of fireproofing and hollow bricks, with an output in that year valued at $965,047. By 1907 this had increased to

---

[1] Mr. G. P. Putnam, of the Atlantic Terra-Cotta Company, gives the date as 1846, and the firm name as A. Hall & Sons.

$4,250,638. The oldest of these was that of Henry Maurer & Son. Four of the others were operated by the National Fireproofing Company, which has its headquarters at Pittsburg, Pa., and whose original plant (now inactive) in New Jersey was the factory at Port Murray, Warren County, which used Hudson shale. In 1900 this company acquired the Perth Amboy Works, known as the Old Pardee Works; in January, 1901, the fireproofing factory at Lorillard was taken over, and in July, 1901, the Raritan Hollow and Porous Brick Company at Keasbey.

Other factories are at Sewaren, Spa Springs (begun in 1869 and passed through many hands) Piscataway and South River. As late as 1902 a plant was established at Woodbridge.

The rapid growth of this industry in New Jersey is due to several causes. It is based on an almost inexhaustible supply of clay, which in former years had little or no value, and even at this day would probably not be put to any use other than that for which it is now dug. Furthermore, these clay deposits are in general close to tide water, so that the product can be shipped either by boat or rail to the large eastern markets.

Floor and Wall Tile. The manufacture of floor and wall tile seems to have begun in New Jersey about 1882 when the Harris Manufacturing Company was established in Trenton. It was soon after changed to the Trent Tile Company, and is still in operation (Ref. 8, p. 362). In 1885 the Providential Tile Works was established in the same city (Ref. 8, p. 367), and this was followed four years later by the establishment of the Old Bridge Enameled Brick and Tile Company at Old Bridge (Ref. 41, p. 23) and the Elterich Art Tile Works at Maywood. This latter in 1892 became the Maywood Art Tile Company (Ref. 41, p. 231). Another works, the Pardee Tile Works, has also been in operation for some years at Perth Amboy.

Except in the case of some of the buff and red floor tile, all the raw materials used are obtained from other States, so that the tile industry cannot be regarded as founded on the New Jersey clays. The clays mostly used come from Florida, North Carolina, and England, while the product itself is shipped not only to various States but also to foreign countries.

Roofing Tile. Some roofing tile have been made by Henry Maurer & Son, at Maurer, but the production has not been important or regularly kept up.[1]

Conduits. Conduits form a line of clay products the use of which has greatly increased in the last few years because of the increased use of electrical power transmission and the necessity of placing many of the cables underground. The occurrence of suitable clays in New Jersey and the proximity of the deposits to the large eastern cities to which shipments could be conveniently made by water, have served to encourage the industry.

According to Mr. J. C. Rossi, the manufacture of conduits was begun about 1898. The clays used were in general a mixture of red-burning plastic clay and a low-grade fire clay, all obtained from the Cretaceous beds of Middlesex County.

In 1904 there were three plants located at Perth Amboy, South River and Clayville, running exclusively on this product. Conduits are also occasionally made at the fireproofing factories.

New Jersey was not the first State to produce this line of wares, the oldest works being in Ohio.

Fire Brick. The manufacture of fire brick represents one of the oldest branches of the clay-working industry in New Jersey, and is of more importance than is commonly imagined. The New Jersey clays were first used for fire brick after the War of 1812 (Ref. 4, XXVI, p. 363), and one of the earliest records, according to Dr. Cook (Ref. 36, p. 1), shows that clay was taken from Woodbridge to Boston in 1816, and used for manufacturing fire brick. The quantity or price was not given, but four years later there is a record of a Boston party who received 50 tons of New Jersey clay, paying 25 cents per ton for it (Ref. 36, p. 1).

The value of the clays of the Woodbridge district does not seem to have been widely recognized for some years, however, although in 1855 the statistics given in the New Jersey Geological Survey Report on Clays, in 1878, show that clay for making 50,000,000 bricks was then being taken annually from the pits at Woodbridge, Perth Amboy and South Amboy.

Perhaps the oldest factory in the State was that known as the

---

[1] Pan tiles associated with common brick have been found on site of a house built by the Dutch in 1668.

Salamander Works (no longer in existence), where brick were made as early as 1825, and in 1833 they were being manufactured at Perth Amboy by John Watson (Ref. 36, p. 1). Trenton was added to the list in 1845, the yard being owned by Davies until 1867; at first horse power was used and 600 to 800 bricks made daily, but later steam power was installed and the output increased to 2500 per day (Ref. 37, p. 246). The works of W. H. Berry at Woodbridge began operations in 1845, and have continued up to the present day, changing the name to J. E. Berry in 1896. This was followed by the establishment of works of Henry Maurer & Son at Maurer in 1856, of M. D. Valentine & Bro. at Woodbridge, in 1865, and Sayre & Fisher at Sayreville in 1868. Others were later started at Woodbridge, Trenton, South River, Keasbey, Ostrander, Spa Springs and Jersey City.

All obtained their supply of clays from the Cretaceous beds of Middlesex County.

Pottery. The State of New Jersey can probably lay claim to having one of the oldest potteries in the country, for E. A. Barber, in his work on the Pottery and Porcelain of the United States, notes that the remains of an old kiln fire hole were found a mile or two below South Amboy, and that it is probably a relic of the earlier pottery ware made on this continent, "and most probably built by the Dutch. . . ."

As early as 1685, pottery, now such an important product of the New Jersey clay-working industry, was manufactured by Dr. Daniel Coxe, a former Governor of West New Jersey. He was probably the first to make white ware in the Colonies, erecting a pottery at Burlington, and it is presumed that he used South Amboy clay (Ref. 8, p. 54).

Barber gives the following "quaint and interesting reference to it as copied from an inventory of property offered for sale in 1688."

"I have erected a pottery at Burlington for white and chiney ware a greate quantity to ye value of 1200 li have already been made and vended in ye Country, neighbour Colonies and ye Islands of Barbadoes and Jamaica, where they are in great request. I have two houses and kills with all necessary implements, diverse workmen, and other servants. Have expended thereon about 2000£."

Later, about 1800, a stoneware potter, by the name of Van Wickle, established a pottery at Old Bridge, now Herbertsville (Ref. 36, p. 1), using some of the Cretaceous clay from Morgan's bank at South Amboy. In the same year stoneware was made from local clays at Perth Amboy (Ref. 6, p. 115), and a man named Price was making stoneware from South Amboy clay at Roundebout (now Sayreville) in 1802 (Ref. 36, p. 1).

Three years later (1805) an earthenware pottery was established at Flemington by Mr. Fulper (Ref. 4, XXXI, p. 365), and this is still in operation making stoneware.

Another stoneware pottery was started at Elizabeth (Ref. 8, p. 117) in 1816, but changed later to a yellow and Rockingham ware works. Still later it passed into the hands of L. B. Beerbauer & Co., and was used for making ironstone china, which necessitated the importation of clays from other States.

In 1825 the Jersey Porcelain and Earthenware Company was incorporated in the town of Jersey, Bergen County, and in 1829 became the American Pottery Company (Ref. 12, p. 404).

A few years later, or in 1833, David Henderson organized the American Pottery Manufacturing Company, and this factory, during the next seven years, produced ware with a buff or cream colored body, which was much used. It is interesting to note that these works were the first in America to use the English method of transfer printing in decoration.

About 1843 the name of the factory was changed to the Jersey City Pottery Company, and it is stated by Barber (Ref. 8, p. 117) that many of "the best potters of the old school in the United States learned their trade at this factory." The pottery subsequently passed into other hands, and in 1892 the old buildings, which had stood for 65 years, and from which many fine pieces of work had been turned out, were finally demolished.

Looking back over the period described above, it will be seen that all of the wares made could have been wrought from New Jersey clays, except the white wares, which required kaolin. But whether this was obtained from Pennsylvania or England the records do not inform us.

Trenton, now the most important potting center, was the site of a pottery at an early date. An old history of Trenton,[1] now in the hands of the State Gazette of that city, states that the first pottery in Trenton was built by John McCulley, in 1779, on North Warren Street, about where St. Mary's Cathedral now stands. It remained there until 1816, when it was removed a little further west to Bank Street, continuing there until Mr. McCulley's retirement in 1852. He died in 1858. The product consisted of red flowerpots and pie dishes.

From 1850 to 1860 Trenton began to assume its importance as a pottery center of the United States. Beginning with a few small potteries, which made the lower grades of pottery, and were able to use New Jersey clays exclusively, it has rapidly developed into one of the two great pottery centers of the country, manufacturing the higher grades of ware, whose composition calls for the almost exclusive use of plastic and other raw materials, obtainable only outside of the State or country.

The Trenton industry appears to have had its birth probably about 1852, at which time Hattersly's Pottery was in operation, with one small kiln six feet in diameter. The developments since that time can, perhaps, be best listed chronologically as follows (Ref. 129, p. 305):

1852. Taylor and Speeler began manufacture of yellow and Rockingham ware, adding white granite in 1856 (Ref. 36, p. 254).

1853. R. Millington and J. Astbury organized first sanitary-ware pottery in America.

1853. Wm. Young's Sons began manufacture of C. C. ware, the first in Trenton (Ref. 8, p. 454). This was a leased pottery located on the present site of the City Pottery Works. The firm was succeeded by the Willetts Manufacturing Company.

1857. Wm. Young leased Hattersly Pottery for a term of five years, but later built his own pottery.

1859. Rhodes and Yates. First pottery to make white granite and C. C. ware exclusively.

1859. The Trenton China Company began operations (Ref. 8, p. 238), and F. Frey of Switzerland introduced the art of decorating china with gold and colors (Ref. 36, p. 256).

1859. Glasgow Pottery established by John Moses in 1859. This was run by Mr. Moses and his sons until a few years ago when it was bought out by Thos. Maddock and Sons Company. Most of the old plant has been torn down, giving way to the new buildings of the latter concern.

[1] E. C. Stover, private correspondence.

1862. Greenwood Pottery Company organized, started by W. Tams and W. Barnard, and operated in turn under name of Stephens, Tams & Co. and Breasley & Co., the present name being adopted in 1868.

1863. Etruria Pottery built by Bloor, Ott and Booth; succeeded by Bloor, Ott and Brewer in 1864. Shortly after changed to Ott and Brown. Later it became the Cook Pottery.

1865. Union Electrical Porcelain Company.

1868. Coxon and Thompson started a pottery, which has since become Empire Plant of Trenton Potteries Company.

1869. James Moses bought the Mercer Pottery from Mr. Thompson.

1869–1889. Union Pottery Company.

1869. James Mayer founded the Arsenal Pottery.

1870. Maddock began manufacture of sanitary or plumbers' ware (Ref. 8, p. 228).

1873. East Trenton Pottery Company.

1879. International Pottery Company began operations on site of Speeler's old pottery.

1879. New Jersey Pottery organized, but reorganized in 1883 under name of Union Pottery Company.

1879. Burroughs and Mountford Pottery established in what was formerly the Eagle Pottery.

1879. The Willets Manufacturing Company bought the Wm. Young's Sons' Pottery.

1880. Prospect Hill Pottery started by Dale & Davis.

1881. Trenton China Company established.

1881. Enterprise Pottery Company established.

1881. Crescent Pottery established.

1882. Thos. Maddock and Sons took the old Millington and Astbury Pottery.

1884. Delaware Pottery started.

1889. Ceramic Art Company organized.

1890. Greenwood China Company started.

1891. Imperial Porcelain Company organized.

1892. Keystone Pottery Company began operations.

1892. Trenton Potteries Company began operations and purchased the Crescent, Delaware, Empire and Equitable potteries. Also built the Ideal.

1893. Maddock Pottery Company organized and purchased plant formerly owned by the Trenton China Company.

1893. Economy Pottery Company.

1894. Bellmark Pottery Company.

1894. American Porcelain Works.

1894. Hart Brewer Pottery Company, started originally as Isaac Davis Pottery, and passed in turn into the hands of Fell and Throp and then of the present owners.

1894. Trenton Fire Clay and Porcelain Company. Succeeded Trenton Terra Cotta Company.

1895. Economy Pottery Company.

1895. John Maddock and Sons.
1896. Monument Pottery Company.
1896. Artistic Porcelain Company.
1897. Cook Pottery Company.
1897. Sanitary Earthenware Specialty Company.
1899. Star Porcelain Company.
1900. Diamond Porcelain Company.
1901. Elite Pottery Company.
1901. Acme Sanitary Pottery Company.
1902. Fidelity Pottery Company, successors to the Egyptian Pottery.
1902. Hudson Porcelain Company.
1903. Duncan MacKenzie Sons' Company, successors to Union Electric Porcelain Company.
1903. Morris and Wilmore Company.
1903. Electrical Porcelain and Manufacturing Company.
1904. C. B. Walton Company.
1905. National Porcelain Company.
1905. Resolute Porcelain Company.
1905. Sun Porcelain Company.
1908. Standard China Works.

A more striking evidence of their growth is shown by the fact that: In 1852 there was one pottery with one kiln; in 1874 there were 12 potteries with a large "ironstone" china production (Ref. 40, pp. 42–3); in 1879 there were 19 potteries with 57 kilns, producing about $2,000,000 worth of wares annually; in 1883 the number of potteries had increased to 23 with 110 kilns, and in 1903 there were 41 potteries with 258 kilns.

Up to 1863 the products included white, sanitary, yellow, and Rockingham ware; in 1903 they included china, C. C. ware, white granite ware, sanitary ware, belleek, and electrical porcelain.

The technical advances that have taken place in the pottery industry at Trenton have been well summarized by E. C. Stover (Ref. 137, II, p. 147), who states that one of the early improvements was the production of a ware that would not craze, following which came the introduction of belleek. Later a superior quality of hotel china was introduced, which has secured a wide and enviable reputation. The production of a good quality of sanitary ware was another important development, and the manufacture has grown, so that at the present day Trenton is, without question, at the head of this branch of the pottery industry in the United States. The Trenton potter has not stopped, however, at a satisfactory body, but makes successfully the most complicated forms of sanitary appliances, much of this ware being exported.

Electrical porcelain was first made in 1891.

Still another important advance has been made in the manufacture of fire-clay bath tubs and sinks which are made in one firing.

The first solid porcelain lavatory made in one piece was produced by the Trenton Potteries Company in 1896, while the first solid porcelain bath tub was made by O. O. Bowman & Son in June, 1894. In these lines of work Trenton also leads, having the largest single pottery in the world devoted exclusively to the manufacture of these articles. The product comes into successful competition with the foreign wares.

Trenton has assumed its importance as a pottery center, not because of the wealth of raw materials in the immediate neighborhood, but rather because of its central location as regards transportation facilities, for probably the only New Jersey materials used by the majority of the Trenton potters are sagger and wad clays. It owes its initial growth, however, to the establishment of a few small potteries, which served as a nucleus and used local clays. As these grew, they branched out into other and better grades, and hence had to look elsewhere for raw materials.

Outside of Trenton the manufacture of pottery has been developed at a number of scattered localities, most of these making either earthenware or stoneware. For the former the local clays are commonly employed, while for the latter the Cretaceous stoneware clays of the Middlesex district form the main source of supply.

Clay-Mining Industry. Although an enormous quantity of clay is dug annually to supply factories located within the State, an additional large tonnage is mined each year to supply factories located in other States, many of the largest firms in New York, Pennsylvania and adjoining States drawing on the New Jersey pits for their supply of raw materials.

New Jersey is the largest producer of clay in the country, and the clays shipped away are used in the making of stoneware, sewer pipe, terra cotta, pressed brick, fire brick, stove linings, saggers, abrasive wheels, tiles, crucibles, zinc retorts, hollow ware, electrical porcelain, etc.

The clay-mining industry is by no means a recent development, having already assumed considerable proportions in 1878, when Dr. Cook wrote his classic work on the New Jersey clays.

References to the mining of clay are found at a still earlier date, however.

Clay called "fuller's earth" was used by the soldiers in 1776 for cleaning their belts (Ref. 36), and in 1816 fire clay was shipped from Woodbridge to Boston (Ref. 36, p. 1). A few years later, viz., 1835, the New Jersey clays were being shipped to Philadelphia for satining wall paper (Ref. 36, p. 1), and in 1854 their use for alum manufacture is noted.

The statistics printed annually by the United States Geological Survey do not give the quantity of clay shipped from New Jersey to other States, but in 1902 the New Jersey Geological Survey Report (Ref. 129, p. 34) states that the quantity amounted to 152,013 long tons. This represented about thirty per cent of the clay mined in New Jersey which was sold raw. The States taking these shipments included Pennsylvania, New York, Ohio, Maine, Connecticut, Massachusetts, Maryland, New Hampshire, West Virginia, Rhode Island, and Wisconsin. Some was even shipped to Canada.

The quantity of clay mined and sold raw in 1907 is given by the United States Geological Survey as follows:

Kind.	Quantity, short tons.	Value.
Ball clay............................	3,666	$16,918
Fire clay............................	318,603	485,613
Stoneware clay.......................	21,108	44,704
Brick clay...........................	18,876	16,517
Miscellaneous........................	75,885	103,496
Total.........................	440,138	$675,248

The value of clay products manufactured in New Jersey since 1894 is given below.

VALUE OF CLAY PRODUCTS OF NEW JERSEY FROM 1894 TO 1907.

Year	Common brick	Front brick	Ornamental	Architectural terra cotta	Fireproofing	Hollow brick	Tile not drain	Fire brick	Miscellaneous brick and tile
1894	$1,601,096	.....	$257,300	$88,000	$206,471	.....	$701,995	$502,430	$619,263
1895	1,097,063	$387,737	179,828	763,420	285,165	.....	850,014	456,825	716,122
1896	950,113	340,919	188,819	618,502	721,694	.....	143,292	604,983	90,539
1897	1,188,191	670,282	170,721	539,512	987,637	.....	191,735	277,670	169,386
1898	1,315,922	568,106	15,852	635,007	762,370	.....	292,644	519,688	479,436
1899	1,809,906	609,819	43,368	660,304	653,144	.....	37,123	633,158	1,269,875
1900	1,449,694	426,692	4,112	647,884	873,706	.....	508,392	1,072,535	701,857
1901	1,675,746	473,138	11,514	920,664	610,864	.....	486,122	780,327	823,430
1902	1,506,254	552,000	11,470	861,730	905,047	.....	795,153	819,580	909,970
1903	1,500,295	548,553	14,970	1,364,094	1,256,002	$69,652	734,159	949,392	654,596
1904	1,842,075	687,469	(a)	1,412,023	947,253	264,393	548,097	908,882	744,102
1905	3,090,809	852,744	1,975	1,614,263	1,017,774	290,301	585,130	1,393,448	1,197,747
1906	2,610,686	806,887	1,951	1,682,022	1,399,233	85,962	1,163,401	954,081	1,185,388
1907	2,289,883	825,767	4,605	1,722,067	1,039,868	119,659	1,059,085	947,472	1,020,488

Year	Total brick and tile	C. C. ware	White granite, semi-porcelain	China	Bone china, Delft, Belleek	Sanitary ware	Electrical porcelain	Miscellaneous pottery	Total pottery	Grand total
1894	$3,976,555	.....	.....	.....	.....	.....	.....	.....	.....	$3,976,555
1895	4,736,174	.....	.....	.....	.....	.....	.....	.....	$162,946	4,899,120
1896	3,658,861	$358,175	.....	$2,600	.....	$376,151	$109,000	$223,116	1,060,042	4,728,003
1897	4,195,134	460,608	.....	49,800	.....	1,036,445	14,200	424,600	1,985,713	6,180,847
1898	4,568,925	733,958	$923,273	424,060	52,500	1,477,192	182,000	237,459	4,030,442	8,706,357
1899	5,716,707	751,444	814,704	494,870	42,000	1,850,225	154,867	762,516	5,070,566	10,787,273
1900	5,664,772	544,249	1,528,546	345,112 [1]	38,800 [1]	1,807,953 [1]	285,466	702,525	5,252,651	10,928,423
1901	5,781,805	443,445	1,546,574	665,948	237,835 [1]	2,194,354 [1]	342,479	460,438	5,900,073	11,681,878
1902	6,420,304	581,267	1,431,270	680,368	.....	2,792,322 [1]	358,496	349,236	6,192,959	12,613,263
1903	7,101,713	409,029 [1]	1,575,892	805,691	71,000 [1]	2,774,484 [1]	385,398	293,732	6,315,226	13,416,939
1904	7,354,294	325,959	1,575,804 [1]	357,804 [1]	162,500	2,853,621 [1]	302,293	663,287	5,949,753	13,304,047
1905	10,044,191	(c)	1,288,926	810,917	129,000	3,420,291	540,206	453,994	6,655,334	16,099,525
1906	10,079,611	1,436,246		1,065,986		3,742,045	783,549	254,832	7,282,658	17,362,269
1907	9,019,834	1,225,691		1,135,885		3,615,685	744,068	264,295	6,985,626	16,005,460

(a) Included under miscellaneous brick and tile.   [1] Some additional in miscellaneous pottery.   (c) Under miscellaneous pottery.

NEW MEXICO.

With the exception of the adobe clays for brickmaking and smooth alluvial clays for making pottery by Mexicans and Indians, the plastic materials of New Mexico have been little developed.

The fire and semi-fire clays around Socorro were worked in 1894 by the Socorro Fire Clay Company for making building brick and fire brick (Ref. 4, XXI, p. 30), but the plant is said to be idle at the present time.

At about the same time (1894) the penitentiary authorities at Santa Fé were working the local clays for making brick and earthenware. Somewhat later the Cretaceous shales near Las Vegas were developed for dry-press brick. The mining of semi-refractory clays in the Gallup district began in 1898 at the Clark Coal Mine at Clarkville, four miles west of Gallup, the production amounting to about 12,000 tons annually. It was shipped to the United Verde Copper Company at Jerome, Ariz., to be used in lining copper converters (Ref. 114, p. 299). Four years later, or in 1902, the Rocky-Cliff Coal-Mining Company also began mining the clay near Gallup for the same purpose, and at present it is the chief clay industry of the district, the only other being a local plant near Gallup (Ref. 114, p. 300). The industry, however, probably owes its start to the coal-mining work, the clays being a side development. In the San Juan district brick have been made since 1900 when a small brick plant was put in operation at Farmington. In 1901 building brick in small amount were made at Fruitland, and in 1903 red building brick were being manufactured at Flora Vista, Aztec, Jewett and Shiprock, all simply to supply a local demand.

With only a small local demand, and with long hauls to important markets, it is understandable that up to the present time there should have been but little development of the clays of this territory.

The statistics of production since 1894, given below, show the low rank of New Mexico.

VALUE OF CLAY PRODUCTS OF NEW MEXICO FROM 1895 TO 1907.

Year.	Value.	Year.	Value.
1895.............	$18,325	1902.............	$68,879
1896.............	(a)	1903.............	142,039
1897.............	33,270	1904.............	108,764
1898.............	41,940	1905.............	141,722
1899.............	108,090	1906.............	152,599
1900.............	41,898	1907.............	180,284
1901.............	81,345	....	....

(a) Figures for this year not given separately by the United States Geological Survey.

NEW YORK.

It is only natural that somewhat complete records should be found of the early clay-working industry of New York, since every phase of its commercial activities has been chronicled by numerous historians. Indeed, the early records are better than the later ones. As has been done in the case of several other States, an attempt will be made to classify the facts according to products.

Bricks. Clay working appears to have been under way early in the seventeenth century, and we are told that Governor Stuyvesant had introduced brickmaking in New York City between 1630 and 1646 (Ref. 4, XXXIII, p. 266), while a large yard was also located at Fort Orange (Ref. 1, 1, p. 222).

It is also recorded that Wouter Van Twiller of Amsterdam, a governor appointed by the Dutch West India Company, proceeded, on his arrival at Manhattan Island, to erect for his own use a substantial brick house, and several smaller dwellings for the officers, but the bricks used in these buildings were brought from Amsterdam and were of such good quality that few were broken on the long and rough voyage (Ref. 141, p. 30). Some of these early importations still exist in some of the old Dutch houses. The importation of bricks either did not continue, or was too expensive or insufficient to meet the demand, for between 1647 and 1664 the establishment of another brickyard on Manhattan Island is recorded (Ref. 27, p. 80). Moreover Stone (Ref. 26, p. 56) notes that in 1661 "breweries, brick-kilns, and other manufactories carried on a successful business."

The next date recorded is 1742, when the establishment of a brickyard on the site of the present City Hall Park is noted (Ref. 1, I, p. 226).

That brickmaking continued in New York City for some time after this is shown by the fact that in 1822 the New York City yards were still running and equipped with machines turning out 25,000 brick per day of 12 hours with a selling value of $5 to $8 per 1000 (Ref. 1, II, p. 340). All of these yards used the surface loams which were to be had at many points. As the city grew, these yards were gradually crowded out, although it is not known at just what date they were discontinued.

But there was an abundance of brick clays to be had at other points not far distant, for the Hudson River between New York and Albany is bordered at many points with deposits of excellent brick clay, easily accessible for working, and the product from which could be sent by water to New York City.

These plastic resources were taken advantage of at an early date, and even before the Revolution some slight attempts at the manufacture of brick were tried in Rockland County where the clay was found, but the product was only for local use (Ref. 30, p. 171). One yard was certainly in operation at Haverstraw in 1792, and the brick from it were used in the chimney of the old Treason House (Ref. 30, p. 171). Another one was running at Tarrytown in 1799 (Ref. 147, p. 78).

Green (Ref. 30) gives the following interesting account of the Rockland County industry.

" The first kiln of bricks for a *regular* market ever prepared in this County, was baked about 1810, under the management of a company from Philadelphia, and the yard then opened was on the bank of the Minisceongo. The enterprise ended in failure and the work was abandoned. In that year the total number of bricks made in this county was only 94,371,646. Five years elapsed before a second attempt was made. Then in 1817, James Wood, a native of England, who had learned the trade of a brick maker in his native land, and who had been in the brick-making business in Sing Sing and at Verplanck's Point, attracted to Haverstraw by the vast quantities of brick clay and the apparently unlimited supply of wood, leased from the DeNoyelles a piece of land on the river shore, directly opposite their family burying ground, and started the first successful brick yard in the county."

The use of coal dust for burning bricks was accidentally discovered. An English friend of Wood sent him a small quantity of anthracite coal, which was then being developed in Pennsylvania as a curiosity. "On burning it he found that while the combustion gave forth intense heat, there was little smoke."

Attempts were then made to mix coal dust with the bricks in the upper layers of the kiln, where the heat had been insufficient, with the result that they were burned as hard as those in the lower layers, a condition never before attained. This discovery is said to have revolutionized the industry along the Hudson Valley. Wood also invented a machine for mixing coal dust, clay and sand.

The next yard after Wood's was established by the Allison family a short distance north of the foot of the present Main Street in Haverstraw, and in a brief time several yards were opened at Grassy Point, and below Caldwell's Landing.

By 1834 these yards were in a somewhat precarious condition, but in that year David Munn took hold of the business at Grassy Point and made a success of it. In 1838 six yards at Grassy Point and Haverstraw were turning out 12,000,000 brick annually (Ref. 30, p. 173). In 1852, an impetus was given to the brickmaking industry of Rockland County by the invention of the Automatic Brick Machine of R. A. Ver Valen. For some time previous, Hall's Improved Machine had been in use, and the introduction of the new machine of superior efficiency started litigation which resulted in Ver Valen's favor.

From the small beginning around Haverstraw the industry gradually spread to Newburg (where brick had been made at least as early as 1822) (Ref. 32, p. 272), Fishkill, Rondout, Hudson, Coeymans, etc., until now the Hudson Valley belt represents the largest brickmaking district in the United States, if not in the world.

It seems from the available data that brickmaking began in Albany, at the upper end of the Hudson Valley district, almost as soon as it did in New York City, for a tile kiln existed there in 1653 (Ref. 1, 1, p. 224).

Howell and Tenney relate that in 1656–1657 Johan de Hulter came over from Amsterdam and made brick in Albany, being one of the first to ply his trade in this part of the New World. In 1657 his wife sold the kiln to A. J. Ilpendam (Ref. 170, pp. 582–584). Other plants are referred to in the years of 1656, 1662 (Ref. 29, p. 582), and in the period from 1708 to 1746 (Ref. 29, p. 582, and Ref. 1, vol. 1, p. 225). In 1708 John Bryant began making brick in Albany County, and sold them by the pound (Ref. 170, pp. 582–584). This business grew until he employed 100 men and had the largest plant in the State. It was sold in 1743 to Angus McDuffie (Ref. 170, pp. 582–584).

The Albany industry was still prospering in 1799 (Ref. 29, p. 587). It was in this year that John Stanwix began molding brick, and the yard has been continued by his heirs for many years (Ref. 170, pp. 582–584).

Since then, while the industry has continued, it has never expanded to great proportions, there being even now only five or six yards located at Albany.

The brickmaking industry spread north and west from Albany, operations beginning at a number of localities. It is definitely known that yards were in operation in Cohoes in 1832 (Ref. 35, p. 61).

By 1837 yards were described as being in operation near Huntington, Long Island (Ref. 148, p. 91), Jamaica, Long Island (Ref. 148, p. 136), Stuyvesant, Stockport, Hudson, New Lebanon, Staatsburg, and Poughkeepsie (Ref. 148); Lyons, Lockville, Walworth Corners, Rochester, North Penfield, Fairport, Mendon, Pittsford, and Albion (Ref. 148).

By 1842 the industry around Buffalo, now of such importance, had also become well established (Ref. 4, XXVI, p. 199), although it is not known in just what year it began. By 1845 there were yards also in operation at Watertown, Half Moon, Horseheads, and Glens Falls. All of these were producing hand-molded bricks made from surface clays.

The Hudson Valley industry had in the meantime expanded so that by 1843 brickyards had become established at practically all of the localities where they are now in operation (Ref. 149), and even at this early date improvements had been made in the methods of grinding and molding by machinery. That the brickmaking industry was growing rapidly is shown by the fact that the 1860 Census gives 205 yards for this State.

Prior to 1880 all of the brick made in the State were from the soft surface clays of Pleistocene Age, but in 1888 the Horseheads Brick Company at Horseheads and the Elmira Shale Brick Company at Elmira began the use of shale for brick manufacture,[1] using the Devonian shales so widely distributed in the southern part of the State. The use of these deposits has never expanded much, however. Since that time they have been developed at Hornell for common and paving brick, at Jewettville for dry-pressed brick, and at Cairo for paving brick (made at Catskill). The Salina shales near Syracuse have also been worked for brick. The Devonian shales have been utilized for other types of ware, as will be mentioned later.

At the present day the Hudson Valley and Buffalo are the two prominent brickmaking districts, but others have been in operation for a number of years, as around Rochester, Syracuse, Rome, Utica, etc. Pressed brick and paving brick, although manufactured to some extent for at least twenty years, have never attained much prominence in New York.

A word more should be said about the pressed-brick industry, which, as stated above, has never reached great prominence in New York State. For many years a number of the common brick works have repressed a few brick on hand-power represses, but factories devoted exclusively to the manufacture of pressed brick have been few. This has been due largely to the lack of raw materials, and not absence of markets. Some years ago a factory was in operation on Staten Island, and a dry-press brick works was running at Canandaigua, but is now idle.

As a result of these conditions, the Pennsylvania, Ohio, and New Jersey factories find the markets of New York State wide open to them.

Architectural Terra Cotta. The manufacture of this ware was established by the New York Architectural Terra Cotta Company at Long Island City in 1885. This was accomplished only after

---

[1] Private communication from R. G. Eisenhardt.

several unsuccessful attempts to gain a foothold, as architects showed considerable prejudice to the use of these products (Ref. 8, p. 388), but the industry is now on a firm basis. In the early years of its history, the works tried some clay from Long Island and Staten Island, but at the present time relies almost exclusively on New Jersey for its raw material. Terra cotta has been manufactured also at Tottenville, Staten Island, Corning, N.Y. (since 1896), and Glens Falls, N.Y. (as early as 1893), but the works, with the exception of the last, are dependent upon New Jersey and Pennsylvania for their clays.

Roofing Tile have been made only at Alfred Center and Alfred Station, from the Devonian shales, since 1891.[1]

Sewer Pipe. The manufacture of these has never reached large proportions. They were made in Rochester as early as 1879, and have also been produced at Buffalo and Angola. The first two works used New Jersey clays in part, and the third, which has been discontinued, employed Devonian shale.

Fire Brick. Although New York possesses few fire clays, it is probable that the State was not far behind New Jersey in the manufacture of fire brick, since the clays could be so easily obtained from the neighboring State. The industry probably began on Staten Island partly because Cretaceous fire clays occur there in limited quantities. It is known definitely that gas-retorts, probably the first in America, were made in Brooklyn in 1854, and that in 1828 fire brick were manufactured in Utica (Ref. 34, p. 277) and in 1829 in Albany (Ref. 1, II, p. 240).

Other works have since been started at several localities in the State, notably at Troy, but, as can be readily understood, the fire-brick industry can never become of great importance, since all the raw materials must be transported a greater or less distance to the factory.

Pottery. Stone states (Ref. 26, p. 59) that a pottery was established on Long Island in 1661, and engaged in making a ware thought by historians to be equal to Delft. Since the true Delft has a white-ware body, the Long Island material must have been made either from some local pocket of white-burning clay or from New Jersey materials, which seems to the authors doubtful.

[1] Two factories have been started at Malden in the last four years.

Nothing more is heard of the pottery industry until 1735 when a pottery was established by John Remmey, a German, in New York City. This was located on "Potters Hill," near the old City Hall (Ref. 150, also Ref. 6, p. 63). The firm was later known as Remmey & Crolius and the Crolius Pottery.

From other sources we are informed that in 1742 the J. Crolius pottery stood at the end of "18th" Street, in the middle of the street where the Hall of Records now stands, and the directory of 1791 mentions two potteries, known respectively as Crolius' Son, and Remmey's, the location of both being given as Potters Hill.

On a map published in 1813, showing New York City in 1742-4, there are several potteries shown at the intersection of what are now Reade and Cross streets. After the Revolution, Reade Street was extended east to Broadway and Potters Hill was leveled; Crolius moved to Bayard Street and continued in operation there until 1848 (Ref. 6, p. 131).

The development of the pottery industry around New York City was rapidly followed by that at other points. Indeed, it was to be expected that when communities developed, small potteries might spring into being to supply a local demand, and so as early as 1809 stoneware was being made by Paul Cushman of Albany. His wares bore the interesting inscription "Paul Cushman Sto(n)eware Factory, 1809, one half mile west of the Albany Gaol."

Two years before this, or in 1807, an important development began at Athens, in the starting of a pottery by Nathan Clark. Mr. Clark was born at Cornwall in 1787, and learned the business of potting at some factory, not positively known, but thought possibly to be that of Crolius in New York City. The business which he founded at Athens, soon after the birth of that town, was highly successful, and was continued by his successors up to 1890 (Ref. 150).

Clark's early productions were made of local clays, but these proving unsatisfactory, the raw materials were obtained from New Jersey. The product was largely salt-glazed earthenware, but some of the earlier productions were also slip glazed. About 1840 the firm was changed to Clark & Fox, Clark retiring a little later, but subsequently buying the works back from Fox. Mr.

Clark's energies were not confined to Athens, for he established branch potteries in the western part of the State, one of these being at Mount Morris and another at Lyons. Moreover, several of his apprentices left his employ and set up independent works at points farther west in the State (Ref. 150).

There seems to have been considerable activity in the pottery industry in the early half of the nineteenth century. Thus a man named Seymour operated a stoneware plant in Troy from 1809 to 1865, and in Albany from 1800 to 1810. Paul Cushman, as already mentioned, was producing salt-glazed stoneware. Fenton's pottery was established at Ellicott, and a kiln of ware valued at $200 to $500 was burned every two weeks. In 1826 Whittemore came into partnership with him (Ref. 33, pp. 119–120).

The first porcelain made in this State is said to have been that made by Dr. H. Mead of New York City in 1816 (Ref. 8, p. 115). One of the early potteries in the interior of the State was the Central New York Pottery, established at Utica in 1819, and making earthenware (Ref. 8, p. 114). A few years later, in 1831, the present Shepley & Smith pottery at West Troy was established by Perry (Ref. 8, p. 178), and in the following ten or twelve years a number of stoneware potteries were running in Albany. No mention is made of the character or source of their raw materials, and it is not unlikely that some of their clays were brought in from New Jersey. Potteries continued to be established in this region, another one starting at West Troy in 1850.

There were a number of stoneware works in operation in other parts of the State between 1830 and 1850, the localities including Rochester, Penn Yan, Lyons, etc., but the sources of their raw materials are not in all cases known. The factory at Penn Yan drew its supply from New Jersey, and that at Lyons, run by J. Fisher & Co., but later changed to the Lyons Stoneware Company, drew a part of its clay at least from the Perth Amboy district (Ref. 150).

Additional stoneware and red earthenware potteries recorded as running about 1850 were at Albany, West Troy, Sherburne, Poughkeepsie, Brooklyn, Greenpoint, Volney, Stillwater, Huntington, Greenport, Ellenville, and Dundee. One of these, the

Porter and Frazer Pottery of West Troy, is that established by Perry in 1831 (Ref. 150).[1]

No doubt some of these obtained their clays from New Jersey, and in the case of some located at Canterbury, Ellenville, and Poughkeepsie, this information is so given (Ref. 149, p. 145), but it is possible that the Long Island pits supplied some of the material, for the existence of stoneware clays in that region had been pointed out as early as 1837 (Ref. 147). In fact, the clays at Mosquito Cove, Long Island, had been worked for tobacco pipes in 1801 (Ref. 150, p. 260, and Ref. 151, p. 200).

Of some importance to the pottery industry was the development of the natural glaze clay found at Albany, and known as the Albany slip. It is not known just what date its use was discovered or begun, but in the State Geological Report for 1843 (Ref. 149, p. 141) it is stated that the Albany clay had long been used in the glazing of stoneware and shipped all over the country.

Mr. M. V. B. Wagoner, of the Empire Clay Mining Company of Albany, the firm now supplying this clay, informs us that it was mined in 1846 by a man named Orcutt, who owned a pottery in Albany.

The Greenpoint Pottery, of such historic interest to porcelain collectors, was established by Cartlidge and Ridgeway in 1848, and made porcelain hardware, buttons, etc. (Ref. 4, XXIV, p. 24), and in 1850 in their factory there was done some beautiful transfer work equal to the Trenton or East Liverpool work of to-day (Ref. 4, XXIII, p. 123). Soon after this pottery was established a number of others were running in New York City. The Bochs in 1850 began making porcelain hardware in the city (Ref. 8, p. 162), while Morrison and Carr in 1853 made china, majolica, bone china and parian ware (Ref. 8, p. 179). In the case of all of these nothing is said regarding the source of the raw materials, although they certainly did not come from New York State. They may have been obtained from New Jersey and Pennsylvania.

In 1860 Thomas C. Smith bought a pottery from a company of Germans, who had been making the English bone china for three years. When Mr. Smith purchased this factory he had no

---

[1] Comparison of this statement with one by Barber given above shows that two different potteries appear to have been started by Perry.

intention of continuing the business, but during a journey abroad shortly afterwards he became interested in the large factories he visited, and on his return decided to utilize the knowledge he had acquired in endeavoring to manufacture true porcelain in America. The result was that in 1864 the bone china was abandoned and the true hard porcelain substituted, and then the name Union Porcelain Works was adopted.

Mr. Smith was the first to establish the industry in this country upon a successful basis, and succeeded in turning out and placing upon the market a true porcelain of recognized commercial value. The product of the Union Porcelain Works is tableware, electrical insulators, hardware trimmings, and some objects of art. The tableware and hardware trimmings were manufactured at the beginning, but the insulators not until about 1890.

Since that time the pottery industry has developed at several other points, the year 1861 seeing the establishment of another pottery at Albany (Ref. 29, p. 587), and 1871 the beginning of an important white-granite industry at Syracuse, viz., the Onondaga Pottery. This works has continued to the present day, having added bone china to its wares (Ref. 6, p. 422), but does not use any New York clays.

Other white-ware potteries have been established in New York City, Buffalo, and Syracuse, but they bear no relation to the development of the New York clays.

Of equal importance is the establishment of a pottery at Syracuse by Mrs. A. A. Robineau, at which true hard porcelain of highly artistic character is being produced.

There are probably few educated persons in this country who are not familiar with the Rogers groups of statuary, which have done so much to encourage a taste for sculpture in American households, and the story of whose development by the late John Rogers is of considerable interest.[1] Mr. Rogers became interested in making clay statuettes when a boy of about sixteen years, through seeing a friend in Boston, Mass., modeling clay figures. He at once procured some clay for himself from a Charlestown, Mass., pottery, whittled some modeling sticks and made his first figure.

[1] The authors are indebted to Mrs. John Rogers and Dr. George F. Kunz for this information.

He would have been glad to have made this his business at once, but his family were unwilling, as they had no faith in his being able to earn a living from such work, and moreover it was necessary that he should support himself at once. So at their urgent desire he went West and worked at various occupations for many years, but not finding any of these congenial, he returned to the East in the spring of 1860, after having lived in the West for some years, and came to New York. In his trunk he carried " The Slave Auction," and with this subject he started his regular business of making his " Rogers Groups of Statuary." The factory was located in Center Street, New York City, and the clay obtained from several sources, mainly from New Jersey. Mr. Rogers continued in business until 1895, when his health failed, but during the thirty-five years of his business he modeled a number of subjects which are widely known. His best-known groups included: "Coming of the Parson," "The Returned Volunteer," "Taking the Oath," "The Wounded Scout," "Weighing the Baby," etc. He also modeled an equestrian statue of Gen. J. F. Reynolds for the city of Philadelphia, which now stands at the entrance to the City Hall.

Electrical Porcelain. New York is one of the few States in which electrical porcelain is manufactured. This appears to have been started in 1890 by the firm of Pass & Seymour at Syracuse. At that time the business was confined principally to the manufacture of parts for insulation purposes, as sockets, etc., to which the manufacture of insulating tubes was added a little later. This same firm also produced porcelain high-tension insulators in 1903.

Electrical porcelain insulators have also been made at Victor since at least 1900, and for several years the General Electric Company of Schenectady has produced the same line of wares. They have also been manufactured by the Union Porcelain Works of Brooklyn. With few exceptions the clays used have all been obtained outside of New York State.

New York is among the leading States in the clay-working industry, ranking fifth in 1907. Its high standing is due largely to the enormous output of the Hudson Valley brick region. The variety of clay products manufactured in the State of New York is shown in the statistics presented in the following table.

VALUE OF CLAY PRODUCTS OF NEW YORK FROM 1894 TO 1907.

Year.	Common brick.	Vitrified paving brick.	Front brick.	Drain tile.	Sewer pipe.	Architectural terra cotta.	Fireproofing.	Hollow brick.	Tile not drained.	Grand total.
1894	$3,945,022	$136,697		$62,955	$10,000	$508,000	$ 828		$64,704	$5,164,022
1895	4,396,027	121,898	$290,910	56,740	133,000	336,000			143,405	5,880,496
1896	4,141,973	259,550	298,515	292,954	85,289	484,113	72,410		99,060	6,414,206
1897	3,657,750	309,564	263,166	25,385	116,000	420,601	56,410		150,360	5,615,504
1898	4,381,257	302,680	260,135	74,072	89,224	367,854	87,152		83,910	6,622,537
1899	5,275,194	342,845	324,645	41,921	51,293	417,350	108,961		91,645	8,076,412
1900	4,266,715	341,611	249,078	89,019	94,293	676,408	93,994		105,519	7,660,606
1901	4,947,599	343,343	254,696	73,554	96,770	754,911	98,947		140,800	8,291,718
1902	5,021,132	322,250	249,573	110,301	209,105	(a)	123,497		125,680	8,414,113
1903	5,305,522	220,296	248,760	140,181	134,360	947,153	(a)	$28,825	150,504	9,208,252
1904	6,783,528	189,281	263,150	139,876	125,510	785,978	132,035	24,050	154,417	10,543,070
1905	10,297,214	149,391	237,305	153,598	(a)	874,722	117,577	11,295	164,445	14,486,347
1906	9,205,981	163,969	351,824	153,237	(a)	967,987	75,651	32,428	101,319	13,876,607
1907	7,056,453	253,664	198,265	180,818	(a)	1,089,278	73,064	47,254	43,726	11,772,874

Year.	Fire brick.	Miscellaneous brick and tile.	Total brick and tile.	Red earthenware.	Stoneware.	Porcelain electrical supplies.	Miscellaneous pottery.	Total pottery.
1894	$298,578	$137,238	$5,164,022		$44,033 (b)			
1895	302,407	65,022	5,845,463					$44,033
1896	345,485	23,124	6,102,473	$49,200	51,533	$55,000	$156,000	311,733
1897	339,740	93,263	5,432,239	179,265	179,265		4,000	183,265
1898	386,624	46,737	6,079,645	29,723	76,620	90,785	424,693	621,821
1899	227,814	544,552	7,426,220	34,555	33,344	125,234	457,059	650,192
1900	360,933	217,711	6,495,281	25,207	37,008	(a)	1,103,110	1,165,325
1901	293,944	109,704	7,214,358	27,472	48,596	310,214	691,078	1,077,360
1902	402,006	1,170,711	7,484,682	31,873	54,535	391,319	451,704	929,431
1903	629,245	129,328	7,934,174	29,959	52,351	474,842	424,484	981,636
1904	381,784	24,884	9,228,432	33,650	41,131	438,792	801,065	1,314,638
1905	427,873	431,197	12,858,617	32,240	51,540	617,663	926,287	1,627,730
1906	451,783	484,101	12,008,260	34,034	70,131	663,886	1,100,296	1,868,347
1907	538,721	507,133	9,838,376	32,896	87,471	626,032	1,188,099	1,934,498

(a) Included under miscellaneous.　(b) Rockingham and yellow ware.

NORTH CAROLINA.

The early clay industry of North Carolina as of the other southern States was carried on in small, scattered yards. From 1663 to 1729 good brick are said to have been made in the State (Ref. 54), and in 1744 Ed. Heylyn took out patents to manufacture pottery from an "earth" furnished by the Cherokee Indians, a decomposed granitic rock, which he shipped to the Bow potteries in England (Ref. 8, pp. 59–60). Fort Caswell on the coast was built of local brick in 1820 (Ref. 4, XXIV, p. 499). In the North Carolina Geological Survey Report for 1856 (Ref. 55) occurrences are noted of porcelain clay in Lincoln County, fire clay in Gaston County, and clay for pipe bowls in Forsyth County, and in the Report for 1875 (Ref. 56) are mentioned fire clay and kaolin from Greensboro. It is not known that any of these deposits were worked, however.

The history of the development of the kaolin deposits is not without interest. Previous to 1888 miners getting out mica in the State frequently came across masses of kaolin and called it " bull tallow." In that year, however, a Mr. Dutton of Boston in searching for gold discovered the kaolin deposit and realized its value. He sold it to the Harris Kaolin Company, which has since mined it and shipped it in large quantities, their principal mines[1] being in Webster, Jackson County. The kaolin mining is the most important of North Carolina's clay-working industries.

Small potteries have been running in the region around Lincolnton and other points for a number of years, but they are of minor importance and often temporary character. Brickyards were in operation at many points in the State by 1896, and a sewer-pipe works was running at Pomona.

The value of North Carolina's output of clay products since 1894 has been as follows:

---

[1] Private communication.

VALUE OF CLAY PRODUCTS OF NO. CAROLINA FROM 1894 TO 1907.

Year.	Common brick.	Front brick.	Miscella-neous.[1]	Red earthen-ware.	Stoneware.	Other pottery.	Total.
1894	$226,882	....	$59,798	....	....	....	$286,680
1895	311,088	$5,605	90,690	....	$3,600	....	400,983
1896	370,129	5,060	48,310	$1,880	13,075	....	438,454
1897	303,305	8,588	43,431	10,170		$3,700	369,194
1898	347,468	4,200	59,968	1,311	12,815	4,020	429,782
1899	682,282	14,412	51,845	(a)	25,403	260	774,202
1900	737,577	4,025	155,938	1,937	16,498	....	815,975
1901	682,469	8,070	60,787	2,015	17,470	527	771,338
1902	692,813	8,375	79,821	658	13,854	....	795,521
1903	728,802	8,223	111,239	612	13,620	....	862,496
1904	760,161	6,300	117,503	638	13,362	....	897,964
1905	878,539	12,725	115,578	387	12,932	....	1,020,161
1906	1,041,078	4,410	125,080	713	11,057	....	1,182,338
1907	1,150,685	7,925	146,990	2,382	7,840	....	1,315,822

[1] Includes mainly vitrified paving brick, and also a scattered production of drain tile, sewer pipe, fireproofing, and fire brick. (a) Included under miscellaneous.

NORTH DAKOTA.

The history of the clay-working industry of North Dakota as far as is known is given in the fourth report of the North Dakota Geological Survey (Ref. 113, p. 298). "The clay industry of the State is confined almost entirely to the production of bricks. Common brick were probably first manufactured at Fargo, some time in the seventies. The industry spread through the Red River Valley, so that in 1885 plants were in operation at Fargo, Grand Forks, and Minto. Grand Forks took the lead in production, two plants being started in the early eighties, one by Wm. Bridge and another by W. P. Alsip. The industry developed rapidly there, and at present four plants are in operation at Grand Forks. Brick have also been made at several other places in the valley, namely, at Walhalla and Grafton, and at present are manufactured at Drayton, Hillsboro, Fargo, and Abercrombie. Brick plants were early started at Mandan and Jamestown on the Northern Pacific, and at Minot and Williston on the Great Northern railroad. All these plants and several others manufactured common brick by the soft-mud process, using surface clays and burning the brick in scove kilns."

Cretaceous clays were probably first used at Dickinson, where

as early as 1892 common brick was manufactured from the Laramie
clays.   Brick were also made later at New Salem from these clays.
With the building of the Soo railroad the coal mines in Ward
County were developed and brick plants were established at Kenmare, Donnybrook, Burlington and Velva, all using the Laramie
clay.   Those at Kenmare and Burlington are still in operation.
A stiff-mud machine was installed at Kenmare in 1903, and common brick have been made since then on a large scale, being burnt
in updraft and round downdraft kilns.

Pressed brick were first manufactured at Dickinson on the site
of the present plant in 1893 by the Dakota Land and Improvement Company.   The plant was in operation almost two years.
The high-grade, light-burning clays were used with a dry press,
but the brick were probably burned in scove kilns.   Brick were
also made at this time by the stiff-mud process from the same clays
several miles north of Dickinson.   The pressed-brick plant was
idle from 1897 to 1898, when Professor Brannon of the State University bought up the plant and first manufactured front brick on
a permanent basis.   The Dickinson Pressed- and Fire-Brick Company was organized later and developed the same property more
fully.   Since then pressed-brick plants have been established at
Hebron, Mayo, Kenmare, and Wilton.   Repressed front brick
are also made at Richardton.   The Hebron plant used the Tertiary light-burning clays and manufactures fire brick as well as
front brick.   It is interesting to note that the brown lignite coal
of North Dakota makes a very satisfactory fuel for burning brick,
as it burns with little smoke and furnishes a uniform and sufficiently
high heat.   The principal demand for this fuel, except for domestic
use, is from the brickyards of the State.

VALUE OF CLAY PRODUCTS IN NO. DAKOTA FROM 1894 TO 1907.

Year.	Value.	Year.	Value.
1894	$52,400	1901	$76,708
1895	48,000	1902	123,214
1896	59,625	1903	127,085
1897	62,420	1904	147,579
1898	72,900	1905	232,432
1899	168,124	1906	269,873
1900	92,399	1907	287,919

OHIO.

The history of clay-working in the Central States appears to be confined almost entirely to the nineteenth century, although the clay-working industry was no doubt established before that time. Among the Central States Ohio stands out with great prominence, having for some years outranked all other States in the production of clay products. This, perhaps, is not surprising when we consider the vast supplies of Carboniferous fire clays, of Carboniferous and Devonian shales, and of surface clays within its boundaries, these raw materials serving as a basis for the manufacture of large quantities of fire brick, sewer pipe, stoneware, paving brick, pressed and common brick, tiles, etc. In addition to these there are other ceramic industries, such as white-ware factories, which, although not using Ohio clays, nevertheless find other conditions favorable to their existence. Most of these are clustered around East Liverpool.

Widely distributed as are the raw materials, there are several important districts in which many important plants have clustered. Prominent among these are the Ohio Valley, especially near East Liverpool, Zanesville and vicinity, the Akron district, Cincinnati, etc.

The published records which the authors have seen indicate that the clay-working industry of Ohio seems to have begun at a later date than it did in the Eastern States, but it developed more rapidly.

On account of the importance and diversified character of the ceramic industry in Ohio, it seems best to classify the record by products, and describe the developments chronologically as far as possible.

Brick. Many small brickyards working surface clays existed, no doubt, at an early date in the State of Ohio, but little attention seems to have been given them in the published records.

It is known, however, that Captain William Dana came to Marietta, Ohio, from New Hampshire in 1788, and carried on a profitable business making bricks, which were the first known to have been made in the territory (Ref. 157, p. 499).

The industry no doubt continued at scattered points, but no records are available until 1804, when brick molding was under way in Union township, Ross County (Ref. 158, p. 267).

Brick kilns are also known to have been in operation in 1806 at Salem, Perry township (Ref. 159, p. 223); at Fairfield not later than 1807 (Ref. 159, p. 140); and at Cadiz in 1807 (Ref. 160, Vol. 2, p. 169). The first brick house in Highland County was that of Richard Evans of Clear Creek, built in 1809 (Ref. 158, p. 361), while in 1814 a brick cotton factory was constructed at Salem (Ref. 159, p. 223). The first brick house in Palmer township, Washington County, was erected by Jabez Palmer in 1828 (Ref. 157, p. 666). None of these early enterprises, however, were more than temporary efforts.

J. W. Crary, Sr., was making brick in Cincinnati as early as 1829 (Ref. 67), and three years later in 1832 mention is made of a contest between hand molders in Cincinnati, two of whom are said to have made 25,470 and 24,700 brick respectively in one day from sunrise to sunset (Ref. 4, XVIII, p. 338, and Ref. 126, p. 362). Evidence that brickmaking had been under way for some time is shown by the statement in the Ohio Geological Survey Report of 1838, which notes that the industry was well established, bricks being made extensively in the State (Ref. 73, p. 25). They were, moreover, being shipped to other States (Ref. 161, p. 309). Atwater (Ref. 161, p. 316), in writing of the industry at this time (1838), says: "In some parts of the State brick houses predominate. In the remainder of the State brick is preferred as the cheapest, most durable and best. The materials for brick are near the spot where they are needed. . . . The farmer and his family can make the brick without hiring any of the work done" (Ref. 161, p. 316).

Cincinnati, already referred to, was also the locality at which the first dry-press machine is said to have been tried (Ref. 45, II, 1846, p. 20). The reference states that it was the first one tried in the country, but other records throw doubt on this. Cincinnati seemed to continue a center of brick production, for by 1859 it had 60 brickyards employing 500 hands with a yearly production of $285,000 worth of brick. Indeed, twelve years prior to this, or in

1847, the number of brick houses were said to exceed those built of wood (Ref. 160, Vol. II, p. 32).

Columbus brickyards were by 1853 producing 18,000,000 brick annually (Ref. 167, p. 330). Akron is noted as producing brick in 1856, the yard being established by the Robinson Clay Products Company, and this plant is still in operation. Brick plants are mentioned as in operation at Waverly in 1861 (Ref. 168, p. 753) and at Chillicothe in 1866 (Ref. 158, p. 207).

The pressed-brick industry was, however, slow in developing. Mr. P. L. Simpson of Chicago[1] informs the authors that a dry-press machine, the first of which he has any knowledge, was built in Cleveland, Ohio, between 1865 and 1868, and installed near the present site of the Garfield monument. The material used was a surface clay and proved a failure, so that the machine had to be moved to Evansville, Ind., where it also failed, and was then moved to Nashville, Tenn. Curiously enough the first installation of the machine at Cleveland was almost directly over one of the great deposits of red shale peculiarly adapted to dry-press methods, but it was not until 1888 that this material was discovered by a Chicago man and hauled to Chicago, where it was worked on dry-press machines. But even in 1884, the pressed-brick industry was not highly developed, as Prof. Ed. Orton Jr. (Ref. 140, p. 704) speaks of it as "representing one of the newer departments of building-material manufacture." Zanesville was at that time the most important locality, the clay used being probably the Lower Freeport. Eight years later, in 1892, the pressed-brick industry was well established, the Columbus Brick and Terra Cotta Company, North Baltimore Pressed Brick Company, Akron Vitrified Brick Company, Oakland Pressed Brick Company (of Zanesville), and the Findlay Hydraulic-Press Brick Company being the most important ones. The Akron Vitrified Brick Company, which is located at Independence, was the only one using red shales. The Oakland plant at Zanesville began by using a red surface loam, but later mixed it with the Middle Kittanning shale. The factories at Union Furnace and North Baltimore were pioneers in the manufacturers of different colored pressed brick (Ref. 135, p. 236).

[1] Private communication.

In 1893 the Ohio shale of the Devonian had been used only at Columbus (Ref. 135), for the manufacture of common brick, but since then the shales of this formation have assumed considerable importance around Cleveland for making this class of structural clay products.

The Medina clay-shales were worked in connection with drift clays for tile as early as 1873 in Miami County, but there are no published records to indicate that they have been used since that date (Ref. 135).

The Bedford shale of the Lower Carboniferous was in use in 1893 at one point (Akron) for making red-pressed brick (Ref. 135), and since then it has developed into one of the important brick shales of the State. It is now worked at Bedford, Akron, Independence, and a number of other localities for pressed-brick manufacture (Ref. 139, p. 392). It is also used at Willow Station for common brick (Ref. 139, p. 392).

The Lower Mercer clay and shale were of importance as early as 1893, having been used in Stark, Tuscarawas, Muskingum, and Hocking counties. The Putnam Hill or Brookville clay, also of the Allegheny or Lower Coal Measures, is likewise of importance, having been utilized at a number of localities, especially Zanesville (Ref. 139, p. 395).

At Shawnee, Ohio, where there are now several works making pressed brick, the Upper Mercer clay is being used for making buff, gray, speckled and iron-mottled flashed brick.

The most important pressed-brick region of Ohio at the present day is in the Hocking Valley.

Terra Cotta. Ohio has never assumed any prominence as a producer of architectural terra cotta, but considerable ornamental terra cotta, such as lawn vases, statuary, etc., and useful terra cotta, like chimney tops, have been produced, even as early as 1867, at Wellsville (Ref. 159, p. 284). It is also referred to in 1884 (Ref. 140, p. 719).

Hollow Brick, Fireproofing and Conduits. As early as 1884 (Ref. 140, p. 708) fireproofing was much used, Toronto, Jefferson County, and Columbus, Franklin County, both being important localities of manufacture.

Hollow bricks were then made at only one place in Summit County, and E. Orton, Jr., stated at that time (Ref. 140, p. 707) that "the use of this article is so limited as to scarcely deserve description."

It is not surprising, however, to find at the present day that Ohio leads in the manufacture of hollow-building tiles or blocks, because these are much used in the Central States, and Ohio contains the proper raw materials for making them. In 1907 the value of hollow block produced in this State amounted to $314,545, which was slightly below 1906. Much the same grade of material is used for fireproofing, and while the value of this ware produced in 1907 amounted to $691,531, it was a poor second to New Jersey, which is much better located with respect to large markets, such as those afforded by the Eastern cities.

Fireproofing is manufactured at a number of localities in Ohio, many of the plants belonging to the National Fireproofing Company of Pittsburg, which was incorporated in 1899, and has works at East Palestine, Columbia County; Osnaburg, Waynesburg, and Greentown, Stark County; Magnolia, Carroll County; Delaware, Delaware County; Haydenville, Hocking County. Some of these plants also make conduits; in fact, those first made in this country were produced at Aultman, Ohio,[1] probably as early as 1893.

Wall, Floor and Roofing Tiles. The Ohio clays are used for both floor and roofing tile, but wall tile made within the State are manufactured from white-burning clays not obtainable in Ohio.

One of the early floor-tile factories, namely that of the American Encaustic Tiling Company, was erected at Zanesville in 1875 (Ref. 8, p. 353). This plant, which is said to be the oldest and largest in the country, has continued in operation up to the present time.

There were also at this period three works making artistic panel and encaustic tile, the largest being the American Encaustic Tiling Company mentioned above. The clays of the Putnam Hill horizon were the main reliance of the factory at Zanesville. The Mosaic Tiling Company began at Zanesville in 1895, with the

[1] Private communication from J. C. Rossi.

manufacture of inlaid mosaic tile. This was discontinued in 1899 for the manufacture of ceramic mosaic tile, and in 1900 wall tile was added. For the floor tile the local red and buff clay were used to some extent, but for the wall tile china clays and ball clays were shipped in from other States and also from England.

The Ohio Tile Company, which started at Hamilton in 1901, was the outgrowth of a works known as the Hamilton Tile and Pottery Company, and produces enamel dull-finish tile and terra vitrae of brick, but the product is made almost entirely from clays mined outside of Ohio.

The Zanesville Tile Company began in 1905 manufacturing floor, wall, and enamel tiles, from domestic clays not obtained in Ohio, and this plant is still in operation.

A peculiar style of wall tile for exterior work is that made by the Fisher Veneer Tiling Company of Zanesville.

Roofing tile appear to have been made in Ohio at as early a date as pottery, but the former were made for private use, and the latter for market. Thus, it is recorded that John Robinson was making roofing tile at Germantown, Ohio, in 1812, and one of the buildings roofed with these was standing as late as 1907. In 1827, the Zoarites, who founded a colony at Zoar in Tuscarawas County, engaged in the making of clay roofing tile for use on their own buildings. These tile, which had rounded lower ends and were known as "beaver-tails," were made by these people simply for their own use (Ref. 4, LI, p. 584).

The actual manufacture of roofing tile as a commercial venture does not appear to have begun in Ohio until 1873, when John Conrade of Zanesville commenced the manufacture of roofing tile under the J. B. Hughes patents. They were of the interlocking type. Three years later, or in 1876, H. B. Camp of Cuyahoga Falls commenced the manufacture of roofing tile of the French diamond pattern. The industry was conducted on a small scale, however, and Mr. Camp soon turned the business over to J. C. Ewart of Akron, Ohio (Ref. 4, LI, p. 584).

It was a year before Mr. Camp began, however, that Merrill and Ewart started the manufacture of roofing tile at Akron, Ohio, using the Sharon shales of the Coal Measures, and by 1892 theirs was the largest roofing tile works in the country. Indeed it is still in operation, but since 1902 has been known as the Akron Roofing Tile Company.[1] This plant was referred to in the Ohio Geological Survey Report for 1884 (Ref. 140, p. 706).

In 1893 the Carboniferous clays were being worked for roofing tile manufacture at three points (Ref. 135), viz.: At Akron, by Merrill and Ewart; at Bellaire, by the Bernard Tile Company, no longer in operation; and at New Philadelphia, by the Repp Roofing Tile Company, not running at the present time.

Since that time others have started as follows: National Roofing Tile Company at Lima; Ludowici-Celadon Company, New Lexington, using a clay that lies just above the Putnam Hill Limestone; Cincinnati Roofing Tile Company, Cincinnati, organized in 1895 and still running.

In the year 1905 a merger of the Ludowici Roofing Tile Company and the Celadon Roofing Tile Company was effected, the new company, with headquarters at Cleveland, Ohio, being known as the Ludowici-Celadon Company, and controlling factories in several states.

Sewer Pipe. Ohio at the present day ranks first in the production of sewer pipe, and its manufacture was perhaps the most important development in the Ohio clay industry between 1850 and 1860 (Ref. 7).

In 1850 a Mr. Hill found that the clay on an East Akron farm was suited for sewer-pipe manufacture, and the first shale sewer-pipe was made in 1851 (Ref. 7).

Two years later (1853) two Scotchmen who were engaged in making chimney tops at Anderson, W. Va., crossed the river and began sewer-pipe manufacture from Ohio River fire clays, their plant being erected at Newburg (now Toronto) (Ref. 7).

In 1868 the first steam press for sewer-pipe manufacture was invented, and in 1869 and 1870 sewer-pipe factories started up at Freemans, Elliottsville, Columbus (Ref. 167, p. 331), and Wellsville (McClave). All of these are now abandoned, the first two being razed to the ground. In the case of the Ohio River plants their abandonment[2] was due to their absorption by the American

---

[1] Private communication.　　[2] Letter from E. Orton, Jr.

Sewer Pipe Company, which organization bought up all the plants along the river, improved the best ones, and dismantled or closed down the others.

The Columbus plant was closed down mainly because of the poor character of the raw materials, which could only be worked profitably with the greatest care. The works has since been used as a paving-brick plant, but is now idle.[1]

In 1879 Robinson Bros. & Co. built a plant in Akron for making sewer pipe. The clay, known as the "Akron shale" (Sharon shale), was mined near the works, and the industry has continued up to the present time, but with considerable enlargement, so that its present output is about 2000 cars per annum.[2]

There are no detailed published data showing the development of the sewer-pipe clays and industry in different parts of the State, but by 1884 there were three important districts, as follows: Jefferson County with 8 works, Akron district with 6, Columbus district with 2, as well as some scattered plants. Ohio was even then the leading producer of sewer pipe, followed by Missouri, New Jersey, Illinois, Pennsylvania, and Indiana in the order named (Ref. 140, p. 711).

In 1890, or about 11 years after the establishment of the earlier mentioned plant of Robinson Bros. & Co., the same firm purchased the fire-brick plant owned by the Wentz-Wagner Company, 3 miles north of Canal Dover, and incorporated as the Crown Fire Clay Company. While used primarily for making fire brick it also has a large addition for manufacturing sewer pipe from the shales and clays near the works.

Still later, in 1898, the same firm purchased the plant of the Royal Fire Clay Company of Midvale, Ohio (which had been in operation since 1891), and incorporated it as the Royal Sewer Pipe and Fire Brick Company. This was remodeled for making sewer pipe, and has a present capacity of 5000 car loads per annum.[3] The product is made from local clays.

This was followed in 1903 by the purchase of the Canton and

---

[1] Private communication.
[2] Private communication, B. W. Robinson.
[3] Private communication, B. W. Robinson.

Malvern Fire Brick Paving Company (built in 1880), at Malvern, Ohio, which was after remodeling used for making fire-clay pavers up to April, 1907, when it was changed over to a fire-clay sewer-pipe plant, with an annual output of 1800 car loads per annum. In 1903 these various companies were consolidated to form the Robinson Clay Products Company.

Later, in June, 1906, the company began the construction of a sewer-pipe plant at Akron, which will have an annual capacity of 5000 car loads. This is worthy of mention, as the works are equipped throughout with electric motors, doing away with shafting and belting.

Returning to 1893, we find that the sewer-pipe clays were by that time being quite extensively used. Orton in his report (Ref. 135, p. 215) lists 35 sewer-pipe plants, most of which used fire clays. They were scattered over the Carboniferous area of the State. One plant, that at Barberton, was at that time said to be the finest in the world (Ref. 135, p. 214).

A notable event in 1900 was the formation of the American Sewer Pipe Company, which purchased a number of factories in Ohio and neighboring States. Some of these were closed down, while others were strengthened and are still running. The Ohio plants taken in were at East Liverpool, Walkers, Empire, Freemans, Elliottsville, Toronto, Uhrichsville, Akron, Barberton, Columbus, and Lisbon.

The clays used for sewer-pipe manufacture have been almost exclusively the Carboniferous fire clays and shales. Orton in 1893 (Ref. 135) states that the shale of the Devonian had been used for this purpose at Columbus (having been in operation in 1884 [Ref. 140, p. 661]), and this continued until 1900, although the material had to be treated with the greatest care on account of its high carbon contents.[1]

The Sharon shales, overlying the Sharon coal, became of importance in the early nineties, and according to E. Orton (1893) " had lately become the basis of one of the largest sewer-pipe industries in the United States at Akron and vicinity." At about this same time the Lower Kittanning clays were also assuming importance. Around Uhrichsville the Lower Kittanning or No. 5 underclay is

---

[1] Private communication.

used for the manufacture of sewer pipe by three concerns. Two of these, the Uhrichsville Sewer Pipe Company and the Diamond Fire Clay Company, are owned by the American Sewer Pipe Company, while the third, the Buckeye Sewer Pipe Company, is an independent plant. The approximate dates of establishment of the first two were 1888 and 1887 respectively.

Paving Brick.[1] The manufacture of regular vitrified paving brick in Ohio appears to date from the year 1887, for the factory of the Malvern Clay Company, at Malvern, started in that year, is said to have been the first plant to manufacture paving brick from fire clay,[2] the supply coming from the No. 6 vein of the Sandy Valley in the Canton district. This preceded the plants making paving brick from shale by about one year at least. These Malvern clays are still extensively used, and as late as 1904 the industry was expanded by the organization of the Big Four Brick Company.

The first brick plant at Canton producing pavers was that of Captain Williams (Ref. 4, XXXIII, p. 18), which was succeeded very shortly by the Metropolitan Company. They used the "Canton shale."

Prior to 1888 the paving bricks made around Canton were manufactured at an ordinary building-brick plant, but since that time several factories have given their entire attention to it, using the stiff-mud process of molding.

The manufacture of shale pavers was begun at Gloucester by the Wassall Brick Company in 1889, and in the next year paving-block manufacture was undertaken at Nelsonville by the Nelsonville Brick Company. At that time there are said to have been but two other factories in Ohio making paving blocks. The material used at Nelsonville is the fire clay underlying the No. 5 or Lower Kittanning coal.

Paving blocks were made at Zanesville at least as early as 1891 by the South Zanesville Sewer-Pipe and Brick Company,

---

[1] While most of the important localities are referred to under this subheading, there are some necessary omissions, for the reason that information regarding them was not obtainable.

[2] C. J. Deckman, private correspondence.

from a mixture of shale, fire clay, and potter's clay.[1] In 1902 the making of paving brick was undertaken at Youngstown by the Bessemer Limestone Company, the material used being a shale overlying the limestone at that locality.

The same year (1902) witnessed the organization of the Peebles Paving Brick Company at Portsmouth, at which place pavers had been made, however, since 1892. Still later, or in 1905, the Carlyle Paving Brick Company was started, and all these plants, as well as some at Sciotoville, are said to use a Sub-Carboniferous shale.

E. Orton, Jr., in referring to the paving-brick industry (Ref. 135, p. 132), states that by 1893 the clays used for paving brick were shales, impure fire clays and river clays. The shales used at that time included the Lower Mercer, Putnam Hill, Freeport, Kittanning, and Cambridge Limestone formations (*ibid.*, p. 134). The alluvial clays, which have never assumed importance, were first taken up about 1885 at Middleport (*ibid.*, p. 140), but in 1893 the majority of pavers were made from fire clay, the great shale measures being but little developed. Around Canton the Putnam Hill and Lower Kittanning clays were then being utilized for paving-brick manufacture.

Orton at that time pointed out that the Lower Barren Measures carried vast deposits of shale, which were just beginning to be understood and appreciated, and might possibly be of value for pavers. These are now extensively used for the manufacture of paving brick.

The Devonian shales were developed later. They have been utilized at Collinwood, Cuyahoga County, since 1900, and at Wickliffe since about 1896. Other openings have been made at Carrolton, Carroll County, and Conneaut, Ashtabula County, while in 1905 their use was begun at Willow, Cuyahoga County, by the Newburgh Brick and Clay Company.

Since 1893 the manufacture of paving brick from the Carboniferous shales and clays has increased tremendously, and the production has been swelled slightly by pavers made from other formations, so that in 1907 Ohio produced 264,571,000 brick

---

[1] Private correspondence.

valued at $2,672,600, being the leading State, and far outranking all others.

This output of Ohio represents about 30 per cent of the total product of the country, and over 27 per cent of the total value. The prominence of Ohio in the production of this line of clay wares is due largely to the natural advantages which it possesses. And yet it was not the pioneer in the manufacture of this grade of wares. It has not been possible to mention more than a few of the more important localities regarding which, or from which, information could be obtained. Other plants of size are located at Logan, Athens, Fultonham, Trimble, Massillon, and smaller ones at a number of other localities, the large majority of them situated within the Carboniferous area of the State.

Fire Brick. The first refractory material used in the State was sandstone, which was superseded by fire-clay brick as soon as the blast furnaces began to use "stone coal" (Ref. 140, p. 686), but the exact date of this change is not known, although it was not later probably than 1850.

McClave (Ref. 7) states that fire brick were made at Toronto as early as 1830, but we have no accurate information on this point.

According to Mr. Thomas Kemp of Strasburg, Ohio, fire brick were made near Steubenville about 1857 or 1858. They were manufactured entirely of plastic clay and were not of very high grade, but were used in the construction of blast furnaces at that time. These same clays are now being worked by the National Fire Brick Company on the Ohio River to make top linings for blast furnaces.[1]

Sciotovillle, a locality supplying refractory clays of high grade, supported a fire-brick plant at least as early as 1861, when the firm of Reese & Sons was established. Two others, Watkins, Porter & Co., and Farney, Murray & Co., organized about 1865, but in 1870 all three were consolidated under the name of the Sciotoville Fire-Brick Company (Ref. 168, p. 316). The product of these Sciotoville factories no doubt came into great favor, for by 1869 it was said to be supplanting the Mount Savage bricks that had hitherto been shipped in from Maryland (Ref. 76, p. 136).

[1] Private communication.

Another factory the Minor Fire-Brick Company, was erected at Empire in the Strasburg district in 1869.[1] Webster had also a plant in operation in the same year (Ref. 168, p. 375).

That the industry had not assumed prominence by 1870 is shown by J. S. Newberry, who in his report of that year (Ref. 77, p. 50) says, "Nearly every coal seam in the series is underlaid by a bed of fire clay of greater or less thickness," which was probably a somewhat too optimistic statement to make. "In Summit County only a single stratum is worked, — the Springfield clay underlying Coal No. 3, — but there are now in that county something like forty potteries supplied from this source."

"In Holmes, Stark, Tuscarawas and Columbiana counties there are many beds of fire clay of excellent quality. Most of these are like the Springfield clay, eminently plastic, and well adapted to the manufacture of stoneware." . . . "Quite another quality of fire clay and of more rare and peculiar properties is that mined by Mr. Holden, at Mineral Point, Tuscarawas County. This is not at all plastic, and yet it is exceedingly resistent to the action of fire. As a consequence, it is destined to be largely employed in the manufacture of fire brick; fragments of this clay being cemented by just enough of this plastic clay to hold them together.

"Practically this clay corresponds to the ' cement,' or once burned clay, employed in precisely the same manner by the fire-brick makers of New Jersey.

"The manufacture of our fire clays is an industry yet in its infancy, but one destined to great expansion. Our furnace men are paying for Mount Savage or Amboy fire brick from $80 to $90 per thousand, while, by the judicious use of the best materials we have, brick nearly or quite as good may be furnished at a little more than half this price " (Ref. 77, p. 50).

By 1870 there were three fire-brick plants in operation at Sciotoville (Ref. 77, p. 169), and one in Webster (Ref. 77, p. 166). The Lower Kittanning clay of the Hanging Rock district [known as the Newcastle vein (Ref. 140, p. 122)] was being worked as early as 1871, and is still being mined (Private correspondence). Two years later (1873) good fire brick are said to have been made in

[1] Private correspondence.

Springfield (Ref. 78, p. 221). The fire clays were developed at Oak Hill, Jackson County, in 1872 (Ref. 168, p. 668), and at Letonia in 1875 (Ref. 159, p. 244). The latter, however, appear to have been utilized mainly for stoneware.

By the middle eighties the refractory-ware industry seemed to have gotten on a pretty firm footing, and a number of fire-clay horizons had been developed.

The No. 1 bricks at that time came mainly from the Portsmouth district, but also from Logan and Mineral Point (Ref. 140, p. 700). The lower grades of fire clay, producing a No. 2 brick, were made chiefly in the Ohio Valley. The Sciotoville clay, of the Sub-Carboniferous, already famous in Kentucky, had likewise been opened up by this time (Ref. 140, p. 661). Manufacturers did not, even then, confine themselves to fire brick alone, but also utilized the clays for other types of refractory wares, such as retorts, which were being made in some quantities at Dover and Cincinnati (Ref. 140, p. 700). Glass pots were manufactured at Steubenville, but the raw materials were drawn only in part from Ohio, German and Missouri clays making up a large part of the mixture.

The Lower Mercer clay was worked north of Dover (Ref. 140, p. 663), but the plant has since changed over to sewer pipe. Fire brick were made at Union Furnace by the Columbus Brick and Tile Company in 1886 (Ref. 4, XXXI, p. 20) from local clays, and the Cleveland Fire Brick Company was organized in the same year (Ref. 4, XVIII, p. 26), but had to ship its clays in from the southern or southeastern part of the State. As late as 1893 the statement was made by Edward Orton, Jr. (Ref. 135, p. 218), that the fire-brick business was not in an over-healthy condition, and that many fire-brick manufacturers had gone over to the paving-brick business. This period represented a decline, however, following over-expansion during a time when there were numerous small iron furnaces calling for many brick. With improvements in blast-furnace practice, there was a concentration towards fewer furnaces of greater capacity, so that temporarily at least less brick were called for.

At that time (1893) the main fire-brick industry was located in the Ohio Valley from Steubenville to Wellsville (Ref. 135, p. 233). The important refractory clay horizons had also become pretty well known by that date, in fact some of them had been developed some years previous to this. Thus, the Mineral Point clay had been used in glass-pot manufacture for a number of years (Ref. 135, p. 231). The Sciotoville clay of the Sub-Carboniferous was used at Sciotoville and near Logan, Hocking County, for fire-brick manufacture (Ref. 135), as was also the Tionesta clay at Union Furnace.

But it was the Kittanning shale which even in 1893 was the great clay horizon of the State, and which in its importance far outweighed that of any other clay bed in the geological section of Ohio. Indeed, Orton at that time pronounced it as of probable equal value to all other sources of the Coal-Measure clays combined (Ref. 135). He says: "The Kittanning clay-horizon proper is seen at its best where it enters the State from Pennsylvania, and again where it leaves the State in its extension into Kentucky. In both of these localities of the Ohio Valley, viz., in Columbiana and Jefferson counties, on the one side, and on the other, in Lawrence County, it shows large volume and excellent quality. A second, or flint-clay phase, is found at a few points in Stark, Tuscarawas and Carroll counties, known as Mineral Point clay, and was then (in 1893) largely worked at Canal Dover. The Lower Kittanning clays were even then used not only for fire brick, but also for other purposes.

The Middle Kittanning clay had been developed at one point, viz., Oak Hill, Jackson County, while the Lower Freeport was worked at one locality for refractory wares, viz., Moxahala, Perry County. These same formations are worked at the present day, but some of the fire-brick factories located in the southeastern and southern part of the State obtain their clays in part from Pennsylvania and Kentucky.

The region between Strasburg and Mineral Point is of considerable prominence at the present time, for it is between these two points that there are important deposits of flint and also plastic clay underlying the No. 5 coal, as previously referred to in connection with Mineral Point. This clay has been developed extensively since 1860, and there are now six plants manufacturing fire brick from it in this district. They are as follows:

National Fire Brick Company, Strasburg, O.	60,000 daily capacity.
Robinson Clay Product Company, Parrel.	40,000
Dover Fire Brick Company, Strasburg.	30,000
Columbia Fire Brick Company, "	30,000
Federal Clay Product Company, Mineral Point.	20,000
C. E. Holden, " "	mostly special shapes.

A plant was erected at Canal Dover by David Miller, Henry Harriff, and a Mr. Ross in 1868, but as all the best clay had to be hauled by team from Strasburg to Canal Dover, the plant was reorganized by Cleveland capital and moved to the former place, where it was operated under the name of the Dover Fire-Brick Company.

In 1880 Mr. Thos. Kemp, who was one of the pioneer operators in this section, built the plant of the Wentz-Wagner Company located three miles from Canal Dover. This plant was later sold to the Crown Fire-Brick Company, and is now controlled by the Robinson Clay Products Company of Akron, Ohio.

Nine years later, or in 1889, Mr. Kemp and the Stowe-Fuller Company organized the National Fire-Brick Company located near Strasburg, which has been expanded until now it is the largest fire-brick plant in the State.

In 1904 the Columbia Fire-Brick Company was organized and located near Strasburg. All of these plants are in the northwestern section of what is termed the Strasburg field, and the development of the fire-brick business in that section has been greater than at the Mineral Point end of the field, because the flint-clay beds are said to be heavier and workable to better advantage there.

This same general region is of importance, not alone as a producer of fire brick, for in the same valley there are a number of other clay plants, many of them working the clay under the No. 5 coal, and utilizing it in the manufacture of sewer pipe, building brick, paving brick, fireproofing, etc.

The operations of the Harbison-Walker Refractories Company are referred to in some detail under Pennsylvania, but this corporation also controls several plants in Ohio. These with their approxi-

mate dates of establishment are as follows: Portsmouth and
Kentucky Fire-Brick Company, operating one plant at Portsmouth
since 1888, and another at South Webster since 1883; the Scioto
Star Works at East Portsmouth built in the seventies, and the
Blast Furnace Works at Sciotoville, recently dismantled on
account of unfavorable conditions for competing with other
works.

The three important fire-brick producing districts in Ohio at
the present day are the Canal Dover area including Strasburg,
the Ohio River from Steubenville to East Liverpool, and the
Portsmouth section (Private communication).

Pottery. The most important development of the potting
industry in Ohio has been largely in those counties underlain by
the Coal Measures, whose clays were much used by the early
potteries, but as the manufacturing enterprises developed and
higher grades of ware were made, clays were brought in from
other States.

In the Carboniferous area mentioned the greatest expansion
seems to have occurred in the Ohio Valley, notably around East
Liverpool, which is mentioned under a separate head. A second
important center is at Zanesville.

We are not able to state just when the first pottery in Ohio
was established, but in the year 1806 Richard Iliff started one at
the Eagle Spring, near the Court House in Highland County.
When Hillsborough was laid out he moved into town, and was
later succeeded by Fisher and McClain. A. Gossett, who learned
his trade under Iliff, and who retired from business in 1880,
carried on a pottery during the War of 1812, and it is stated that
his ware was substituted for queensware for table dishes, tea sets,
etc. (Ref. 158, p. 364).

It seems probable that common pottery was made at several
other localities in Ohio as early as 1812; in fact, one works is
credited to Salem (Ref. 159, p. 223) and another to Steubenville
(Ref. 160, Vol. II, p. 258).

Steubenville had two earthenware factories in 1817 (Ref. 70,
p. 239), and Field in 1829 says that there were potteries in Lee
and Williamson which had been in operation for "many years"

(Ref. 71, p. 197), but no mention is made of the character of the ware or the kind of clay used.

At Wellsville, which now has a number of potteries, potting was introduced about 1826 by Joseph Wells, who made red earthenware and stoneware. Previous to 1850 Rockingham and yellow ware were attempted, but did not succeed (Ref. 159, p. 284). In 1837 earthenware was not only made in Ohio, but was shipped into other States (Ref. 72, p. 309).

The published records up to this date are evidently incomplete, for in 1838, when the first Ohio Geological Survey was published, pottery clays were already being worked at Springfield, Milton, Canfields' Corners, Zanesville, Zoar, New Philadelphia, and Newport. One of these localities, Zanesville, was destined to become a famous clay-working center. All of these potteries appear to have used the coal underclays. At Springfield there were then (1838) 5 potteries for stoneware turning out annually 80,000 gallons (Ref. 73), but now there is only one plant near there.

In the next decade, or up to about 1850, the foundation of Ohio's prominence in clay-working was greatly strengthened, the chief factor being the establishment of the industry at East Liverpool, and this locality will be referred to in more detail later.

During the early forties pottery-making in Cincinnati was also quite active, and in 1841 the Cincinnati pottery is said to have produced $12,000 worth of ware with the employment of 11 hands (Ref. 74, p. 56). About 1842 W. Bromley was running a pottery in the same city (Ref. 8, p. 273), and previous to 1850 a man named Kendalls ran a stoneware and Rockingham-ware factory at this locality.

In 1849, Hill, Foster & Co. made the Old Black Mill at Middlebury (now East Akron) into a pottery (McClave), while some three years after this there was established at Akron the firm of Whitmore, Robinson & Co., for making Rockingham and yellow queensware, this being the first concern to make that class of ware in that section. The factory was located in what was then known as Middlebury, but is now a part of the city of Akron. This plant has since been remodeled until it now constitutes the

No. 1 plant of the Robinson Clay Products Company. In 1870 the manufacture of stoneware, such as butter jars, churns, jugs, etc., was added to the output. The clay for all grades of ware came from Akron township. This clay is said to have been used previous to this by several small potteries located at Mogadore, but these have since discontinued, probably because they could not compete with larger and more modern plants which have been constructed in that part of the State. Another important producer at this locality is the United States Stoneware Company, which was established in 1865 for the manufacture of stoneware. Its clays are obtained from North Springfield, Ohio.

By the year 1869 extensive potteries were in operation in Muskingum and Perry counties using the underclay of the Coal Measures in those districts (Ref. 76, p. 136). As can be seen by reference to the Ohio Geological Survey Report for 1874, ordinary brick and pottery were so extensively made that any attempt to enumerate all the plants would be useless.

Steubenville is located in an active pottery-producing belt, and this ware had been made in that district as early as 1812 as mentioned above, but no important plant appears to have been started until 1879, in which year the Steubenville Pottery began operations, making semi-vitreous china, but drawing all its clays from other States. It was in this same year (1879) that the Wheatley Pottery of Cincinnati started, but its steady production of art pottery did not begin until some years later.

A most important event in the early eighties was the founding of the Rookwood Pottery in Cincinnati by Mrs. Maria Longworth Nichols (now Mrs. Bellamy Storer). The clays at first used were from Ohio, but in later years the raw materials from other States were largely drawn upon. The underglaze decorations of the Rookwood ware have remained unsurpassed for many years. The earlier wares had reds, yellows, and browns as the principal colors, covered by a bright glaze. Matte glazes were introduced about 1890, and the latest type of these, the "Vellum" matte, was first shown at the St. Louis Exposition.

More recently the factory has added architectural faience to its output.

In 1884 (Ref. 140, p. 682) East Liverpool and Cincinnati were the two white-ware districts of Ohio, and there were also at this time three important stoneware districts which in the order of their importance were Akron, Summit County, Roseville, Perry County, and Rock House, Hocking County (Ref. 140, p. 669). The clay used at Akron was the Sharon shale, and that at Roseville the Brookville and Kittanning (Ref. 140, p. 664). The earthenware production had also assumed some importance by this date, the industry being supported mainly by the Carboniferous clays.

According to E. Orton, Jr. (Ref. 140, p. 676), a mixture of Lower Kittanning clay and Lower Barren Measures shale was employed at East Liverpool for making door knobs. Other important earthenware manufacturing centers were in Hamilton and Columbiana counties, the former producing mainly kitchen utensils, the latter, in addition, door knobs.

These same two districts were also important producers of yellow and Rockingham wares, the highest form of pottery made within the State exclusively from Ohio clays (Ref. 140, p. 678), a condition which exists at the present day. In the former district, which included East Liverpool, there were nine large yellow-ware works, all using Lower Kittanning clays.

The Cincinnati district at this time (1884) had ten potteries, the clays all coming from the Kittanning and Ferriferous limestone formations of Lawrence County (Ref. 140, p. 678).

The sagger clays used in yellow-ware manufacture at this time came from Ohio, but those employed in the making of saggers for white-ware had to be brought from New Jersey (Ref. 140, p. 680), and this still holds true to some extent.[1] The best natural stoneware clays in the State at that time were said to be those of Springfield township, Summit County, and occurred with the Quakertown seam of coal. These supplied the potteries at Mogadore, Tallmadge, Cuyahoga Falls, and Akron. The Lower Mercer clay also occurring there was avoided as being of no value, although the same formation in southwestern Hocking County yielded a good stoneware material (Ref. 140, p. 662).

Some idea of the early importance of the pottery industry can be

[1] Private correspondence.

gained from the statement that in 1882 Ohio produced earthen-ware alone valued at $419,028.

The growth of the stoneware industry is perhaps best indicated by the statement that in 1893 there were no less than forty potteries in operation with an annual capacity of 24,350,000 gallons (Ref. 135, p. 117). The ware from these factories was shipped all over the country, even to the Pacific coast (Ref. 135, p. 118). East Liverpool was then the most prominent yellow-ware district, but factories were also located at Wellsville, Akron, East Palestine, and Cincinnati (Ref. 135, p. 121), and yet up to this time there were only two china potteries (*ibid.*, p. 127), and one ornamental-ware pottery (*ibid.*, p. 128).

The information regarding the raw materials used for pottery manufacture at this time (1893) is rather scant, but the follow-ing is given by E. Orton, Sr. (Ref. 135). The Quakertown clay and shale were worked in Summit County to furnish potteries in Springfield, Portage County, and for the Mogadore potteries and others in Stark County. The plastic clays from the Kittanning horizon were worked on a large scale for making Rockingham, yellow and stoneware, and formed the foundation of the great pot-tery industries of Eastern Ohio.

The appearance in 1893 of a detailed report on the clay-working industries of Ohio gives a clear idea of the state of development of the ceramic industries at that time, and shows that fifteen years ago the variety of pottery products manufactured in the State was nearly as great as it is now. The product included earthenware, stoneware, yellow and Rockingham ware, ornamental pottery, C. C. ware, white granite, and china. The last three, of course, were not made from Ohio clays.

Aside from the developments mentioned since 1893 around East Liverpool and Zanesville (pp. 184–188) there have been several others, including the production of semi-porcelain by the Carroll-ton Pottery Company since 1903; of playing marbles by the Colonial Sign and Insulator Company of Akron for a few years, beginning 1896; of vitrified porcelain by the Pope-Gosser China Company at Coshocton, in 1903; and the establishment of several potteries at Roseville, Wellsville, Crooksville, and other places. This

does not mean, however, that the industry was newly established
at these points, for stoneware was made at Crooksville at least as
early as 1885–86 (Langenbeck).   White-granite ware was produced at Wellsville by the Pioneer Pottery Company in 1878, but
they were succeeded by the Wellsville China Company making
semi-porcelain in 1900.   Of the several works in operation at
Roseville, the Ransbottom Stoneware Company making stoneware
from clays outside of Ohio began in 1901, and the McCoy Pottery
Company, using native clays, in 1899.   Some works, as Pace Bros.
& Sons' Pottery Company, have been in operation here (Roseville) since at least 1875, making earthenware, and since 1895, at
least, cooking utensils, all from local clays.

East Liverpool.   The industry at this locality seems to have been
founded by Mr. James Bennett who had come over from England
and worked in Jersey City potteries until 1837, and then at Troy,
Ind., which locality he left later and went up the Ohio River looking for a good pottery site.   At East Liverpool he found good clay
and decided to erect a pottery for manufacturing yellow and Rockingham ware (Ref. 8, p. 192).   He thus laid the foundation of the
East Liverpool industry about 1839.

Since Bennett was not able to finance his undertaking, he
interested Anthony Kearns and Benjamin Harker, the firm building a pottery 40 by 20 feet.   The first kiln (of mugs) was purchased
in part by I. W. Knowles and taken down the river, while the
remainder were peddled by Bennett in a wagon.   The entire lot
is said to have netted him $250 (Ref. 159, pp. 180–184).

In 1841 Bennett sent for his three brothers in England, and they
are said to have made the first Rockingham ware in the United
States (Ref. 8, p. 194).   They all moved to Birmingham, Pa., in
1845 (Ref. 159, pp. 180–184).

In 1840 Benjamin Harker operated a small pottery in a log
house, and was followed in 1841 by Hancock's Pottery (Ref. 8,
p. 156), making yellow and Rockingham ware (Ref. 6, pp. 253 and
276).

The following year, or 1842, James Salt, Frederick Mear, Joseph
Ogden, and John Hancock rented the Mansion House property for
pottery purposes, being succeeded in 1879 by Croxall and Cart-

wright (Ref. 159, pp. 180–184). The Goodwin Pottery, making yellow and Rockingham ware, was organized in 1844.

Since then the industry at and around East Liverpool has steadily expanded. Beginning with the manufacture of the lower or medium grades such as yellow ware, the production of C. C. ware may be said to have sprung from it by the constant improvement of these wares and by the bringing in of better material from other States (Ref. 126), so that by 1907 the value of the pottery produced in that district amounted to $5,727,974, or 19 per cent of the United States production. It should be added, however, that the development

FIG. 3. — Original Bennett Pottery, East Liverpool.

of the pottery industry at this, the second greatest potting center in the United States, is due not to the existence of all the raw materials at that point, but partly because of its central location for bringing in the raw materials and shipment of the product. Of course, the early potteries found their clays close at hand, and served as a nucleus around which the others grew. The chronology of events as far as we have been able to obtain them for this district are, in addition to those already given, as follows:

1845. Thomas Croxall & Bros. purchased Bennett's pottery and ran it for some years (Ref. 159, pp. 180–184).

1846?. James Taylor, after starting a pottery with George Harker, went with Henry Spieler to Trenton, N. J., and built one of the first Trenton potteries (Ref. 159).

1847. Wm. Brunt, Sr., began making yellow ware (Ref. 159).

1850. Woodward, Blakely & Co. started, but by 1879 the site of their factory was occupied by Wm. Brunt, Jr., & Co., West Hardwick & Co., and Vodrey Brothers (Ref. 159).

1850. The plant of the present G. F. Brunt Porcelain Company was started for manufacturing clay door knobs from the local Carboniferous clays. Some years later it was operated under the name of Henry Brunt & Sons.   In the year 1891 the manufacture of electrical porcelain was begun, and since then this has comprised the entire output.   The firm was changed to Brunt & Thompson in 1895, and in 1897 to the G. F. Brunt Porcelain Works.   It was incorporated under the present name in 1907.   No Ohio clays are used in the ware.

1850. William Brunt Pottery established, but was the outgrowth of a plant manufacturing Rockingham ware and yellow ware.   The present factory produces semi-porcelain.

1854. Knowles, Taylor & Knowles started (Ref. 6, p. 337) making yellow ware.   The firm is still in operation but makes a much higher grade of product; in fact, this was the first firm to permanently establish the whiteware industry in this city (Ref. 6, p. 337), although Mr. J. N. Taylor states that a good white ware was made here by William Bloor as early as 1861.[1]

1856. The Croxall Pottery began the production of Rockingham and yellow ware, succeeding another firm which had been in operation since 1845. The local Carboniferous clays were used.

1857. Vodrey & Brother began making yellow and Rockingham ware, which they continued until 1879, at which time the manufacture of white granite and semi-porcelain was begun.   The firm name was changed to the Vodrey Pottery Company in 1896.

1864. Manley & Cartwright started a one-kiln plant for Rockingham and yellow ware.   Several years later in 1872 the firm name was changed to Manley, Cartwright & Co.   In 1880 on the retirement of Mr. Manley, the firm once more changed its name, this time to Cartwright Brothers.   The manufacture of Rockingham and yellow ware was discontinued in 1887 and semi-granite and C. C. ware taken up.   The firm was incorporated under its present name in 1896.

[1] This same fact is noted by Mack (Ref. 159).

1868. C. C. Thompson Pottery established as a yellow-ware pottery, and in 1882 added C. C. ware to its output.

1873. R. Thomas & Sons Company began the production of door knobs only, and in 1884 added electrical porcelain to its product.

1873. Establishment of Laughlin Brothers Pottery, which was changed to Homer Laughlin in 1879, and to Homer Laughlin Company in 1897. Beginning with two kilns the plant has expanded until now it has 32 at East Liverpool and 30 additional ones at its Newell pottery on the West Virginia side of the river. It is an interesting example of the expansion of an individual works. The clays employed are both domestic and foreign.

1877. Manufacture of whiteware taken up by the Goodwin Pottery Company.

1879. Harker Pottery Company began the making of whiteware.

1879. Dresden Pottery started (Ref. 8, p. 209).

1887. Sebring Pottery Company took over Agner & Gaston Pottery.

1890. East End China Company organized for manufacture of semi-porcelain.

1890. Hall China Company began manufacture of white granite and later semi-porcelain.

1892. West End Pottery Company founded, manufacturing white granite and semi-porcelain.

1898. French China Company started, but in 1901 taken over by the Smith-Phillips China Company, making semi-porcelain wares.

1899. National China Company started production of semi-vitreous wares.

1900. Sevres China Company took over factory of former Sebring Pottery Company and made semi-porcelain.

1902. Anderson Porcelain Company began making electrical porcelain.[1]

From this brief chronological record it will be seen that all of the early potteries established at East Liverpool were engaged in the manufacture of yellow and Rockingham ware, and made these from local clays. The introduction of whiteware necessitated the bringing in of white-burning clays from other districts, not one pound of Ohio clay going into the composition of the body, so far as we are able to ascertain. East Liverpool at the present time is, therefore, receiving clays from Tennessee, Kentucky, Florida, Georgia, North Carolina, Pennsylvania, and England.

The introduction of whiteware about 1879 was followed at

[1] There are several other firms located at East Liverpool, most of them of comparatively recent establishment, but they have not furnished any information, and hence cannot be included in the above list.

about the same time by the introduction of decorated commercial ware with underglaze decorations. This was by Homer Laughlin (Ref. 8, p. 209).

The development of the semi-vitreous china in the East Liverpool industry is said to have occurred about 1890, by the introduction of better clays, somewhat different mixtures and harder firing. It is therefore an outgrowth of the white-granite industry, and is known under several different names, such as semi-vitreous china, semi-vitreous porcelain, semi-porcelain, and porcelain granite.[1]

It may not be out of place here to mention the developments which have occurred at East Palestine and Sebring. In 1897 the Sebring Pottery Company started a factory at East Palestine. Two years later it began operations at Sebring. The works at East Palestine were then taken over by the Ohio China Company, while the original plant at East Liverpool passed over to the control of the Sevres China Company, as already mentioned. The French China Company of East Liverpool, formerly owned by the Sebring Pottery Company, is now run by the Smith and Phillips Porcelain Company. There are now located in the city of Sebring a group of potteries engaged in the manufacture of the better grades of white ware, and all belonging originally to the Sebring Pottery Company. Farther west in Columbiana County, at Salem, the Salem China Company began semi-porcelain manufacture in 1890.

Zanesville. According to the older reports of the Ohio Geological Survey, potteries were in operation in this district as early as 1838, but there seem to be no detailed records until a much later date. Atwater in his History of the State of Ohio, published in 1838 (Ref. 161), makes the interesting statement that "the clays in this vicinity (Zanesville) are equal to any now used in England, France or Germany for earthenware, and we should not be disappointed if Zanesville should be the very first town on this continent to firmly establish the manufacture of real Liverpool ware" (Ref. 161, p. 342).

Many of the early potteries were located near Roseville in this district and were operated by farmers, who shipped their wares from Putnam by boat to market.[2]

---

[1] Private correspondence.   [2] K. Langenbeck, private correspondence.

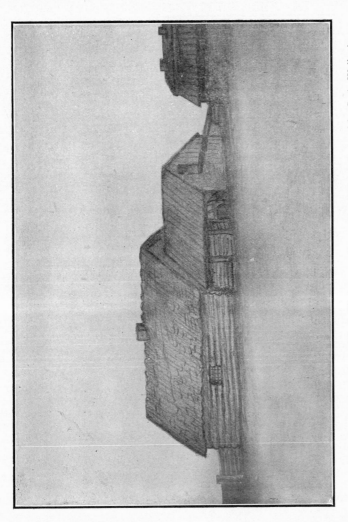

PLATE VI. — Original plant of S. A. Weller near Zanesville, Ohio.   (Loaned by S. A. Weller.)

The Zanesville district did not reach its prominent position as a potting center until a later date than East Liverpool, and, unlike the latter, has always drawn to a large extent on local clays.

In 1872 the S. A. Weller Pottery Company had its beginning as a small log-cabin pottery seven miles from Zanesville, and equipped with one kiln. The product consisted of common red earthenware made of local clays. Since then the works have been moved to Zanesville and greatly expanded, so that it now includes 25 kilns all fired by natural gas, a fuel much used in some of the Ohio clay-working establishments. The present ware includes several types of art pottery known under the name of *Louwelsa*,[1] *Aurelian*, *Jap-Birdinal*, *Eocean* and *Sicardo*. The last named is of special interest as being a good example of luster work.

Another large establishment, that of J. B. Owens, began the manufacture of flowerpots, stoneware, etc., adding the making of art pottery and underglaze decorative pottery in 1895.

Some years before this, or in 1883, the local clays were used in an attempt to make floor tile, but the venture was unsuccessful, and after lying idle for a while the plant was converted into a stone-ware pottery and was taken over by the Zanesville Stoneware Company in 1887. This plant has continued in operation up to the present time, using local clays for the manufacture of common stoneware articles, and in addition since 1898 the same clay has been employed for special stoneware products, such as water filters, cooking utensils, etc. The glazes, however, are not of local materials, salt glaze being applied from 1887 to 1892, Albany slip following up to 1897, and Bristol glaze up to 1907, when solid color glazes were introduced.

The Roseville Pottery was organized in 1892, using the local red and buff-burning clays for the manufacture of flowerpots, cheap jardinieres, etc., this being the same clay that has been used in this district for brick manufacture. In 1898 the factory was moved to Zanesville, where the local clays are employed for making so-called underglaze, *Rozane* ware. The higher grades of art pottery manufactured at this plant are, however, composed of

---

[1] The *Louwelsa* is practically the same as the *Lonhuda* ware formerly made at Steubenville, Mr. Weller having purchased the factory where it was made in 1896.

PLATE VII. — Present factory of Homer Laughlin Company, East Liverpool, Ohio.

Tennessee, Georgia, and Pennsylvania clays, of white-burning character, necessary partly because the ware is covered with a transparent glaze. In addition to the large factory at Zanesville, the company operates a smaller plant for making red and white cooking utensils, and still another at Roseville for cheap earthenware cooking utensils from native clay. A second plant at Roseville, making majolica pitchers, etc., uses foreign clays, because of the white body required.

Among the other potteries in the district from which it has been possible to obtain some information were the following: Peters and Reed Pottery Company, established in 1898, and making red earthenware from local clay shales of Carboniferous Age; Zanesville Art Pottery Company, which in 1900 changed from the manufacture of roofing tile to art pottery, and using local clays only in part; Ohio Pottery Company, also started in 1900 and making stoneware from clays of the Putnam Hill horizon.

Electrical Porcelain. This product has been referred to under pottery, but should perhaps receive separate consideration, even though the mention be brief. The following works are engaged in this branch of manufacture, and where it has been possible to obtain them, the dates of their establishment are given.

1884. R. Thomas & Sons, East Liverpool.
1891. G. F. Brunt Porcelain Company, East Liverpool.
1896. Akron Smoking Pipe Company, Mogadore. This company originally manufactured clay pipes.
1902. Anderson Porcelain Company, East Liverpool.
      New Lexington High Voltage Porcelain Company, New Lexington.
      Colonial Sign and Insulator Company, Akron, Ohio.
1906. United States Electric Porcelain Company, Findlay. This plant was formerly operated by the Bell Pottery Company in the manufacture of white ware.

The variety of clay products manufactured in Ohio and the rapid growth of the industry (trebling in little more than a decade) are shown in the following table:

VALUE OF CLAY PRODUCTS OF OHIO FROM 1894 TO 1907.

Year	Common brick.	Vitrified paving brick.	Front brick.	Ornamental brick.	Drain tile.	Sewer pipe.	Fire-proofing.	Hollow brick.	Tile, not drain.	Fire brick.	Miscellaneous brick and tile.
1894	$2,136,691	$928,948	....	$92,683	$1,465,586	$3,311,895	......	......	$476,118	$742,304	$1,514,273
1895	1,887,023	787,878	$518,717	57,767	884,638	1,746,503	$59,600	......	797,985	606,175	2,649,741
1896	1,516,088	619,463	337,507	62,982	569,871	2,058,210	279,264	......	805,198	575,748	225,830
1897	1,358,333	597,905	357,613	104,426	737,754	1,495,974	314,800	......	563,353	510,878	306,379
1898	1,701,719	796,935	289,519	23,070	800,003	1,264,756	343,770	......	661,921	528,278	243,001
1899	2,427,684	1,133,509	466,555	42,037	977,773	1,680,724	346,090	......	565,094	976,693	888,421
1900	2,232,090	1,118,106	433,086	45,855	715,874	2,243,286	351,884	......	690,257	1,340,775	559,992
1901	2,725,512	1,443,537	612,718	49,021	707,409	2,735,703	357,284	......	996,005	1,287,059	612,176
1902	2,001,847	1,643,532	674,822	46,027	894,713	2,646,134	757,613	......	1,156,371	1,327,982	1,491,371
1903	3,002,506	1,860,971	633,101	42,522	1,149,990	3,295,635	347,105	$518,544	1,072,103	1,501,936	636,528
1904	2,768,456	2,222,931	755,870	64,544	1,143,957	3,495,917	476,276	312,549	1,005,611	1,186,966	605,408
1905	3,033,435	2,055,120	1,074,007	18,153	1,291,323	3,559,160	606,246	317,516	1,188,460	1,427,919	716,629
1906	3,243,157	1,955,360	1,025,590	38,218	1,520,748	3,087,360	793,179	365,842	1,523,410	1,670,630	900,312
1907	3,012,485	2,672,600	1,033,434	24,468	1,433,341	3,792,352	601,531	314,545	1,586,174	1,668,728	577,976

Year	Total brick and tile.	Red earthenware.	Stoneware.	Yellow or Rockingham ware.	C. C. ware.	White granite, semi-porcelain.	Porcelain electrical supplies.	Miscellaneous pottery.	Total pottery.	Grand total.
1894	$10,668,498	......	......	......	......	......	......	......	......	$10,668,498
1895	10,086,027	......	......	......	......	......	......	......	......	10,649,382
1896	7,050,221	$606,558	$563,355	$218,392	$1,127,310	......	......	$384,160	$2,899,350	10,609,571
1897	6,347,415	167,396	529,691	271,453	1,644,246	1,709,884	$157,700	936,986	4,720,269	11,067,684
1898	6,652,978	164,893	583,277	187,649	663,530	3,561,759	178,919	841,515	6,137,459	13,167,627
1899	9,504,580	254,370	616,445[1]	159,553	789,044	3,820,402	190,314	1,288,562	6,996,045	16,500,625
1900	9,731,305	144,068	804,261	142,207[1]	1,056,226	5,019,050	247,135	1,207,890	8,573,323	18,304,628
1901	11,526,424	126,149	1,185,537	131,843[1]	726,321	6,230,734	325,664	1,685,670	10,048,561	21,574,985
1902	13,730,610	123,561	1,102,174	129,591	729,526	6,757,661	415,874	1,174,800	10,519,138	24,249,748
1903	14,120,041	162,634	1,064,339	222,904	762,475	6,681,080	486,740	1,709,153	11,088,087	25,208,128
1904	13,978,485	137,705	1,310,302	178,817[1]	422,630	7,286,640	557,027	1,997,211	11,669,298	25,647,783
1905	15,278,968	......	......	177,143	609,478	8,521,944	879,207	1,388,292	13,024,074	28,303,039
1906	17,023,806	206,258	1,581,732	......	......	9,735,072	1,100,979	1,366,318	13,990,359	31,014,165
1907	16,867,631	142,042	1,648,213	......	......	9,419,060	933,256	1,380,728	13,533,199	30,340,830

[1] Some given also under "Miscellaneous Pottery."

PLATE VIII. — American Encaustic Tiling Company, Zanesville, Ohio.

CHAPTER VI.

OREGON.

LITTLE information is available regarding the clay industry of this State. In 1870 (Ref. 115) five brickyards were in operation, making 2,917,000 brick, and in 1880 (Ref. 116) 23 yards, making both fire and common brick. New yards have been established from time to time, but the production of the State has never been large.

VALUE OF CLAY PRODUCTS OF OREGON FROM 1894 TO 1907.

Year.	Common brick.	Front brick.	Drain tile.	Fire brick.	Miscellaneous.[1]	Grand total.
1894	$95,820	....	$29,093	$630	$36,445	$161,988
1895	70,812	$800	4,000	15,486	47,445	138,543
1896	55,719	2,062	14,239	200	54,125	126,345
1897	58,130	4,100	22,993	....	30,575	115,798
1898	90,369	4,275	13,460	2,550	21,210	131,864
1899	191,881	18,460	20,481	(a)	96,552	327,374
1900	168,369	2,690	15,772	1,334	93,220	281,385
1901	172,058	8,469	11,991	962	70,411	263,891
1902	208,647	15,500	18,097	750	75,610	318,604
1903	249,178	42,375	23,331	(a)	110,660	425,544
1904	302,098	21,750	21,553	1,599	99,340	446,340
1905	261,139	14,800	23,718	1,568	79,350	380,575
1906	341,127	33,837	23,424	5,524	102,180	506,192
1907	355,912	49,900	25,631	22,000	92,396	545,839

[1] Includes pottery, fireproofing, sewer pipe, as well as some paving brick and tile (not drain).

(a) Included under miscellaneous.

PENNSYLVANIA.

Owing to the mass of data obtainable regarding the clay industries of this State, it seems advisable to depart somewhat from a strictly chronological discussion and to consider the history of the State by geographic sections. The eastern section includes approximately the eastern third, while the western section takes in the western two-thirds of the State.

EASTERN PENNSYLVANIA.

Brick and Tile. One of the great brickmaking centers of the State and a region concerning which much has been written, especially in regard to early pottery development, is that around Philadelphia. The earliest, though a somewhat brief, record of brickmaking after the Swedes first settled in Pennsylvania, is contained in a petition presented in Philadelphia in the New Amstel (New Castle) court with reference to establishing a brick-yard on some plantation (Ref. 42, I, p. 140). William Penn soon after coming to Philadelphia seems also to have been interested in the industry, for one of his letters, dated July 16, 1683, says, "I have here the canoe of one tree; it fetches four tonns of bricks," which shows that bricks were articles of transportation at that time (Ref. 130, p. 53). In the following year, 1684, it is said (Ref. 42, III, p. 2292) that the people of Philadelphia used brick, made in their local yards, for sidewalk pavements and for building, and that even with the brick selling at $28 per thousand clamored at the kilns for them. They were probably made of surface clays, were burned 40,000 to 50,000 at a time, using one-half a cord of wood per thousand, and burning a week. Pastrius, who founded Germantown, writing in 1684 in his history of the "lately dis-covered Province of Pennsylvania situated on the frontiers of the western world," states that at that time there were sufficient kilns in the neighborhood to supply the demand (Ref. 130, p. 53).

William Penn, writing again concerning Pennsylvania in 1685, speaks of " Divers brickeries going on, many cellars already stoned or bricked, and brick houses going up " (Ref. 130, p. 53). Penn published a letter written by Robert Turner at Philadelphia in 1685 which says, " and since I built my brick house . . . many people take example, and some that built wooden houses are sorry for it. Brick buildings are said to be as cheap, bricks are exceedingly good and better than when I built; more makers fallen in and bricks cheaper. They were before at 16*s.* per English thousand and now many brave brick houses are going up with good cellars" (Ref. 130, p. 53). Turner's house was located on the southwest corner of Front and Arch streets, and was when blown up by dynamite a few

years ago, to make room for " improvements," said to be the oldest
house in the city erected by a citizen (Ref. 130, p. 53). The only
brickmaker whose name we find mentioned is Dr. Pegg, who in
1685 together with others was engaged in brickmaking in the city
(Ref. 8, p. 46), and it was no doubt these brickmakers who furnished the brick for the first Old Christ Church erected in 1695
(Ref. 4, XVII, p. 130).

In 1705 one of the oldest public buildings in the country was constructed of brick in the city of Philadelphia. It was situated on
Second and Market streets, then High Street, and stood there until
1837 when it was demolished (Ref. 130, p. 54). The total expense
of its construction was 616 pounds, the bricks costing 29s. 6d. per
thousand (Ref. 130, p. 54). The general run of bricks, however,
at this time cost 22s. per 1000, and the bricklayer received 3s. 6d.
per day for laying them (Ref. 130, p. 53). The brick houses by
this time were of considerable size, the first three-story one being
erected in 1707, by Thomas Masters (Ref. 130, p. 53).

That the people of those early days were taking notice of the
clays of the region was evinced by a letter written by Lewis Evans
in Philadelphia to an English friend in 1753 in which he says, "The
greatest vein of clay for brick and pottery begins near Trenton Falls
and extends a mile or two in breadth on the Pennsylvania side of
the river to Christine; then it crosses the river and goes by Salem.
The whole world cannot afford better brick than our town is built
of" (Ref. 8, p. 47).

It may perhaps be advisable before taking up Philadelphia in the
nineteenth century, to review the progress made by clay-working
industries in the remainder of southeastern Pennsylvania during
the seventeenth and eighteenth centuries.

No data were obtainable of any clay-working in the State in the
seventeenth century outside of Philadelphia, and not until 1735 do
we read of any activity along clay-working lines in the southeastern
Pennsylvania region save in that city.

At that time Mr. Hüster, a German tile maker, was manufacturing flat shingle roofing tile in upper Salford township, Montgomery
County (Ref. 8, p. 51), and in 1740 the Moravians of Bethlehem
were making similar tile (Ref. 8, p. 51). Brick were made by

Egge & Nonnewacher in Allentown in 1774 (Ref. 4, XXVI, p. 363), and in Reading in 1790 (Ref. 43, p. 198).

A stray notice shows that farther west, around Wilkesbarre, the brickmaking industry was established in 1804 by a Mr. Hamlin, and two of the brick houses erected in 1806 are still standing, or were until a comparatively recent date (Ref. 4, XXVI, p. 363).

In Philadelphia at the beginning of the nineteenth century four-fifths of the houses were constructed of brick, and the industry must have been well established. During the years 1806 to 1809 there were several concerns in operation making brick and pottery (Ref. 8, p. 111). In 1837 the Jarden Brick Company of Philadelphia was established, and continued in business for many years (Ref. 4, XVIII, p. 238).

That the clayworkers were not confining their attention to bricks alone is shown by the fact that in 1840 A. Miller of Philadelphia was advertising for sale fire brick, earthenware, muffles, kaolin, quartz, and feldspar (Ref. 8, p. 108). Five years later in 1845 he made the first floor and wall tile in the United States, the idea being conceived by an apprentice at his works. The tile were of Rockingham ware, and were first used on his own warehouse (Ref. 8, p. 343). Previous to 1840, all brick in Philadelphia, and in fact throughout the country, were hand molded, the quantity made by one man being 2000 to 4000 per day. In a contest in Philadelphia in 1835 between two expert molders, however, working from sunrise to sunset, each is said to have turned out about 25,000 bricks (Ref. 126, p. 362). In 1840 the first brick machine in the city began operations, being one of the pioneer machines of the country It was a soft-mud machine operated by horse power. The operation of such a labor-saving machine was strongly opposed by the brickmakers, who feared it would deprive them of work, and a few years later the machine was destroyed in a riot incited by these men (Ref. 4, XVIII, p. 338). This served only as a temporary check, for in 1847, after the riot, a dry-clay machine was made in Philadelphia (Ref. 126, p. 362). In Reading the industry of common-brick making was well established by 1840, at which time there were nine kilns producing annually 2,777,000 brick (Ref. 43, p. 119), and another yard was started in 1845 by W. H. Parker, using a

residual clay derived from limestone and making a red brick
(Ref. 131, p. 34). Fire brick are said to have been made in Reading in this same year (Ref. 43, pp. 119–121). By 1846, 17 kilns
were in operation, turning out over nine million brick annually
(Ref. 43, pp. 119–121). After the establishment of Mr. Parker's
yard in 1845 eight others were organized previous to 1898, and were
for the greater part using the residual clay in making red brick
(Ref. 131, p. 34).

The condition of the brick industry in Philadelphia in 1857,
according to a brickmaker's statement (Ref. 130, p. 54), may be
summarized as follows: "In the city there were about fifty yards,
twenty-five in the south end and twenty-five in the north, including
Germantown and across the Schuylkill, but there were few if any
bricks made by machinery at that date." "In Washington, where
great quantities of brick are made by brick machine, they do better, but bricks thus made are never equal in quality to hand-made
brick, which bring in the market $1.00 more per thousand. The
red-pressed bricks of Philadelphia had a high reputation, and were
exported to Cuba and shipped to New York City (Ref. 130, pp. 54
and 55). Indeed, for many years large quantities of them were
used in the eastern and central United States. They were made
by hand from local loams and repressed."

We first hear of brick being made in Lancaster in 1862 by
James Pranglen, and by 1898 four yards were in operation, using a
red-burning residual clay (Ref. 131, p. 33). This common red-
brick industry was soon established throughout the Great Valley
region. A yard was also started in Columbia in 1869, and by 1898
yards were in operation in Bethlehem, Allentown, Lebanon, York,
and other towns throughout the Great Valley, using for the most
part the residual clays derived from Cambro-Ordovician limestone
(Ref. 131, p. 34).

Previous to 1872 Hyzer and Lewellan in Philadelphia were making encaustic floor tile, using the wet-clay process. Very soon they
changed to the dry "dust" process (Ref. 8, p. 344), and before
1876 they had taken up the manufacture of fire brick (Ref. 8,
p. 345), but the source of their raw materials is not known.

The paving-brick industry of southeastern Pennsylvania seems to have begun about 1892 when the Montello Clay and Brick Company at Montello began the manufacture of red, vitrified brick from Triassic shales. The same materials were used in 1894 by the McAvoy Vitrified Brick Company, Perkiomen Junction (Pawling P. O.). They employed a stiff-mud machine (Ref. 130, p. 59). Since then paving-brick manufacture is said to have been taken up at Reading, Allentown, Hamburg, and Oaks Station. The Reading and Allentown yards use Cambro-Ordovician shales, the Hamburg firm uses the Hudson River shales, and the Perkiomen Brick Company at Oaks Station the Triassic shale (Ref. 131).

Since 1892 the manufacture of ornamental dry-pressed brick has been taken up at Pine Grove Furnace by the Fuller Brick and Slate Company, and the Mt. Holly Brick and Clay Company at Mt. Holly, the latter firm using the white residual clays from Upper Mill and Henry Clay mines, South Mountain (Ref. 131). The Penn tile works at Bendersville station also began using the South Mountain clays in part for the manufacture of encaustic floor tiles in 1893. The manufacture of enameled brick from a mixture of Clinton (?) clays, and Clearfield County Coal Measure fire clays, was begun at Saylorsburg, Pa., by the Blue Ridge Enameled Brick Company about 1894, and is still running.

The manufacture of pressed brick around Philadelphia has also grown. For many years the red-pressed brick, made from surface Pleistocene loams, were used in large quantities in the eastern cities, but with the falling off in favor of red-pressed brick, and the coming into fashion of buff, speckled, and other brick made from fire clays, some of the Philadelphia yards began the production of these, and have continued making them up to the present day. Their raw materials had to be brought either from the Cretaceous clay belt of New Jersey or the Coal Measure fire-clay districts of western Pennsylvania.

Architectural Terra Cotta. In 1886 Stephens and Leach began the manufacture of terra cotta in West Philadelphia (Ref. 8, pp. 397, p. 197). This works was subsequently run by Armstrong and Conklin, and is still in operation, although it has been absorbed by the New York Architectural Terra Cotta Company of Long Island City, N.Y.

A new factory, that of W. O. Ketcham, was started as late as 1906, drawing its raw materials from northeastern Maryland.

Pottery.   Before the close of the seventeenth century potting had begun in Philadelphia, the first in the State, when in 1690 the City had one potter (Ref. 8, p. 54), and tobacco pipes were being manufactured (Ref. 8, p. 338).   The source of the raw materials is not known.

In the early part of the eighteenth century the tobacco-pipe manufacture was still going on, and between 1712 and 1719 pipes were made and sold in the city for four shillings a gross (Ref. 4, XXI, p. 551).

The china works of Philadelphia, of such historic interest to all china collectors, was established in 1769 (Ref. 12, p. 402).   A newspaper of that year (1769) tells of its erection, and later in the same year gives an advertisement for shank bones to be delivered at Southwark, Philadelphia, the advertisement bearing the firm name Bonnin and Morris (Ref. 12, p. 402). As the kaolins and white clays of Pennsylvania had not yet been developed, this pottery and others later on drew their supply of clay for white-ware manufacture from New Jersey or Delaware.   Bonnin obtained most of his from White Clay Creek, Del. (Ref. 8, p. 99).   The English and Dutch china manufacturers became greatly alarmed at this industry on our continent, and started a brisk competition, shipping over quantities of chinaware (Ref. 8, p. 99), with the result that Bonnin and Morris were soon forced to close down (Ref. 8, p. 90), after vain attempts to obtain assistance in 1771, by petitioning the Assembly for funds and by carrying on a lottery.   Bonnin after the failure returned to England.   His ware was probably blue decorated and soft bone-china (Ref. 8, pp. 91–98).

Before the close of the century, in 1792, two potteries were in operation in the city, one by Miller and one by Curtis, both probably making common earthenware (Ref. 8, pp. 104 and 107), and using supposedly local clays.

The town of Lancaster had three potteries (Ref. 1, 1, p. 238) as early as 1740, and somewhere in the State, probably in this southeastern region, the Dutch were making the ware known as " Tulip

Ware " (Ref. 6, p. 115).[1] The Vickers were making earthenware in Chester County from 1753 to 1765 (Ref. 8, p. 103), and in 1762 slip-decorated ware was made in Montgomery and Bucks counties, while the Wrightstown (Bucks County) pottery was established by a Mr. Smith in 1763 (Ref. 8, pp. 68–69). In no case is the character of the raw materials mentioned, but it is doubtful if they were brought any distance. Before the close of the century, in 1792, earthenware was also made at Bucksville, Bucks County (Ref. 8, p. 71).

The healthy condition of the industry is well indicated by the statistics of 1811, which show that there were 30 kilns and 16 potteries in the city of Philadelphia alone (Ref. 42, III, p. 2232), and it was said " earthenware equal to Staffordshire could be made if workmen could be found " (Ref. 44, p. 75). This was rather a bold assertion, but chinaware was made at that time by D. Freytag, and it was said to be finer than any then being produced in the United States (Ref. 8, p. 115).

The J. C. Remmey and Šon Pottery, now one of the two large controlling companies in Philadelphia, was established in New York in 1684 and in Philadelphia in 1810. They have probably always manufactured stoneware, and in 1898 (Ref. 130, p. 49) their chief product was chemical stoneware, the raw materials coming from New Jersey and Maryland.

The history of the Tucker china in the city began in 1812. At that time Ben Tucker had a china shop in the city and sold imported chinaware. His son, W. E. Tucker, became interested in decorating the ware, and had an experimental kiln behind the shop. He began soon to experiment with native clays and bone, and succeeded in making porcelain. In 1825 he purchased an old water works plant and converted it into a pottery. The following year, 1826, he bought a feldspar quarry in New Castle County, Del., and began making porcelain. Just as the former attempt at chinamaking in the United States had been a cause of alarm to the English manufacturers, so did this one, and in an endeavor to

[1] Dr. J. M. Clarke, in a paper on "The Swiss Influence on the Early Pennsylvania, Slip-Decorated Majolica " (Albany, 1908), has pointed out that the Germans and German-speaking Swiss were known under the general name of " Dutch," but that the designs and slip glazes on these wares were of Swiss origin.

overthrow the enterprise certain English workmen employed by Tucker were bribed to partially cut off the handles of the ware before burning it, and to commit other underhand acts against their employer. These troubles were almost discouraging to Mr. Tucker, and in 1830 he attempted to obtain $20,000 as a grant from Andrew Jackson, the President of the United States, but failed. The kaolin for his works he purchased of Israel Hoppe, New Garden township, Chester County, Pa., and his feldspar from Delaware. In 1832 he began the manufacture of fire brick, using the South Amboy clay. Mr. Tucker ran this pottery until 1828 (Ref. 8, pp. 127–139).

During the same period, 1812–1840, many brickyards and potteries were springing up in Philadelphia. A pottery making red and black ware was operated by a Mr. Haig in 1812 (Ref. 8, p. 116). In 1837 the American China Manufactory was being operated in the city by a Mr. Hemphill, John Pennington of West Grove furnishing him with clay (Ref. 8, p. 140).

During the first half of the nineteenth century, 1800–1850, in the southeastern district outside of Philadelphia several interesting facts are to be noted. In 1820 kaolin was discovered by Israel Hoppe while digging a post hole on his farm at New Garden, Chester County. He shipped a quantity of it to the Tucker pottery in Philadelphia, and also used it for fire-brick manufacture.[1] This represents the beginning of the Pennsylvania kaolin industry. A pottery was in operation as early as 1820 in Bird-in-Hand, Lancaster County, making probably earthenware (Ref. 8, p. 340).

There appears to be little mention of new developments for the next 25 years, but it is certain that the use of the pottery clays continued to grow, and that many of the potteries established by 1825 kept running for a number of years. In the year 1856 the making of tobacco pipes in Manheim, Lancaster County, is referred to, while two years later, or in 1858, white ones were made in Philadelphia (Ref. 8, p. 340). No doubt there was a brisk demand for this kind of ware in the populous Dutch districts.

The Phoenixville Pottery, Kaolin and Fire Brick Company, which began operations in 1867, was succeeded a few years later

[1] Private communication.

by Schrieber and Co., who made terra-cotta heads, etc.   Later on, under different owners, the works produced white ware (1877), majolica (1879), and hard porcelain (1882) (Ref. 8, pp. 267–269), but whether they ran entirely on Pennsylvania clays is not known.

The present Philadelphia City Pottery was established in 1868, and also the Port Richmond Pottery (Ref. 8, p. 251), while in the same year (1868) terra cotta was being made in Reading by Fox, Hagg, & Co. (Ref. 43, p. 119). This no doubt refers to terra-cotta vases and not architectural terra cotta.

In the latter half of the nineteenth century southeastern Pennsylvania, so well supplied with common-brick plants, began to develop its better classes of clay, such as the white clays of the Great Valley and South Mountain areas and the kaolins of Delaware and Chester counties. Mr. Israel Hoppe, already mentioned, shipped in 1852 some of his kaolin of New Garden to the Trenton potteries, being obliged to cart it 12 miles to Newport, Del., for shipment.

He sold this property in 1856 to H. Spencer, who erected a large washery and sold his clay to paper manufacturers or to Trenton and East Liverpool potters.

An interesting type of residual white clay deposit is that found in the Great Valley and South Mountain district. This clay is the decomposition product of hydro-mica slates intercalated in Cambro-Ordovician limestones and in Cambrian slates. At present the largest markets for the clay are for the paper trade and for potteries. As far as we know, these clays were first used at Mertztown, where they were mined and shipped as early as 1874 by the Star Clay Company. Associated with the white clay at a number of localities is a limonite ore which has been mined from time to time. Since 1874, fifteen or twenty companies have been engaged in mining this clay, the chief centers of development being Mt. Holly Springs in Cumberland County, Mertztown in Berks County, Ore Hill in Huntingdon County, Hunter's Run, and Glen Loch in Chester County (Ref. 131, p. 16). Among those now operating are the Philadelphia Clay Company, Mt. Holly Springs Brick and Clay Company, Harrisburg Clay Company, etc. The clays are used in white-brick manufacture, wall paper, asbestos goods, floor tile, white cement, and antiphlogistine. For some of these purposes the clay has to be washed before shipment. In 1883 the kaolins of Delaware County were being mined in Oley township and sold to the paper mills at Pleasantville for $7 to $15 per ton. In fact, kaolin was being extensively mined throughout the county (Ref. 46, D3, p. 367).

WESTERN PENNSYLVANIA.

Brick, Tile, and Terra Cotta. The earliest mention we find of the clay-working industry in western Pennsylvania is the statement (Ref. 4, XXXIV, p. 266) that the first brick house west of the Alleghenies was erected in Kaskaskia in 1750. There seems to be some dispute, however, as to whether the brick used were imported from Holland, as many of the early brick were, but there is no good reason to doubt that the early Dutch settlers made brick in Pennsylvania soon after their arrival, and the brick for this first house are supposed by some to have been made at Fort Duquesne, now Pittsburg. This is very possible, because brick were being made at that locality in 1760 (Ref. 4, XXXIV, p. 266). The history of the industry presents a blank for about eighty years, and the next record we have is that in 1840, John Glass located a brick works on Block House Run, near New Brighton. This is now operated by the A. F. Smith Company.

The oldest brickyard still in operation in Pittsburg is that of R. Knowlson & Son, which was established in 1845. Common red-building brick continues to be the chief clay product made in Pittsburg, and since the establishment of Knowlson's yard at least 25 other ones have begun operations, using in most cases clays and shales of the Lower Barren coal measures (Ref. 132, p. 168), while throughout Allegheny County similar conditions prevail. A marked change has also taken place in methods of manufacture, the hand-mold and horsepower pug-mill having been replaced almost entirely by machinery (Ref. 132, p. 134).

Between 1850 and 1890 there was a steady growth in the brick industry of Western Pennsylvania, but there are few recorded details.

In 1892 the Fallston Fire Clay Company erected a plant on Brady's Run for the manufacture of face brick, using the Lower Kittanning, Lower Freeport and Clarion clays, as well as shales of the Allegheny series. Pressed brick were also produced at Kittanning, Vanport, Layton, and Bolivar in 1898 (Ref. 132, p. 118), the manufacture of these having continued up to the present.

In 1900 the old plant of the Keystone Pottery Company at Rochester, organized in 1890, was transformed into a brick plant by the Miller Brick Company. Two years later, or in 1902, the Beaver Clay Manufacturing Company erected a plant at New Galilee, using the Lower Kittanning clay for face-brick manufacture, while several years previous to this two plants were erected at Darlington, and are still in operation, but these make both paving and face brick.

In the northern part of the State we find that the Devonian shales have been used since 1891 at Bradford, McKean County, for the manufacture of red dry-pressed brick. They were developed by P. B. Broughton & Co. This appears to have been the first utilization of shales in this part of the State. A terra-cotta plant, started by the Northeastern Terra Cotta Company at the same place in 1906, is utilizing the Carboniferous (?) clays from Freeman in McKean County.

One other important phase of the industry around Pittsburg is that of encaustic tile. In 1867 one Keys, who was managing a brickyard in Pittsburg, conceived the idea of making tile, and in 1871 succeeded in his experiments. In 1876 the business was organized as the Pittsburg Encaustic Tile Company, and in 1882 became the Star Encaustic Tile Company, which now manufactures a full line of unglazed tile. The company uses Conemaugh shale from near the works, Kittanning clays from New Brighton, and some Florida ball clay (Ref. 132, p. 29).

The tile works of the Beaver Art Tile Company was established at Beaver Falls in 1887, to manufacture glazed tile, 85 per cent of the clay then used coming from the local Kittanning deposits, with some kaolin from outside the State (Ref. 132, p. 47). This plant was erected by Isaac A. Harvey in 1868, who made "Liverpool ware," and was later operated by Elijah Webster, who came from East Liverpool to Beaver Falls and made door knobs. It was still later used by J. Graff, who made yellow ware, after which it remained idle until taken up by the present company. The earlier occupants are said to have used a portion of sagger clay from the Bolivar horizon in Brady's Run.

In 1898 sewer pipe and flue linings were also being made at New Brighton, and in 1889 the Pittsburg Terra-Cotta Lumber Company was incorporated for making fireproofing and terra-cotta lumber from the local shales occurring near the works (Ref. 132, p. 137). This firm name was changed in 1899 to that of the National Fireproofing Company, which owns clay lands and plants also in Ohio, New Jersey, Maryland, and Massachusetts.

Paving brick and fire brick are but little manufactured in the county in which Pittsburg lies. There were in 1898 but four paving-brick concerns there, Kountz Brothers Company of Harmarville, established in 1892, using the shale, and the Blatchford-Meeds Brick Company at Barking, whose date of beginning is unknown.

About 1890 Park Brothers began the manufacture of paving brick in Crow's Run, near Monaca, using Lower Kittanning clay, and in the same year the Brady's Run Fire Clay Company erected a plant on Brady's Run for the same purpose. This works, now known as the Pennsylvania Clay Company, utilizes both Lower Kittanning and Freeport clays.

Refractory Wares. In 1839[1] the firm of S. Barnes & Co. of Rochester was established for the manufacture of fire brick, and now makes high-grade furnace brick, using Lower Kittanning plastic clay with Clarion County flint clay (Ref. 132, p. 65). This is perhaps the third or fourth oldest fire-brick factory in the United States. In the next year (1840) John Glass was engaged in mining fire clay and mortar clay around New Brighton.

The fire-clay industry around Bolivar is a most important one. It seems to have had its birth in 1842, and is therefore one of the oldest centers of fire-clay working in the United States. The pioneer in the industry was James Glover, who came from Mt. Savage, Md., in that year, discovered the Bolivar fire clay, and

---

[1] An early development is mentioned under Clinton County.

was engaged in the fire-clay business for twenty years. The first brick at Bolivar were made by himself and his family in a small factory operated by water power along Two-mile Creek. He transported the brick to Pittsburg by boat, and went out personally soliciting orders for the product. After much difficulty he succeeded in disposing of his first boat load. The bricks were found very satisfactory, and the people soon began to inquire for the Bolivar Scotchman and his brick (Ref. 132, p. 81). Glover continued in business until 1862, when he sold out and moved to Louisiana. Three years after the establishment of the plant at Bolivar (1845), Kier Brothers began the manufacture of fire brick at Salina, using the Bolivar clay (Ref. 132, p. 73). The fire-brick works of the Star Fire-Brick Company was established in 1865 and is still in operation, using clay probably from Clarion, Clearfield, and Cambria counties (Ref. 132, p. 70). Several fire-brick works are also located in Pittsburg, and glass pots are made there, but the clays are shipped in mostly from central Pennsylvania.

During the latter half of the nineteenth century while the pottery industry around New Brighton, and the common brick industry in Allegheny County, were taking such rapid strides, the rest of western Pennsylvania was making great advancement, especially in the fire-clay industry. Many of the Beaver Valley potteries and others manufactured fire brick as a side issue, but a number of firms made it their chief business, using the Kittanning fire clay. One of the oldest of the fire-brick works was that of Pendleton & Brother established in 1856 at Rochester and on the Ohio across from Beaver. Both of these are out of business. Another early works was that of Jos. Soisson & Co., in Connellsville. From 1859 to 1862 Mr. Soisson operated a plant at Portage No. 8 on the old Pennsylvania canal. In 1862 the canal passed into the hands of the Pennsylvania Railroad, and the works were discontinued. The company now operates three fire-brick works, near Connellsville; the oldest, the Volcano, having been established in 1864 (Ref. 132, p. 91). In 1867 the first fire-brick company was established at Black Lick, and since then several companies have been in operation, but now there is only one (Ref. 132, p. 74). The following year, 1868, the Vanport Brick Company began manufacturing fire brick in Vanport; and at White Church (Wymp's P. O.),

Fayette County, D. H. Emme commenced mining fire clay, at first hauling it to the Monongahela River and shipping by boat. The clay was used for making glass pots around Pittsburg (Ref. 132, p. 97).

The Sharon fire-clay bed at Benezette opened in 1854 was worked by Reed & Harrison, 1873–1876, and the product was shipped to Pittsburg, where it sold for $3.50 a ton (Ref. 46, RR, p. 260), and the McClure Coke Company at Darent Station began operating at Lemont Furnace, making fire brick for coke ovens (Ref. 132, p. 97). In 1876 the Brookville fire clay was worked for fire brick at Sandy Ridge, Blue Ball, Woodland, Hope Station, Benezette, Parkville, Queens Run, Farrandsville, Johnston, and Black Lick (Ref. 46, HH, p. 146). The Kittanning clays in 1878 were mined around New Brighton, in Ohio township, at Freedom, Marion, Pulaski, and Rochester (Ref. 46, Q).

The fire-brick works of Welch, Gloninger & Co. were established in 1882 (Ref. 132) at Vanport, using the Kittanning fire clay. In the same year we note the mining of Savage Mountain fire clay along the Baltimore and Ohio Railroad in Somerset County. The run of the clay made good second-grade product, but one-half of it was used by the Savage Fire-Brick Company at Hyndman and Keystone Junction (Ref. 46, T[2], p. 336) for a good grade of fire brick. At Layton in 1898 three fire-brick concerns were in operation, one, the Layton Fire Clay Company, having been established previous to 1890. Clay for glass pots was being shipped from here to Pittsburg, this having begun in 1887 by Mrs. Wurm (Ref. 132, p. 90). It was about this time also, that James H. Welsh located a fire-brick plant at Monaca, which is still being operated. Three years later, or in 1900, the plant of W. H. Wynn & Co. was organized at West Decatur, the clays coming from what is known as the Morgan Run Clay Belt, of Clearfield County. They occur in the Brookville formation.

The largest fire-brick manufacturing company in Pennsylvania as well as in the United States is the Harbison-Walker Refractories Company, organized in 1902, and successors to the firm of Harbison & Walker. The details of the history of this group of factories are given below.[1]

In 1865 J. K. Lemon organized the Star Fire-Brick Company.

[1] Supplied by Mr. Wm. Walker.

This plant was located at Pittsburg, Pa., and the clay used was shipped from Bolivar, Pa. This clay at the present time is considered as only second quality, and is quite inferior to the best flint clays now used in the manufacture of high-grade brick. The first brick were sold for mill use, and the price obtained in September, 1865, was $40 per thousand.

In 1870 Mr. S. P. Harbison, who had been made general manager of the business, started a systematic investigation of fire clays and their adaptability for making brick suitable for different refractory purposes. The result of his investigations showed that the Bolivar clay was not sufficiently refractory for a high-grade brick, and the source of his supplies of clay was changed from Bolivar to Elk, Clearfield, and Cambria counties. After considerable search and many tests he came to the conclusion that the highest grade existed in more uniform quantities and quality in Clearfield and Cambria than in Elk County.

It was necessary for Mr. Harbison to locate a plastic clay to be used in connection with the flint clays, and the best that could be found was located at Kittanning, Armstrong County, Pa. There was also a highly refractory grade of soft clay found in certain deposits in connection with the hard clay from Clearfield and Cambria counties.

Mr. S. P. Harbison, then in need of capital to extend his business, induced Mr. Hay Walker to join him in 1875, and Mr. Walker's son, Hepburn Walker, became active in the management of the business on the formation of the new partnership.

The first silica brick were made at the Star Works, then known as Harbison & Walker, in 1887, and competed successfully with the Dinas or Welsh brick, which up to that time had been almost exclusively used in the United States. The only silica brick made in the United States prior to that date were those manufactured by Isaac Reese & Sons Company at Manorville, Pennsylvania.

In 1884 Harbison & Walker bought the Woodland Fire Brick Company, Ltd., with two works at Woodland, Clearfield County, and with this purchase secured a considerable area of flint clay. Prior to this time the works had been in operation about thirteen years.

By 1886 the capacity of the Star Works at Pittsburg had increased from 8000 to 80,000 brick per day; this, with the Woodland capacity added, giving the company a capacity of about 115,000 daily.

In 1893 Harbison & Walker bought the Cambria Fire Brick Company's works and clay properties located at Figart, Cambria County, and this was followed in 1897 by the erection of the Widemire works at Stronach Station, Pa., with a daily capacity of about 35,000 brick, and also considerable clay land.

Two years later, or in 1899, the company started a plant at Clearfield with a capacity of 75,000 brick daily, and another works at Hays Station with a combined fire-clay and silica-brick capacity of 160,000. Following this, in the year 1901, the company purchased the plant of the W. H. Haws Fire Brick Company, near Huntingdon, Pa., for the purpose of increasing its silica-brick output. In the same year a new plant was erected at Figart for the purpose of making special shapes.

In 1902 T. L. Chadbourne, a lawyer and promoter, conceived the idea of forming a combination of fire-brick manufacturers, with the result that the Harbison-Walker Refractories Company was incorporated. This included not only the works already mentioned, but also the following:

Isaac Reese & Sons Company, in business for upwards of 30 years, with works at Retort, Center County, and Manorville and Cowanshannoc, Armstrong County.

Phillipsburg Fire-Brick Works, operated by Messrs. Wigton, and started about 1893.

Wallaceton Fire-Brick Company, Wallaceton, Clearfield County, operated by Alex. Paterson, and established about 1888.

Clinton County Fire-Brick Company, with works at Millhall, Center County, and Monument, Center County. These are referred to under the Clinton County field.

American Fire-Brick Company of Mill Hall, Pa. A new works.

Fredericks-Monro Company, Farrandsville. Referred to under the Clinton County field.

Clearfield Fire-Brick Company, owned by the Bigler family for about 25 years.

Fayette Manufacturing Company, organized in 1893 with

works at Layton, Fayette County, and Chester. Manufacturers of magnesia brick.

Basic Brick Company of Johnstown. · Organized in 1894 and manufacturing silica brick.

Between 1903 and 1907 the works at Johnstown, Manorville, and Cowanshannoc were dismantled, and additions made to plants located at better points to take care of the capacity of the plants which had been dismantled.

In 1906 a plant was erected at Templeton, Armstrong County, for the manufacture of gray, buff, and Pompeian face brick.

Clinton County.[1] This clay field has generally been called the Lock Haven field, as the original manufactures and developments were made around and near the town of Lock Haven in Clinton County. This section was among the first to make a good grade of fire brick west of New Jersey. Professor Rogers (Ref. 152, p. 155) makes the following statements regarding it: " Under a vein of clay 6 feet thick on Minnersville Hill at Farrandsville is found a vein of fire clay, which is found to be of superior quality for the manufacture of fire brick. This clay is from 6 to 7 feet thick; is destitute of grit and furnishes an admirable fire brick. They are manufactured at Farrandsville on an extensive scale, about 6000 to 9000 brick being made every week, and commanding about $45.00 per hundred. These are principally used on the spot for furnace and other work. The furnace now in operation is built of stone and lined with these brick. It is 54 feet high; the diameter of the boshes was originally 17 feet, but was lately reduced to 13 feet. The above furnace was the first hot-blast furnace in America, and was built by Benjamin Perry."

In 1836 Hollenbach, McDonnel, Whitefield and Herron began operations for the manufacture of fire brick at Queens Run, a few miles west of Lock Haven, and continued in the business for several years, when the plant was sold to Mackey, Graffus and Scott of Lock Haven. It was run for several years under this firm name, when it again changed to Mackey, Fredericks and Company, and after that to John Williams and Company, finally becoming Fredericks, Monroe and Company. In 1862 this last firm moved

---

[1] The notes on this district have been supplied to us by Mr. C. B. Stowe of the Stowe-Fuller Company of Cleveland, Ohio.

the plant to Farrandsville, and engaged in the making of fire brick on the former site of the original plant, continuing until 1903, when the property was sold to the Harbison-Walker Refractories Company, as mentioned on another page.

The Queens Run Fire-Brick Company was organized in 1883 by Bickford, Merrill and Morrison, the plant being located at Lock Haven, and the clay brought by boat from Queens Run. The ownership of this plant has changed several times, until it is now a modern works of about 50,000 daily capacity.

The best clays in the Clinton County district are said to occur in the tops of the series of hills or mountains to the west and southwest of Lock Haven, the clay running in a bed from five to seven feet thick and underlying the coal. The best developed area extends from Queens Run to Farrandsville, and thence southwest to Monument. The clay in this territory is controlled by the Harbison-Walker Refractories Company, Queens Run Fire-Brick Company, Lock Haven Fire-Brick Company, and Pennsylvania Fire-Brick Company.

The clays are both flint and plastic in their character. Fredericks, Monroe and Company at Farrandsville and the Queens Run Fire-Brick Company at Lock Haven were the first plants in this district of any capacity, and the reputation which the bricks from these works won, has been a factor in the establishment of other works in this district since 1873. These include the Clinton County Fire-Brick Company at Millhall, which was afterwards sold to the Harbison-Walker combination, and the American Fire-Brick Company of Lock Haven, likewise disposed of later to the same corporation.

The Pennsylvania Fire-Brick Company at Beech Creek was built in 1900 by people formerly connected with the Queens Run Fire-Brick Company, who use clay from the same district. In 1903 the Lock Haven Fire-Brick Company was bought by the Stowe-Fuller Company and Mr. Chas. Kreamer, who owned a large tract of clay on the Scootac, within a short distance of Queens Run and Farrandsville, and in the center of the best clay district of that section. This plant is of modern construction, and the clay is brought by rail from the mines on the Scootac. Clay from this neighborhood is also shipped to Williamsport for the Burns Fire-Brick Company located there.

The fire brick from this district are said to have been put into the first blast furnace in Pennsylvania. The capacity of the several plants in the Lock Haven district is about 300,000 fire brick per day. Some of the clay, especially that around Farrandsville, burns to a beautiful speckled brick for building purposes. A silica-brick plant was started at Alexandria, Huntingdon County, by the Federal Refractories Company in 1904.

Pottery. As early as 1827 a pottery was in operation in Pittsburg a city later to become such an important market for clay wares (Ref. 6, p. 115). E. Bennett and Brother, who are also referred to under Ohio, operated a pottery in Pittsburg in 1844, but the source of their clays is unknown (Ref. 6, p. 43).

At New Brighton the pottery industry is now of some importance. There were by 1898 three large stoneware factories in operation there, and one other at Fallston near by, a large white-ware factory at Beaver Falls, a flowerpot factory, and factories making hollow ware. It is said (Ref. 132, p. 37) that the first clay mined in Beaver Valley was used by Mackensie and Brothers in a pottery at Vanport, which industry was continued until ten years ago by the Mackensies and Fowlers. Mr. A. F. Smith of New Brighton, his son and his father, had been closely connected with the clay industry in the Block House region for many years. They were early settlers, and realizing the possibilities of the great beds of the Productive coal measures, with its potter's clay, bought up much land, and for many years have been mining and shipping clay to many points in the United States and Canada. This was some time previous to 1862, as in that year Mr. Smith induced Thomas Elverson to begin making Rockingham and yellow ware in a small pottery on the hill above the present New Brighton works. This pottery, owned by Mr. Smith, was idle a number of years, but in 1897 had resumed operations (Ref. 132, p. 38). The concern started by Mr. Elverson was the leader of the line of large works since established in the valley. After a number of changes in the firm, it was in 1890 merged into the Pittsburg Clay Manufacturing Company. The company uses native Kittanning clays and Albany slip (Ref. 132, p. 39). In 1878 Sherwood Brothers established a pottery in New Brighton, using Kittanning clay, taken from their own property (Ref. 132, p. 39). Since then the American Porcelain Company has been organized (1895), making porcelain-lined bathtubs, refrigerators, etc.; the Pittsburgh Clay Company has started a sewer-pipe plant, using Kittanning clay; and the Oak Hill, Enterprise and Beaver Valley potteries have been established, all in the early nineties (Ref. 132).

The Mayer Pottery Company was established in 1881 in Beaver Falls. Previously the works had been owned by the Harmony Society, a quaint German religious society. The Mayers manufacture white and decorated ware, using kaolins from Delaware and Chester counties in the State, and from Florida and North Carolina, with imported ball clay. The whole plant is operated by water power (Ref. 132, p. 46, and Ref. 6, p. 379).

From 1890 to 1895 the Keystone Pottery Company operated a pottery at Rochester. It was destroyed by fire in 1895. The ware, like much of the western Pennsylvania pottery, found a ready market in the New England States; Portland, Me., being an important point to which much was shipped.

Some of the early potteries established in western Pennsylvania since 1850 were the New Geneva Pottery (1854), using a surface clay, and a pottery at Greensboro, Greene County, started in 1857. This latter pottery under various managements continued until 1897, using a surface clay (Ref. 132, p. 25). Potteries have been established more recently at Port Marion and at Kittanning. The Wick China Company, started at the latter place in 1890, uses mostly imported clays, but formerly employed Brandywine Summit kaolin in its ware, and uses Kittanning fire clay for making saggers (Ref. 132, p. 128).

In 1889 Scott Bros. erected a plant on Block House Run which has since been merged into the American Porcelain Company.

Three years later the Rochester and Beaver Valley Pottery Companies were organized, and are still in operation.

From what has been said, it is easily seen what an important position western Pennsylvania occupies, for its extensive deposits of Carboniferous clays have been the main cause of the great development of the ceramic industry there. Fuel is also near at hand, and the metallurgical industries of this region consume a large percentage of the fire-brick product.

The statistics of production since 1894 are given below.

VALUE OF CLAY PRODUCTS OF PENNSYLVANIA FROM 1894 TO 1907.

Year	Common brick.	Vitrified paving brick.	Front brick.	Ornamental brick.	Drain tile.	Sewer pipe.	Architectural terra cotta.	Fire-proofing.	Hollow brick.	Tile, not drain.	Stove lining.
1894	$4,173,274	$521,357	......	$75,281	$61,952	$347,202	$61,000	$75,000	......	$67,300	......
1895	3,570,536	305,035	$1,018,682	48,032	13,320	360,475	263,000	120,508	......	95,529	......
1896	4,118,206	402,182	662,188	30,545	49,039	323,239	142,200	104,401	......	122,707	......
1897	3,178,190	336,413	873,057	61,830	11,461	283,451	157,000	92,880	......	110,620	......
1898	3,424,154	513,391	671,671	76,043	14,164	224,385	147,000	98,717	......	136,706	......
1899	4,537,305	702,782	959,000	57,299	26,719	204,400	139,100	110,210	......	(a)	$106,851
1900	4,484,590	481,670	596,559	57,279	8,420	522,650	180,100	95,957	......	191,878	99,348
1901	5,357,079	670,081	844,087	74,726	7,409	438,998	314,000	101,652	......	188,525	86,190
1902	6,074,352	716,887	966,530	20,972	9,317	550,481	243,800	138,839	......	232,431	116,653
1903	6,174,437	685,274	1,059,805	32,602	11,451	727,465	329,004	191,890	$86,731	207,608	......
1904	5,439,116	766,638	962,765	23,317	8,646	834,646	346,317	139,036	54,154	215,107	......
1905	6,532,814	750,389	1,683,031	37,966	13,509	886,979	405,015	290,762	61,345	310,931	180,353
1906	6,586,374	996,347	1,761,991	40,880	9,113	985,635	367,353	191,489	51,179	389,013	203,674
1907	6,353,799	1,232,718	1,526,565	17,727	10,386	795,991	507,116	185,127	59,646	406,269	179,218

Year	Fire brick.	Miscellaneous brick and tile.	Total brick and tile.	Red earthenware.	Stoneware.	C. C. ware.	White granite, semi-porcelain.	Miscellaneous pottery.	Total pottery.	Grand total.
1894	$1,568,545	$477,135	$7,428,048	......	$208,130	......	......	......	$208,130	$7,428,048
1895	2,250,790	553,124	8,599,031	......	......	......	......	......	......	8,807,161
1896	2,083,414	495,591	8,445,712	$15,800	351,401	......	$48,440	202,000	617,661	9,063,829
1897	1,707,621	356,070	7,171,296	......	426,949	......	276,350	100	703,399	7,874,695
1898	2,846,331	521,836	8,689,645	132,967	245,243	......	......	29,277	932,453	9,714,683
1899	4,921,339	1,035,092	12,935,508	101,251	175,905	......	201,057	689,524	1,167,737	14,103,245
1900	4,587,991	643,252	12,000,875	88,682	255,457	(a)	830,000	216,734	1,390,873	13,391,748
1901	4,791,083	716,913	13,656,730	110,633	320,800	(a)	757,000	476,579	1,665,012	15,321,742
1902	6,080,213	749,592	15,957,160	123,573	373,564	......	1,099,011	230,117	1,826,265	17,833,425
1903	6,537,076	847,470	16,973,772	138,541	393,494	......	1,036,194	305,323	1,873,552	18,847,324
1904	5,477,475	1,042,282	15,421,981	133,125	371,096	......	707,809	187,852	1,399,882	16,821,863
1905	5,771,795	786,841	17,778,122	149,786	309,325	(a)	716,245	171,175	1,346,431	19,124,553
1906	6,854,640	839,205	19,363,794	165,073	312,150[1]	845,366	......	1,088,228	2,410,817	21,774,611
1907	6,907,904	784,830	18,981,743	164,096	380,301[1]	531,634	......	233,787	1,309,878	20,291,621

(a) Under "Miscellaneous."

[1] Includes Rockingham and yellow ware.

RHODE ISLAND.

The Rhode Island clay industry is but little mentioned in the literature. In 1681 a permit was granted in Newport for brick manufacture (Ref. 23, p. 30), and brick were made in Providence in 1698. Brickmaking, however, has never been an important industry in Rhode Island, for as late as 1860 there were listed by the census but six brickyards and no potteries. Even at the present time the production is small and confined mainly to the vicinity of Providence.

The statistics of production are included under Connecticut.

SOUTH CAROLINA.

Interest in the clays of South Carolina began when Josiah Wedgwood, the English potter, was searching for clays. In his "Life" (Ref. 57, 1, p. 367) the fact is noted that in 1765 pottery was being made in South Carolina. In 1768 Wedgwood sent over an agent to get some kaolin which they obtained from Ayoree in the Cherokee district 300 miles from Charleston, and later in that year the first cargo was shipped to England (Ref. 57, 11, pp. 5–6). Previous to 1776 there was a pottery in operation at Hershaw by Bartlam (Ref. 58, p. 590), and in 1797 brick were made at Fayetteville selling for $5 to $6 per thousand (Ref. 1, p. 230). In 1802 a yard for common-brick making was in operation 12 miles from Charleston, and oxen were used in the clay-washing operations, but before the War of 1861 broke out the plant was using a Hall brick machine. In 1877 the yard was converted into a drain-tile plant (Ref. 4, 18, p. 341). The courthouse erected in 1821 in Bennetville was of local brick, and in 1826 Galesborough and Yorkville had similar structures (Ref. 58), while at Edgefield in the same year there was a pottery manufacturing stoneware jugs and pitchers (Ref. 58, p. 526). The State Geological Survey for 1844 (Ref. 59) reports fire clay at Cherokee Ford, and porcelain earth at Pendleton and Pickens.

Brick for furnace linings was manufactured from a fire clay in York in 1848 (Ref. 60, p. 289).

The plastic kaolin of South Carolina seems to have been first recognized as of value in 1856 when Mr. Farar of Bennington, Vt., established the Southern Porcelain Manufacturing Company at Kaolin, S.C. During the war porcelain and pottery insulators for use on the Confederate telegraph lines were made, and also much earthenware pipe. Under several firms this pottery continued in operation until 1877 (Ref. 8, pp. 186–191). It is highly probable that it used the white Tertiary clays. Previous to this establishment the natives around Aiken had used the kaolin for whitewash on their fences (Ref. 8, p. 186). Curiously-wrought grotesque water jugs, supposed by many to have been made in Africa, were, according to Barber (Ref. 4, XXXIV, p. 352), made by slaves in the woods near Aiken in 1862.

In 1862 Col. Davies was manufacturing fire brick and pottery near Bath, the bricks being used in the furnaces casting ordnance and in the powder mills of the Confederates. There was only one other pottery in the South during the war, and that was at Milledgeville, Ga. (Ref. 8, pp. 249–251).

There remains a period of nearly fifty years, for which no records have been found, but it is known that common brickyards have been in operation, and the white Tertiary clays have been mined for some time, but for use mainly in other States.

VALUE OF CLAY PRODUCTS OF SOUTH CAROLINA FROM 1894 TO 1907.

Year.	Common brick.	Fire brick.	Miscellaneous.[1]	Pottery.	Total.
1894......	$229,877	$3,300	$10,120	....	$236,697
1895......	240,785	19,750	16,383	....	276,918
1896......	305,150	....	48,025	$1,100	354,275
1897......	258,897	12,750	18,850	....	290,497
1898......	212,447	6,475	40,310	....	259,232
1899......	551,103	11,220	31,475	11,531	605,329
1900......	665,998	14,321	13,384	17,633	711,336
1901......	546,028	14,925	2,418	11,847	575,218
1902......	560,409	29,800	6,497	16,805	613,511
1903......	612,968	27,240	8,160	9,827	657,195
1904......	665,688	36,960	13,810	15,575	732,033
1905......	671,452	30,720	18,825	28,838	749,835
1906......	748,648	30,564	26,000	25,269	830,481
1907......	760,461	41,318	7,250	14,350	843,379

[1] The figures given under "Miscellaneous" are mainly front brick, ornamental brick, and drain tile.

SOUTH DAKOTA.

Lack of local demand has no doubt been the cause of a slow development of the clay-working industry in this State. Common brick clays have been worked here and there for a number of years, but definite mention is made only of the brick works at Aberdeen in 1888 (Ref. 118), and of a red pressed-brick works at Rapid City (Ref. 119, p. 170). The latter locality is in the Black Hills region, where, as at other points around the border of the hills, the Dakota refractory clays outcrop. Rapid City is, however, the only point where they have been persistently worked, the material being suitable for both pressed and fire brick. The demand for the product is small, however. The statistics of production since 1894 are given below. The product consists mainly of common brick, with a few front and fire brick.

TOTAL VALUE OF CLAY PRODUCTS OF SOUTH DAKOTA FROM 1894 TO 1907.

Year.	Value.	Year.	Value.
1894	$27,002	1901	$59,365
1895	10,740	1902	63,425
1896	53,004	1903	68,825
1897	21,800	1904	63,203
1898	30,770	1905	58,271
1899	46,500	1906	58,175
1900	43,440	1907	40,107

TENNESSEE.

There appears to be no record of brickmaking at an early date in Tennessee, although there were no doubt at least small brickyards. Previous to the Civil War, mention can be found of two potteries in Tennessee. From 1848 to 1856 a pottery at Blountville Court House made glazed earthenware (Ref. 8, p. 177), and it is stated that potter's clay was worked at Porter's Station before the war (Ref. 64, p. 1110). That various potteries were in existence soon after the war is indicated by the fact that in the Tennessee Geological Survey Report for 1869 it is stated that the Tertiary of West Tennessee contains pipe and potter's clay used at various potteries (Ref. 65, p. 431). The same report (Ref. 65, p. 349) also notes that for many years previous to 1869 fire clay of Lower Carboniferous age occurring near the Cumberland Iron Works in Stewart County had been used in making fire brick, much of it being shipped to Hillman's works in Kentucky. At the same time A. Cable at Hickman was making red stoneware and utilizing a black manganese from Hickman in his mixture (Ref. 65, p. 514). Previous to 1879 all brick manufactured in Nashville were made by hand, but in that year Bush & Son put in a Sword machine. In 1886 the Nashville Art Pottery Company made red ware with a brown glaze (Ref. 8, p. 334), and in 1888 a brick plant, now the South Knox Brick Company, was established in Knoxville.

The ball-clay pits of Mr. Mandle at Whitlock, Henry County, were opened in 1897, and large quantities of Lower Tertiary clay are shipped to Ohio, Victor, N.Y., and other points. Shipments of Tertiary clay are also being made at present from Pryorsburg, Graves County, and Peryear, Henry County, and Cretaceous clay from Hollow Rock, Carroll County, the latter being sent to Nashville potteries (Ref. 136).

The Tennessee ball clays have won a high reputation, and are now largely used by American potters, often as a substitute for English ball clay.

At the present time in western Tennessee potteries are in operation at Grand Junction, Jackson, McKenzie, Memphis, Paris, Pinson, and Toone, using Cretaceous and Tertiary clays. Fire brick are being manufactured by Robins & Henderson at Pinson, and by the Fire Proof Brick Company, Peryear, Henry County, while at Gilmore, Madison County, the Southern Brick and Tile Company has been in operation since 1903 (Ref. 136).

The value of clay products produced in Tennessee since 1894 is given below. The production of clay is given in a separate table.

CLAY PRODUCTS OF TENNESSEE FROM 1894 TO 1907.

Year.	Common brick.	Front brick.	Drain tile.	Fire brick.	Miscellaneous.[1]	Pottery.[2]	Grand total.
1894	$417,616	....	$25,900	$30,873	$159,955	....	$634,344
1895	355,420	$25,352	6,850	24,956	109,956	....	522,534
1896	364,463	66,865	8,575	4,372	55,389	$37,661	537,325
1897	406,236	41,351	27,950	35,497	60,889	40,370	612,293
1898	369,944	25,014	13,896	30,547	41,323	39,314	520,038
1899	555,812	58,813	16,695	28,049	220,994	68,490	948,853
1900	609,994	59,493	18,900	32,573	145,763	48,855	915,578
1901	610,968	32,350	15,961	37,100	133,495	64,093	893,967
1902	606,883	35,686	10,323	39,318	170,217	50,698	913,125
1903	789,111	35,965	13,509	50,585	183,172	114,174	1,186,516
1904	946,131	80,906	12,350	53,185	191,629	151,584	1,435,785
1905	1,028,653	103,650	23,116	35,300	138,890	163,670	1,493,279
1906	1,038,266	124,031	19,719	45,379	178,063	214,768	1,620,226
1907	1,036,112	169,616	28,000	40,959	171,960	167,215	1,613,862

[1] Includes vitrified brick, ornamental brick, sewer pipe, fireproofing, and hollow brick.
[2] Mostly stoneware.

QUANTITY AND VALUE OF CLAY PRODUCED IN TENNESSEE FROM 1903 TO 1907.

Year.	Ball clay.		Fire clay.		Stoneware clay.		Miscellaneous.		Total.	
	Short tons.	Value.	Short tons.	Value.	Short tons.	Value.	Short tons.	Value.	Short tons.	Value.
		Dols.		Dols.		Dols.		Dols.		Dols.
1903	(b)	(b)	2,625	3,566	6,913	7,863	1,890	2,363	11,428	13,792
1904	(a)	(a)	23,012	26,074	10,100	10,050	1,800	2,250	47,262	72,599
1905	18,170	38,775	42,662	46,612	4,932	4,362	1,167	1,452	67,531	94,201
1906	25,811	64,522	20,656	23,904	3,188	3,216	9,283	12,755	58,938	104,397
1907	25,653	70,088	4,754	5,541	11,608	13,049	15,747	21,211	58,645	111,287

(a) Statistics not given separately.
(b) Not given alone for this year. Statistics published prior to 1903, not sufficiently detailed to publish.

TEXAS.

Texas, in 1860, had 8 brickyards and 6 potteries. In 1870 returns were obtained by the Census (Ref. 115) from 24 brick-yards producing annually 16,720,000 common brick, while in 1880 there were 113 brickyards producing common, fire, and pressed brick. Brick were being made in 1887 at the following localities: Dallas, Galveston, Paris, San Antonio, and Texarkana (Ref. 117). Cream-colored brick were also made from the river terrace clays at Austin in 1887, and the industry is still successfully carried on. In 1888 new yards were established at Dallas, and yards were reported in Laredo and Waco (Ref. 118).

With the possible exception of the Dallas yards, all of the others were running on the surface clays of Pleistocene age, so that the more extensive and better grades of materials occurring in the Tertiary formations were not opened up until later. That they were developed as early as 1890 is shown by the fact that two firms were in operation in Athens, making pottery and fire brick, which could only have been made from Tertiary clays found there. Since that time there has been a slow development of these Tertiary clays at several points, among them Henderson, Rusk County, Denton, Lloyd County,[1] Adkins, Bexar County, Sulphur Springs, Hopkins County, Elemdorf, Bexar County, etc. By 1901 these clays had been developed at Saspamco, east of San Antonio, for sewer pipe and fireproofing, while clays of similar age, which had been worked for stoneware for several years, were utilized for sewer pipe near Texarkana.

The Cretaceous clay shales of the Eagle Ford formation, so extensively developed in east central Texas, have for some five or six years at least been the basis of an active brickmaking industry near Dallas, and were also developed at a later date near Lamar, Paris, etc.

With the opening up of the coal mines near Thurber, Erath County, there came the development of the Carboniferous shales adapted to red-pressed and paving-brick manufacture, but, although

---

[1] These are Cretaceous.

these are widely distributed in the Carboniferous area of northern Texas, they have been worked at few other points.

In western Texas there have been but few developments, with the exception of small yards started here and there to supply a local demand. An instance of this is the brick works established near Terlingua, to supply bricks for the mercury-roasting furnaces at that locality.

Notwithstanding the fact that scattered through east central Texas there are numerous beds of buff-burning clays, suitable for pressed brick and fire brick, the development of these has been remarkably small, and most of the ware of these two grades comes from other States, St. Louis supplying a large percentage of pressed brick for the larger Texan cities.

In 1892 the Texas Geological Survey called attention to some curious deposits of kaolin in Edwards County, and recently attempts have been made to market the material, but as it lies about 40 miles from the railroad there is some doubt regarding the success of the venture.

In 1907 Texas ranked twelfth, and supplied 1.61 per cent of the total United States production. The statistics of production since 1894 are given below. The " Miscellaneous " column includes an irregular production of vitrified and ornamental brick, drain tile, sewer pipe and fireproofing.

VALUE OF CLAY PRODUCTS OF TEXAS FROM 1894 TO 1907.

Year.	Common brick.	Front brick.	Fire brick.	Miscellaneous.
1894	$895,359	....	$87,360	$82,134
1895	805,772	$103,255	7,060	67,759
1896	665,091	142,500	8,315	51,766
1897	706,312	71,655	23,235	333,627
1898	587,116	8,974	5,435	101,344
1899	947,980	60,061	23,234	107,792
1900	964,743	35,605	14,144	69,061
1901	1,396,889	95,492	23,337	116,471
1902	1,353,489	73,619	17,781	150,723
1903	1,074,051	65,628	22,333	212,902
1904	1,157,130	58,734	30,208	183,524
1905	1,209,898	102,054	14,724	291,481
1906	1,307,199	110,189	45,557	398,018
1907	1,707,812	153,187	75,946	464,443

Year.	Red earthenware.	Stoneware.	Miscellaneous pottery.	Grand total.
1894	....	....	....	$1,028,853
1895	....	$46,600	....	1,030,446
1896	$2,400	55,681	....	915,753
1897	62,210		....	1,197,039
1898	4,750	50,592	....	817,797
1899	5,860	68,192	$8,000	1,221,119
1900	3,242	84,222	....	1,171,017
1901	18,851	71,325	310	1,723,375
1902	8,226	88,176	1,800	1,693,814
1903	6,789	89,347	1,530	1,472,580
1904	6,611	99,860	30	1,536,097
1905	6,114	94,674	....	1,718,945
1906	10,045	98,590	....	1,969,598
1907	6,759	149,414	....	2,557,561

UTAH.

The earliest date we find of clay-working in Utah is that a pottery was in operation in the then Territory in 1850 (Ref. 120, p. 327). In 1870 one brickyard is recorded (Ref. 115), and in 1880, 28 yards, turning out common, pressed and fire bricks.

The Salt Lake Pressed-Brick Company was established in 1891 (Ref. 4, XVII, p. 42d) and is still in operation.

Fire clays are mined near Utah Lake in Utah County, and since 1904 have been used by the Utah Fire Clay Company for the manufacture of fire brick, assay goods, sewer pipe, hollow ware, and building brick.

Although Utah ranked but thirty-third in 1907, with only .4 per cent of the total United States output, it is evident that the above records are incomplete. Common-brick yards are scattered over the State, and pottery and fire brick are produced, but the output of the latter is insufficient to supply the demand of the large smelters, and many refractory brick are obtained from other States. There are no records of extensive fire-clay beds, and the development of the smelting industry does not seem to have induced a corresponding growth in the fire-brick industry, since by 1906 the State had only attained twenty-seventh place in rank as a fire-brick producer.

VALUE OF CLAY PRODUCTS OF UTAH FROM 1894 TO 1907.

Year.	Common brick.	Front brick.	Fire brick.	Miscellaneous.[1]	Total.
1894......	$156,047	....	$4,400	$16,453	$176,900
1895......	69,511	$31,715	5,750	5,610	112,586
1896......	96,161	35,862	5,050	500	137,573
1897......	97,691	11,065	26,625	400	135,781
1898......	134,525	26,582	7,000	12,885	180,992
1899......	159,481	18,467	(a)	38,501	216,449
1900......	174,579	31,039	3,250	25,353	234,221
1901......	134,164	139,591	5,100	12,334	291,189
1902......	236,875	84,979	12,400	24,751	359,005
1903......	265,553	111,825	28,150	34,856	440,384
1904......	255,358	92,902	(a)	71,466	419,726
1905......	311,899	128,754	35,629	68,296	544,578
1906......	368,151	107,255	40,512	118,526	634,444
1907......	357,010	167,581	34,804	73,992	633,387

[1] Includes vitrified brick, ornamental brick, drain tile, sewer pipe and earthenware.

(a) Under miscellaneous.

VERMONT.

The first record found of a clay-working plant in Vermont refers to a pottery begun in Bennington in 1793 by Norton Brothers, which started with the manufacture of red earthenware and in 1800 made stoneware (Ref. 8, p. 104).

The kaolin bed at Moncton was known as early as 1810, and in that year a company was formed to utilize it in porcelain manufacture (Ref. 1, 11, p. 166). A particular account of this bed was given in the "Literary and Philosophical Repertory," 1813–1815 (Ref. 11, p. 53). Another pottery was established in 1812 at Middlebury by Caleb Farrar for the manufacture of earthenware and white ware. The Bennington pottery previously referred to was still being operated by Norton and Fenton in 1839 (Ref. 8, p. 157), and in 1846 this firm began the manufacture of yellow, white, and Rockingham ware (Ref. 8, p. 165). It was in this year and at this plant that the first Parian ware in the United States was made (Ref. 4, XXI, p. 653). The assumption is that the Moncton kaolin was used for these wares. In 1847 Lyman and Fenton established a pottery at Bennington, and this continued until 1860, being the first American factory to make figures of men and animals of soft paste (Ref. 12, p. 404). In the first report of the Geology of Vermont, 1845 (Ref. 11, pp. 52–53), is an account of Mr. Fenton's experiments in using feldspar in his wares, and of some of his improvements in kiln design for which he would take out no patents. He had just erected a large plant and had already turned out $20,000 worth of pottery.

In the same article (Ref. 11, p. 53) kaolin is noted as occurring at East Dorset, Rutland, South Wallingford, Chittenden, Brandon and Moncton, the clay at the latter being derived from graphic granite, but no mention is made of its use. During the year 1843 40 tons of kaolin were taken from the Moncton beds and sold in Burlington at $0.40 per ton (Ref. 11, p. 54). In Adams' Second Report (Ref. 13, p. 229 and p. 250) the Moncton clay is described and called "pipe clay," since it is a bedded deposit and not directly due to the decomposition of feldspar.

Data concerning any clay industry aside from the potteries are extremely hard to obtain. Buell (Ref. 4, XXVI, p. 106) states that the brickmaking industry began in 1840. In 1845 brick and earthenware were being manufactured in Chester (Ref. 11, p. 80), and some inlaid tiles were made at the United States Pottery, Bennington, by the wet-mud process in 1853 (Ref. 8, p. 344). A firm was operating a stoneware and Rockingham ware pottery in Burlington in 1854 (Ref. 8, p. 458). By the year 1861 the clay industry was quite well developed. Fire brick were being made at Bennington, Brandon, and Moncton, enameled ware and iron-stone china at Bennington, and paper clay was being prepared and sold by the Brandon Iron and Car Wheel Company, Brandon (Ref. 14, 803). By this time (1861), as Hitchcock says, it is "use-less to enumerate towns where brick are made, they are so numerous" (Ref. 14, p. 804). The United States Census for 1860, however, reports but three brickyards, one fire-brick concern, one paper-clay factory, and six potteries.

In spite of Vermont's activity in the pottery line during earlier years, it does not at the present time produce much else than brick.

VALUE OF CLAY PRODUCTS OF VERMONT FROM 1894 TO 1907.

Year.	Common brick.	Miscellaneous.[1]	Total.
1894............	$ 92,552	$5,500	$98,052
1895............	97,212	35,332	132,544
1896............	78,920	4,354	83,274
1897............	53,485	......	53,485
1898............	56,578	396	56,974
1899............	92,395	39,130	131,525
1900............	102,699	18,342	121,041
1901............	61,554	16,000	77,554
1902............	60,886	18,000	78,886
1903............	88,801	25,200	114,001
1904............	78,237	21,916	100,153
1905............	86,467	26,500	112,967
1906............	85,755	26,613	112,368
1907............	83,200	26,300	109,500

[1] Made up chiefly of paving brick, drain tile, and stove lining.

VIRGINIA.

Hariol (Ref. 52), in his report on Virginia in 1585, mentions the occurrence of brick clays, but of course little use was made of them so early.

Brickmaking has been carried on in Virginia practically since the first settlers landed. When Sir Thomas Dale arrived in Virginia in 1611 he immediately announced that brick should be made, and soon kilns were erected at Henrico (Ref. 51, p. 135, and Ref. 155, p. 38). From then to 1617 English papers contained advertisements for brickmakers to come over to the colonies (Ref. 51, p. 135), and in 1612 the first stories of many of the houses were built of brick (Ref. 1, 1, p. 220). By 1622 Virginia was exporting brick to the Bermudas, which is by far the earliest record we have of the exportation of brick from the United States (Ref. 51, p. 137).

A stimulus to brick manufacture occurred in 1641, when every one who should build a brick house 24 feet long and 16 feet broad, with a cellar, was given a tract of land (Ref. 155, p. 57). Jamestown by 1676 had 12 all-brick houses, as well as many brick chimneys to wooden buildings. Seven years later, or in 1663, brick were also employed for the construction of a fort (Ref. 155, p. 78).

Although there seems to be good evidence of the establishment of a local brick industry, J. W. Palmer, writing in the *Century Magazine* (December, 1894), speaks of the buildings constructed of bricks brought over from England. While his remarks refer mainly to Maryland, Dr. L. G. Tyler of William and Mary College has strongly disputed this statement (*Century Magazine*, February, 1896), saying that in spite of tradition there is not a case in the annals of importation of bricks brought from England. Moreover, it was easier to import brickmakers than brick.

Writing further, Dr. Tyler says:

Now it seems that brick was made use of almost contemporaneously with the first settlement. To quote the Rev. Alexander Whitaker, who wrote, in 1612, of Virginia: "The higher ground is much like the moulds of France, clay and sand being proportionately mixed together at the top; but if we dig any depth (*as we have done for our bricks*) we find it to be red clay, full of glisten-ing spangles." (Brown's " Genesis of the United States," Vol. II, p. 584.) Again, in the " New Life of Virginia," published by authority of the Council of Virginia at London, in 1612, there is this statement: " You shall know that our colonie consisteth of seven hundred men at least, of sundrie arts and pro-fessions. . . . The Colonie is removed up the river fourscore miles fur-ther beyond Jamestown, to a place of higher ground, strong and defencible. . . . Being thus invited, here they pitch; the spade men fell to digging, *the brick men burnt their bricks*, the Company cut down wood, the carpenters fell to squaring out, the sawyers to sawing, the souldiers to fortifying, and every man to somewhat."

The first brick houses in America made by Englishmen were built at James-town; and in August, 1637, Alexander Stoner, who calls himself " brickmaker," took out a patent for an acre of land in Jamestown Island, " near the brick kiln." That the soil on the Island was prime for making brick was shown by the letter of the council in 1667, who, when the king required the fort at Old Point to be repaired, argued in favor of that at Jamestown, " which hath great comodity of Brick Turfe or mudd to fortifye with all." (Sainsbury MSS.) The fort at Jamestown, like all the rest, was to be homework, since in 1673 there is a complaint on record that the contractors, Mr William Drummond and Major Theophilus Hone, had " made the brick," but had not erected the fort. (General Court MSS.) And in the York County records there is a suit in 1679 " about a house for the safeguard of the bricks made upon Col. Baldry's land for building Fort James at Tyndall's Point " (now Gloucester Point).

In 1649 there was printed a little tract entitled " The Description of Vir-ginia " (published in Force's " Tracts "), wherein it is stated that " the people in Virginia have lime in abundance made for their houses, store of Brick made, and House and Chimnies built of Brick and some wood high and fair, covered with Shingell for Tyles; yet they have none that made them (tiles), wanting workmen; in that trade the Brickmakers have not the art to do it, it shrinketh." Cypress shingles are still preferred in Virginia to clay tile for roofs of dwellings. In the act of 1662 providing for brick houses in Jamestown, not only are " brick-makers " mentioned, but the prices for " moulding and burning bricks." (Hening's Statutes.) And in the York County records, in 1692, John Kingston, " brickmaker," is allowed £7 against the estate of Robert Booth " for makeing and burning Bricks." In the inventories of dead men's personal property there are several mentions of " brick moulds " necessary in making the brick.

The three great public buildings of the colony during the eighteenth cen-tury were the college of William and Mary, the capitol, and the palace. I have the manuscript accounts of the expenses entering into the erection of the first, but among them I cannot find any evidence that the brick was imported. I infer, however, from the items for " brick moulds " that the brick was made on the spot. The committee appointed to superintend the building of the capitol was invested with power to buy certain materials in England; if brick had been one, it would certainly have been mentioned, contributing, as it did, the largest element in the structure. The first capitol building was burned down, however, fifty years later, and a great contest arose as to its future location. Some were for abandoning Williamsburg altogether. Finally it was decided to rebuild at the old place, and in John Blair's diary we read: " Nov. 15 (1751). — Fair. Skelton fired the last kiln for the Capitol." The same fact is noted concerning the other buildings.

In addition I may say that I have carefully examined the files of the Virginia " Gazette " for three years, from 1736 to 1739, recording the ships entered in the James, York, Rappahannock, and Potomac rivers; but there is not a single cargo of brick reported in all that time, except one of 100,000 brick from New England, which came, doubtless, in response to some pressing demand.

How, then, did the idea of houses made of imported brick become so firmly fixed in the popular fancy? I conceive that the impression arose from mistaking the meaning of " English brick." Houses in Maryland and Virginia were, it is true, made of " English brick," but this did not mean imported brick. The statute for building up Jamestown in 1662 called for " statute brick," which meant brick made according to the English statute. In the early days of the colony, previous to the passage of the navigation law, there was a large trade with Holland, and a great many Dutchmen came to Virginia, where they became useful citizens. I find, in the Virginia records, mention made of " Dutch brick," meaning brick made after the Dutch fashion — a large order of brick, such as, I am informed, one sees in the walls of houses in Charleston, S.C. Sometimes, it seems, the colonists preferred Dutch brick, and the reason for the distinction between the two kinds was obvious to them. When in the course of time the circumstances of society had changed, the phrase " English brick " came to be understood as " brick imported from England."

Potteries were never very abundant in the Southern States, but a few small ones for making earthenware were probably in operation in the seventeenth century, as there were potters in Virginia in 1649 (Ref. 1, 1, p. 31). By 1682 many of the small plantations throughout the colonies had their own brickyards manufacturing brick for their own use.[1] Although no doubt many small yards were in operation during the eighteenth century, no mention can be found of any clay-working activity. It is probable, however, that after the establishment of small local yards for brickmaking and for coarse earthenware, no progress was made until after the war of 1861. From 1850 to 1853 a

[1] The starting of a brickyard to make brick for some one building a factory or other like structure, is still a common custom in many of the Southern States.

pottery was operated above Wilson's Landing on the James River. It was moved in 1853 to Philadelphia (Ref. 8, p. 177). Then again in 1860 the census shows that there were 55 brickyards and 15 potteries, but all were, no doubt, of minor importance, and their exact location is not given. In 1875 a stoneware pottery was established in Wise County and ran until 1881 (Ref. 8, p. 177).

Smoking-pipes have been made by the Akron Smoking Pipe Company at Pamplin City since about 1888. Local clays of residual character are used. The Adamant Porcelain Company has been engaged in manufacture of electrical porcelain at Broadway since 1903, and at Harrisonburg since 1904. The factories were older plants that had been remodeled. No Virginia clays are used.

Richmond and Alexandria counties are the two important brickmaking centers at the present day, some of the yards having been in operation for thirty-five or forty years, but the product consists mainly of common brick. Pressed brick have been made for ten or fifteen years at Powhatan near Richmond, but the clay is brought from North Carolina. There has been a scattered development of brickyards in the residual clay belt of the Piedmont region, and the Carboniferous clays of southwestern Virginia have been exploited to a limited extent.

Strong hopes were entertained that the kaolin deposits of Oak Level, Henry County, which were first operated in 1900, would develop into an important resource, but after running for a few years they are now idle. The output of clay products in Virginia since 1894 is given below.

VALUE OF CLAY PRODUCTS OF VIRGINIA FROM 1894 TO 1907.

Year.	Common brick.	Front brick.	Ornamental brick.	Drain tile.	Miscellaneous.[1]	Pottery.	Grand total.
1894	$779,285	(a)	$76,474	$10,705	$71,129	....	$937,593
1895	560,316	$204,078	39,919	4,980	74,243	....	883,536
1896	604,161	195,046	24,283	2,918	42,678	$10,440	879,526
1897	574,269	153,422	29,000	1,800	128,692	7,200	894,383
1898	586,170	225,652	21,591	7,830	34,614	14,026	889,883
1899	765,598	242,137	16,117	5,160	64,052	9,720	1,093,784
1900	934,185	275,847	17,921	3,285	71,147	2,910	1,305,195
1901	1,139,894	267,028	20,429	3,978	3,971	4,047	1,439,347
1902	1,185,362	344,139	....	4,240	40,101	3,991	1,577,833
1903	1,245,861	303,431	27,330	4,750	69,288	22,686	1,673,346
1904	1,292,558	344,891	28,576	5,673	37,030	27,664	1,736,392
1905	1,572,442	352,297	20,363	4,500	44,976	(a)	1,994,578
1906	1,536,312	392,130	....	4,805	32,831	(a)	1,966,078
1907	1,285,374	290,411	8,903	6,250	20,397	(a)	1,611,335

(a) Included under "Miscellaneous."
[1] Mostly vitrified brick, sewer pipe, fire brick, and electrical porcelain.

WASHINGTON.

In 1870 there were five establishments in what was then Washington Territory, turning out 845,000 brick (Ref. 115), and in 1880 but two are reported, turning out 600,000. In 1888, however, a large quantity of brick was made in North Yakima, Seattle, and Tacoma, four new plants having been established in Seattle in that year and two in Tacoma (Ref. 118).

Seattle is the main producing district even at the present day, the building brick, fire brick, and sewer pipe industry there being based in part on Tertiary shales worked at Kummer and Taylor. Red earthenware was produced as early as 1900, but the type of clay and the source of same are not given. Glacial and residual clays have been used for several years at scattered localities.

In 1907 the State produced common, front, and vitrified brick, sewer pipe, drain tile, red earthenware and stoneware.

VALUE OF CLAY PRODUCTS OF WASHINGTON FROM 1894 TO 1907.

Year.	Common brick.	Vitrified brick.	Front brick.	Sewer pipe.
1894......	$153,259	$17,600	....	$209,000
1895......	84,305	32,965	$19,100	85,700
1896......	55,758	31,500	8,390	47,000
1897......	86,607	20,250	10,063	46,500
1898......	148,881	14,777	13,200	43,300
1899......	405,678	14,260	31,790	76,694
1900......	404,687	18,950	31,840	119,809
1901......	477,960	139,162	147,881	118,584
1902......	577,407	74,329	51,771	118,462
1903......	557,147	67,314	65,755	171,133
1904......	665,878	149,559	81,142	215,282
1905......	566,385	143,702	86,388	242,245
1906......	708,968	156,476	122,770	313,880
1907......	846,971	(a)	127,245	482,870

Year.	Fire brick.	Miscellaneous.[1]	Pottery.	Grand total.
1894......	$24,400	$111,310	....	$515,569
1895......	12,500	30,875	....	265,445
1896......	8,300	....	$1,180	161,528
1897......	21,800	9,400	....	190,720
1898......	23,250	7,580	....	250,988
1899......	21,173	28,332	13,350	591,277
1900......	22,988	17,755	9,430	625,459
1901......	24,542	19,169	17,500	944,798
1902	18,662	51,246	13,354	905,231
1903......	13,932	36,884	16,100	928,265
1904......	22,445	44,613	22,000	1,200,919
1905......	24,699	70,513	41,100	1,175,032
1906......	46,525	109,705	41,560	1,499,884
1907......	43,940	390,213	30,695	1,921,934

(a) Included under "Miscellaneous."
[1] Includes scattered production of ornamental brick, drain tile, architectural terra cotta, fireproofing, hollow brick and tile.

WEST VIRGINIA.

It must be remembered that early "Virginia" was much more extensive than its present area, and some of the early history given under Virginia would as properly belong to West Virginia and other nearby States. West Virginia separated from the mother State in 1863.

Probably the first pottery to be established west of the Allegheny Mountains was started at Morgantown some time before 1785 by "Master Foulk." Some years later this became the property of John Thompson, who was an apprentice of Foulk's. The ware made was a porous terra cotta with a yellow lead glaze, but in the early forties Albany slip was used. At the death of G. Thompson (son of John Thompson) in 1890, the plant was closed (Ref. 53, p. 157).

New Cumberland, now the largest brick-manufacturing center in the State, was established in 1839, but nine years before that, or in 1830, the Kittanning fire clays were mined at the mouth of Holbert's Run and shipped to brickyards in Pittsburg, Pa. (Ref. 53, p. 209). Two years later the first brick plant was erected, and in the following twelve years five yards were established in the town, and the production in 1837 was 200,000 brick (Ref. 53, p. 209).

In 1834 a brickyard was put in operation one mile and a half below New Cumberland by Thomas Freeman. It is now the Claymont plant of the Porter Company and uses Kittanning clays. Three years later Porter and Beall built a plant below New Cumberland and shipped brick by water to Wheeling and other points on the Ohio. The plant belongs now to the Standish Brick Company (Ref. 53, p. 211). The industry was still further advanced in 1844 by the establishment of the Aetna Brick Plant of the Mack Company and the starting of what is at present the Sligo Sewer-Pipe Company as a brick plant. When the latter plant began the manufacture of sewer pipe is not stated. Both use Kittanning clays (Ref. 53, p. 211). Near Holbert's Run in New Cumberland can also be seen the ruins of the former kilns of the Kerr and Mahan yard built by James Freeman in 1845 (Ref. 53, p. 211). The American Sewer-Pipe Company is now in possession of a plant below New Cumberland near the site of the old Black-Horse Tavern and known as the Black-Horse Works. This was started in 1844 by J. and W. Porter (Ref. 53, p. 212).

The Clifton sewer-pipe plant was established in 1844 by McCoy and Shawl, the Crescent brick plant in 1856 (Ref. 53, p. 21), and the Union brick plant in 1868, all using Kittanning clays.

One of the earliest potteries, which is still in operation, is the Donahue pottery near Parkersburg. It was built in 1866, and has been under the present ownership since 1874. The ware made is stoneware, and the material used is surface clay (Ref. 53, p. 158). Two years later, in 1868, at Parkersburg, the Copen brick works was established, using the alluvial river clay and making common red brick.

In the Charleston region there have been a number of brick plants in operation at various times, many of which have been unsuccessful on account of poor business management rather than on account of poor quality clays, as there is a large area of the Conemaugh clays of fine quality. It is said (Ref. 53, p. 225) that the first street paved with brick in the United States was one block of Summers Street in Charleston which was paved in 1872 and is still in use. These brick, which were made in Charleston, were not regular paving brick, but simply hard-burned building brick (Ref. 134, p. 451). For a number of years after that Charleston brick were shipped into Ohio, and the first paved streets in Columbus, Ohio, in the early eighties, were laid with them (Ref. 53, p. 225). With the development of the regular paving-brick industry its importance in Charleston diminished, and now no paving brick are made there (Ref. 53, p. 225).

Probably the earliest use of gas as a fuel in kiln-burning began about this time when in 1876 it was first used at the Clifton plant, New Cumberland, the first gas well in the section having been struck in 1862 (Ref. 53, p. 209). In 1876 the Holt brickyard was established at Philippi, Barbour County, and uses the river alluvial clay (Ref. 53, p. 272). This is one of the oldest brick plants using river clay that is still in existence.

The development of the high-grade pottery industry around Wheeling makes an interesting item in the ceramic history of West

Virginia. There the first white ware made in the State was produced by the Wheeling Pottery Company in 1879, whose factory
has been in operation to the beginning of the year 1908. In 1888
the La Belle Pottery started, but was absorbed in 1889 by the
Wheeling Pottery Company. Both plants had been turning out
general ware products, but are soon to be closed indefinitely.[1]

A year later (1900) the newly organized Riverside Pottery
Company purchased the then idle plant of the Ohio Valley China
Company, for the purpose of manufacturing sanitary ware. This
plant was built about 1890 by the West Virginia China Company,
for making vitrified hotel wares, but failed after five years, the
plant being then taken over by the Ohio Valley China Company,
for making true porcelain. Unfortunately, after five years it also
discontinued.

About 1898 the Vance Faience Company (later the Avon Faience
Company) organized and purchased the then idle plant of the
Tiltonville Sanitary Company for making high-grade faience ware.
This was continued until 1903 when there occurred a consolida-
tion of the original Wheeling Pottery Company, the La Belle
Department, the Riverside Pottery Company, and the Avon
Faience Company, all under the name of the Wheeling Potteries
Company. In 1906 the Avon Department began the manufac-
ture of fire-clay bathtubs and lavatories, a growing and important
industry in this country. The fire-clay goods are made from
local clays, but the white ware is chiefly from English clays, with
some American kaolins.

A fourth pottery for white-ware manufacture in Wheeling was
the Warwick Pottery Company established in 1887 and using clays
shipped from outside sources (Ref. 53, p. 165).

In the year 1880 the West Virginia Pottery Company built a
pottery at Bridgeport, Harrison County, and it is still in existence,
being one of two common-ware potteries in the State. The clay
used is located near the works and is a surface material (Ref. 53,
p. 161).

Before the end of this decade, in 1888, the Neale-Morrow Brick
Company was established at Charleston, using an alluvial sandy
clay (Ref. 53, p. 262).

---

[1] Private communication.

. The only other place outside of New Cumberland using the Kittanning clays is the Hammond Fire-Brick Company at Hammond in Marion County. It also holds the distinction of being one of the earliest fire-brick works in the State. It has been in operation for twenty or thirty years, and under the present ownership since 1899 (Ref. 53, p. 220).

Two firms using Conemaugh shale were established in 1899, the Morgantown Brick Company at Morgantown, and the first roofing-tile plant in the State, the Ohio Clay Shingle Company, at Huntington. On the site of the roofing-tile plant a brickyard, the Huntington Paving and Pressed-Brick Company, had been in operation since 1891, using alluvial clays.

From 1890 to the present time the most notable development in the industry has been the utilization of other clay and shale beds not previously worked. Instances of this are the use of the residual clay overlying Silurian limestone for the making of red brick at Charlestown, in Jefferson County, and at Shepherdstown and Martinsburg in Berkeley County (Ref. 53), while the Hamilton shale has been used by a brickyard established at Elkins in Randolph County (Ref. 53, p. 203).

Several new fire-brick works have also been established. The Piedmont Brick and Coal Company, recently started, uses Mt. Savage fire clay and makes fire brick, paving brick, and common brick (Ref. 53, p. 206). The Conemaugh series of shales and clays is utilized in the Thornton Brick Plant at Thornton, Taylor County, which was established 1904 (Ref. 53, p. 223), and was used in 1902–1904 by the Kanawha and New River Brick Company at Charleston, Kanawha County (Ref. 53).

During the same period, 1890–1905, the Monongahela series of shales came into use in Mason, Harrison, and Marshall counties for brick manufacture, and the Dunkard was utilized by the United States Roofing-Tile Company established in Parkersburg in 1903 (Ref. 53, p. 256), while the river clays were utilized more and more throughout the State, local yards springing up in all counties.

The white-ware industry, which is practically coextensive with the great East Liverpool center, was also greatly extended by the establishment of Taylor, Smith & Taylor's Pottery at Chester in 1890 and that of the E. M. Knowles China Company in the same place in 1900 (Ref. 53, p. 165), and the starting of smaller china manufactories at Newell, Hancock County, Clarksburg, Harrison County, Huntington, Cabell County, Cameron, Marshall County, and Mannington, Marion County.

An interesting and important development in the clay-working industries in this State was the establishment of the large pottery of the Homer Laughlin China Company at Newell. This plant began operation in 1907. It has thirty ware kilns and twenty-four muffle kilns, and is probably the largest new plant ever built in this country.

In 1907 West Virginia ranked tenth in the production of all clay products and third in the manufacture of pottery, this being mostly due to the manufacture of sanitary ware.

VALUE OF CLAY PRODUCTS OF WEST VIRGINIA FROM 1894 TO 1907.

Year.	Common brick.	Vitrified paving brick.	Fire brick.	Miscellaneous.[1]	Pottery[2]	Grand total.
1894....	$227,032	$63,964	$500	$379,510	....	$673,006
1895....	208,337	449,388	4,000	664,725	$3,000	892,777
1896....	164,831	177,856	1,500	144,850	410,407	899,444
1897....	164,177	289,886	28,696	112,975	519,520	1,115,254
1898....	157,425	290,266	5,155	127,511	518,218	1,098,575
1899....	269,656	415,089	54,400	127,084	585,310	1,451,539
1900...	708,861	474,880	149,257	44,926	638,841	2,016,765
1901....	348,452	555,389	102,300	81,967	858,642	1,946,480
1902....	527,661	578,777	23,633	222,009	1,166,464	2,518,544
1903....	576,404	576,258	70,802	86,596	1,248,500	2,558,560
1904....	469,501	470,339	11,814	57,690	1,065,205	2,074,549
1905....	476,630	263,449	26,868	56,043	1,195,805	2,018,795
1906....	469,527	578,164	59,757	87,309	1,588,555	2,783,312
1907....	384,007	952,060	34,438	110,750	2,159,132	3,640,387

[1] Includes front and ornamental brick, drain tile, and especially sewer pipe.
[2] Mainly white-granite ware and semi-porcelain as well as sanitary ware.

WISCONSIN.

The brick industry began in Milwaukee probably about 1842, since the first brick house, the Hull house, was erected in the city in that year and was built of local brick (Ref. 4, xxviii, p. 183). In 1843 three firms are reported as beginning to make brick there, J. Messinger starting a yard on Chestnut Street (Ref. 81, p. 164), a man named Sivyer making fire brick (Ref. 81, p. 164), and another of the name of Burnham establishing a horsepower and hand-molding yard (Ref. 4, xxviii, p. 183). If it is true that fire brick were made there, they must have been made from clays mined in other States, as no fire-clay deposits exist in that area. In the sixties new yards were opened in many places, including Kewaskum, Fort Atkinson, Depere and Greenbay (Ref. 82). Soon after, yards were started in Kenosha (1872), Menomonie (1875), and Hika (1876) (Ref. 82). By the year 1877 the famous cream-colored brick of Milwaukee and vicinity were being made extensively in Milwaukee, Ozaukee, Manitowoc, Kewaunee, Appleton, Neenah, Menasha, Clifton, Watertown and Waterloo, while tiles and pottery were manufactured at Whitewater (Ref. 83). In 1888 the Pauline pottery of Chicago moved to Edgerton (Ref. 8, p. 332) and began the production of art pottery largely from local clays, continuing this up to at least the year 1905.

At the present time, common brickyards are established at many points in the State (Ref. 128), making their product from lake, glacial, and residual clays. Pressed brick are also produced at several points, notably at Milwaukee and Menomonie. Common earthenware and drain tile are also produced from, in general, the same type of raw materials. The State is, and always has been, dependent on other States for its fire brick, sewer pipe, paving brick, and many pressed brick. Indeed, large quantities of common brick have to be shipped into the State from Chicago, and come into successful competition with those made at Milwaukee and other points. It was hoped at one time that the State would become an important producer of white paper clays, and a deposit was actively worked for a time near Hersey, St. Croix County, but the plant has been abandoned for several years.

Slip clays have also been shipped in small quantities from the Platteville district of southwestern Wisconsin.

The value of clay products made in Wisconsin from 1894 to 1907 is given below. Common brick is the chief item of the table.

VALUE OF CLAY PRODUCTS OF WISCONSIN FROM 1894 TO 1907.

Year.	Common brick.	Front brick.	Drain tile.	Miscellaneous.[1]	Pottery.[2]	Grand total.
1894....	$1,099,102	....	$85,150	$71,124	....	$1,255,376
1895....	782,552	$123,505	32,314	5,825	....	944,196
1896....	662,617	48,671	27,797	37,410	$12,500	788,995
1897....	640,592	48,670	27,750	7,270	....	724,282
1898....	645,209	61,596	19,457	151,044	....	877,306
1899....	1,073,101	60,213	23,334	641,919	13,145	1,811,712
1900....	963,461	84,601	14,995	9,122	14,000	1,086,179
1901....	1,151,838	54,379	22,727	8,710	9,900	1,247,554
1902....	919,883	70,303	17,763	7,924	10,785	1,026,658
1903....	1,193,360	62,857	34,556	4,237	12,386	1,307,396
1904....	1,230,620	86,688	54,831	107,530	11,325	1,390,994
1905....	1,260,066	49,275	57,576	2,748	12,450	1,382,115
1906....	1,109,386	52,038	51,143	2,605	12,170	1,227,342
1907....	1,019,522	43,387	49,832	6,246	8,832	1,127,819

[1] Includes a scattering of vitrified brick, ornamental brick, sewer pipe and hollow brick.

[2] Mainly earthenware.

WYOMING.

The development of brick clays is recorded in 1880 (Ref. 116), but no doubt small yards were in operation even before that. The clay-working industry has not expanded to any great degree, more because of the small local demand due to the absence of large towns or cities than the lack of raw materials.

A peculiar type of clay, known as *bentonite* and used in soap and paper manufacture, has attracted some attention. It is mined in small quantities.

VALUE OF CLAY PRODUCTS OF WYOMING FROM 1894 TO 1907.

Year.	Value.	Year.	Value.
1894............	$6,850	1901............	$28,950
1895............	8,525	1902............	22,150
1896............	9,659	1903............	22,663
1897............	3,550	1904............	35,845
1898............	3,825	1905............	34,556
1899............	8,450	1906............	74,321
1900............	2,150	1907............	88,340

BIBLIOGRAPHY.

References mentioned by Numbers in Parentheses in Text.

1. Bishop, J. L.   History of American Manufactures.   1861.
2. Maine Historical Society Proceedings.
3. Wheeler, G. A.   " Castine."   1890.
4. The Clay Worker, Indianapolis, Ind.
5. Jackson, C. T.   Geology of Maine.   1838.
6. Jervis, W. P.   Encyclopedia of Ceramics.   1902.
7. Paper by J. N. McClave.   Unpublished manuscript.
8. Barber, E. A.   Pottery and Porcelain of the United States.   2d ed.   1901.
9. Jackson, C. T.   Geology of New Hampshire, First Report.   1841.
10. Hitchcock, C. H.   Geology of New Hampshire, Pt. V.   1878.
11. Adams, C. B.   Geology of Vermont, 1st Report.   1845.
12. Prime, W. C.   Pottery and Porcelain of all Times.   1878.
13. Adams, C. B.   Geology of Vermont, 2d Report.   1846.
14. Hitchcock, C. H.   Geology of Vermont, II, Part IX.   1861.
15. Howe, D. M.   The Puritan Republic.   1899.
16. Corey, D. P.   History of Malden.   1898.
17. Trumbull, J. R.   History of North Hampton.   1898.
18. Haverhill (Mass.) Board of Trade.   1900.
19. Barry, J. S.   History of Andover.   1853.
20. Stone, E. M.   History of Beverly.   1843.
21. Field, Rev. D. D.   History of Berkshire County.   1829.
22. Scientific American, New York.
23. State of Rhode Island and Province Plantations, III.   1902.
24. Shepard, C. U.   Connecticut Geological Survey.   1837.
25. United States Census.   1860.
26. Stone, W. L.   History of New York City.   1872.
27. Lossing, B. J.   The Empire State.   1888.
28. Pierson, J.   Records of Albany Co., N.Y.   1869.
29. Howell and Tenney.   History of Albany Co.   1886.
30. Green, F. B.   History of Rockland Co., N.Y.   1886.
31. Leslie, E. L.   History of Skaneateles.   1902.
32. Ruttenber, E. M.   Orange County (N.Y.) History.   1875.
33. Hazeltine, G. W.   History of Ellicott, N.Y.   1877.
34. Baggs, Dr.   Memorial History of Utica, N.Y.

35. Masten, A. H. History of Cohoes, N.Y. 1877.
36. New Jersey Geological Survey, Report on Clays. 1878.
37. Raum, J. O. History of Trenton, N.J. 1871.
38. Harper's Book of Facts. 1895.
39. New Jersey Geological Survey. 1855.
40. New Jersey Geological Survey. 1874.
41. Furnival, W. J. Leadless Decorative Tiles, etc. 1904.
42. Scharf and Westcott. History of Philadelphia, Pa. I. 1884.
43. Montgomery, M. History of Reading, Pa. 1898.
44. Mease, J. Picture of Philadelphia, Pa. 1811.
45. Scientific American.
46. Second Pennsylvania Geological Survey.
47. Maryland Geological Survey. I. 1897.
48. Maryland Geological Survey. IV. 1902.
49. Vincent, F. History of Delaware. 1870.
50. Booth, J. C. Memoir of the Delaware Geological Survey. 1841.
51. Bruce, P. A. Economic History of Virginia. 1896.
52. Hariol, T. A Brief Report on the New Found Land of Virginia. 1585.
53. West Virginia Geological Survey. III. 1905.
54. Hawkes, Dr. History of North Carolina. II. 1858.
55. Geological Survey of North Carolina. 1856.
56. Geological Survey of North Carolina. 1875.
57. Life of Wedgwood. 1865.
58. Mills, R. Statistics of South Carolina. 1826.
59. Geological and Agricultural Survey of South Carolina. 1844.
60. Tuomey, M. Geology of South Carolina. 1848.
61. Kentucky Geological Survey. 1856.
62. Kentucky Geological Survey, Eastern Coal Field, C. 1884.
63. Kentucky Geological Survey, Geological Features of Jackson Purchase Region. 1888.
64. Killebrews, J. L. Resources of Tennessee. 1874.
65. Safford, J. M. Geology of Tennessee. 1869.
66. Martin, T. H. Atlanta and its Builders. 1902.
67. Crary, Sr., J. W. " Brickmaking." 1890.
68. Williams, J. L. " Florida." 1837.
69. Williams, J. L. View of West Florida. 1827.
70. Ohio Archaeological and Historical Publications. **VI.**
71. Field. History of Berkshire Co., Ohio. 1829.
72. Atwater, C. History of Ohio. 1838.
73. Ohio Geological Survey. 1838.
74. Cist, B. C. Cincinnati in 1841.
75. Cist, B. C. Cincinnati in 1859.
76. Ohio Geological Survey. 1869.

77. Ohio Geological Survey. 1870.
78. Ohio Geological Survey. 1873.
79. WING, T. E. History of Monroe County, Mich. 1890.
80. Michigan Geological Survey. III. 1876.
81. BUCK, J. S. History of Milwaukee. II. 1890.
82. Wisconsin Geological Survey, Bull. VII. Pt. I.
83. Wisconsin Geological Survey. II. 1877.
84. HOLLOWAY, W. R. History of Indianapolis. 1870.
85. Indiana Geological Survey, 20th Annual Report. 1895.
86. Indiana Geological Survey, 1st Annual Report. 1869.
87. Indiana Geological Survey, 2d Annual Report. 1870.
88. Indiana Geological Survey, 12th Annual Report. 1882.
89. Illinois Geological Survey. I. 1866.
90. Illinois Geological Survey. III. 1868.
91. Illinois Geological Survey. IV. 1870.
92. Illinois Geological Survey. V. 1873.
93. Illinois Geological Survey. VI. 1875.
94. Minnesota Geological Survey 1872–82. Pt. I. 1884.
95. Minnesota Geological Survey 1872–82. Pt. II. 1888.
96. Arkansas Geological Survey. 1891.
97. Iowa Geological Survey. 1892–5.
98. Iowa Geological Survey. 1858.
99. Report of Florida Parishes. 1896.
100. Mississippi Geological Survey. I. 1854.
101. Mississippi Geological Survey. 1857.
102. Mississippi Geological Survey, Bull. 2. 1902.
103. Missouri Geological Survey. 1874.
104. BANCROFT, H. H. History of California. I. 1884.
105. BANCROFT, H. H. History of California. VII. 1890.
106. SOULE, GIBBONS and NESBIT. Annals of California. 1855.
107. California State Mining Bureau, Bull. 38.
108. BANCROFT, H. H. History of Utah. 1890.
109. Mineral Resources of Kansas. 1893.
110. Mineral Resources of Kansas. 1898.
111. Mineral Resources of Kansas. 1899.
112. Mineral Resources of Kansas. 1900–1.
113. Mineral Resources of Kansas. 1906.
114. United States Geological Survey, Bull. 315. 1907.
115. United States Census. 1870.
116. United States Census. 1880.
117. Mineral Resources United States Geological Survey. 1887.
118. Mineral Resources United States Geological Survey. 1888.
119. Dakota School of Mines. 1888.

120. BANCROFT, H. H. History of Utah. 1890.
121. GARDNER, J. H. Bull. 6, Kentucky Geological Survey.
122. FOERSTE, A. Bull. 6, Kentucky Geological Survey.
123. SPENCER, J. W. Paleozoic Group of N. W. Georgia. 1893.
124. VEATCH, O. Kaolins and Fire Clays of Central Georgia, United States Geological Survey, Bull. 315, 303.
125. RIES, H. The Clays of Florida, United States Geological Survey, 17th Annual Report, Pt. III, p. 871. 1898.
126. Transactions of the Civil Engineering Society, Vol. 25.
127. Michigan Geological Survey, Vol. 8, Pt. I.
128. Wisconsin Geological Survey, Bull. 15.
129. New Jersey Geological Survey, Final Report, Vol. VI.
130. Appendix to the Annual Report Pennsylvania State College, 1898–99. Pt. II.
131. Appendix to the Annual Report Pennsylvania State College, 1899–1900. Pt. III.
132. Appendix to the Annual Report Pennsylvania State College, 1898–99. Pt. I.
133. Indiana Geological Survey, 29th Annual Report. 1904.
134. WHEELER, H. A. Missouri Geological Survey, XI. 1896.
135. ORTON, E., and ORTON, Jr., E. Ohio Geological Survey, Vol. VII, Pt. I. 1893.
136. CRIDER, A. F. Bull. 285, United States Geological Survey. 1906.
137. Transactions American Ceramic Society.
138. GEER, W. Terra Cotta in Architecture. 1894.
139. RIES, H. Clay, Its Occurrence, Properties, and Uses, New York. 1906.
140. ORTON, Jr., E. Ohio Geological Survey, Economic Geology, V. 1884.
141. DAVIS, C. T. Bricks, Tiles and Terra Cotta, Philadelphia. 1889.
142. WHEELER, H. A. Vitrified Paving Brick, Indianapolis.
143. HAMILTON, P. J. Colonial Mobile. 1897.
144. Alabama Geological Survey, Bull. 6. 1900.
145. Alabama Geological Survey, Report on Valley Region, II. 1897.
146. SELLARDS, E. H. Florida Geological Survey, First Annual Report. 1908.
147. BECK, L. C. New York Geological Survey, Report for 1837.
148. New York Geological Survey, Report for 1838.
149. Natural History of New York, Part IV., 1st Dist. 1843.
150. Report of Director of New York State Museum for 1905, p. 30.
151. MITCHELL. Medical Repository, IV.
152. ROGERS, H. D. Fourth Annual Report, Geological Survey, Pennsylvania. 1840.
153. BRANNER, J. C. The Clays of Arkansas, United States Geological Survey, Bull. 351. 1908.

154. Glass and Pottery World. New York.

155. TYLER, L. G. The Cradle of the Republic.

156. Brush and Pencil. Chicago.

157. WILLIAMS, H. Z., and BROTHER. History of Washington County, Ohio. 1881.

158. WILLIAMS BROTHERS. History of Ross and Highland Counties, Ohio. 1880.

159. MACK, H. History of Columbiana County, Ohio. Philadelphia. 1879.

160. HOWE, H. Historical Collections of Ohio, 3 vols. 1891.

161. ATWATER, C. History of the State of Ohio, 1st ed., Cincinnati. 1838.

162. TAYLOR, J. W. History of Ohio. 1854.

163. CARPENTER, W. H. History of Ohio. 1854.

164. CUTLER, M. Ohio in 1788.

165. WHITTELSEY, C. Early Cleveland (1808 to 1886).

166. HILL, N. N. History of Coshocton County, Ohio. 1881.

167. LEE, A. E. History of City of Columbus, Ohio. 2 vols. 1892.

168. History of Lower Scioto Valley. 1884.

169. ROBERTSON, C. History of Morgan County, Ohio. 1886.

170. HOWELL and TENNEY. History of Albany County, N.Y., Pt. I. 1886.

171. ROWE, J. P. Some Economic Geology of Montana, University of Montana, Bull. No. 50. 1908.

172. Department of Commerce and Labor, Bureau of Census, Bulletin 62. 1907.

INDEX.

247

Hopkins County, Tex., 222.
Hoppe, I., 57, 204; kaolin mines of, 203.
Hornell, N. Y., 152.
Horseheads, N. Y., 12, 151, 152.
Horseheads Brick Company, 152.
Howe, R., 120.
Hudson, N. Y., 150, 151.
Hudson River shales, 137, 200.
Hudson River Valley, N. Y., 10, 149, 150, 151, 152.
Hudson Porcelain Company, 143.
Hudson Valley district, 15.
Huggins and Company, 123.
Hughes, J. B., tile patents of, 168.
Hunter's Run, Pa., 204.
Huntingdon, Pa., 34, 211.
Huntingdon County, Pa., 214.
Huntington, N. Y., 151, 155; W. Va., 237, 238.
Huntington Paving and Pressed Brick Company, 237.
Huron, Ind., 89.
Hüster, early tile made by, 28.
Hüster's Tile Works, 197.
Hydraulic brick-press, 14.
Hydraulic pressed brick, 92.
Hydraulic Pressed-Brick Company, 18, 98, 136.
Hyndman, Pa., 209.
Hyzer and Llewellen, 29, 199.

I.

Idaho, statistics of production, 130.
Ideal Pottery, 142.
Iliff, R., 179.
Illinois: common brick, 81; fire brick, 83; history of, 81; paving brick, 82; pottery, 84; referred to, 10, 14, 17, 22, 24, 25, 26, 27, 28, 33, 36, 37, 38, 40, 48, 52, 98, 99, 121, 124, 125, 170; statistics, 87; terra cotta, 82.
Illinois Brick Company, 12, 81.
Illinois Geological Survey, 81, 84.
Illinois Steel Company, 99.
Illinois Terra Cotta Lumber Company, 86.
Ilpendam, A. J., 151.
Imperial Porcelain Company, 142.
Imperial Porcelain Works, 53.
Importations of brick. See Brick.
Independence, O., 165, 166.
Indiana: history of, 88; referred to, 10, 11, 17, 24, 27, 32, 33, 35, 37, 38, 41, 44, 47, 48, 49, 52, 59, 82, 85, 165, 170; statistics of production, 93.
Indiana Paving-Brick and Block Company, 91.
Indianaite, 59, 89; uses of, 89.

Indianapolis, Ind., 10, 24, 30, 88, 90.
Indianapolis Terra-Cotta Company, 24, 90.
International Kaolin Company, 79.
International Pottery Company, 142.
Iola, Kans., 97.
Ione clays, 70.
Ionia, Mich., 114.
Iowa: history of, 94; referred to, 11, 26, 21, 47, 48, 117; statistics of production, 95.
Iowa City, Ia., 11, 94.
Iowa Geological Survey, 94.
Iowa State College, school of ceramics, 7.
Iron Mountain, Mo., 120.
Ironstone china, 140; Vt., 227.
Ironton Fire-Brick Company, 100.
Irvine formation, clays of, 100.
Isaac Davis Pottery, 142.
Iuka, Miss., 102.

J.

Jackson, Le Roy, 94.
Jackson, Mich., 32, 34, 114; Minn., 117; Miss., 119; Mo., 122; Tenn., 220.
Jackson County, Mo., 59; N. C., 160; O., 176, 177.
Jackson Fire Clay, Sewer Pipe and Tile Company, 34.
Jackson Purchase area, Ky., 98, 99.
Jacksonville, Fla., 79.
Jaffrey, N. H., 46, 131.
Jamaica, N. Y., 151.
Jamestown, N. Dak., 161; Va., 228, 229.
Jamieson, George, 122.
Jap-Birdinal ware, 190.
Jarden Brick Company, 198.
Jasper County, Ind., 90.
Jefferson County, Ark., 68; Mo., 59, 124; O., 166, 170, 177; W. Va., 237.
Jegglin clay pit, 125.
Jerome, Ariz., 147.
Jersey City, N. J., 139.
Jersey City Pottery Company, 140.
Jersey Porcelain and Earthenware Company, 140.
Jewett, N. M., 147.
Jewettville, N. Y., 152.
John, Augustine, 103.
John Francy's Sons Company, 34.
John Lyth and Sons, 33.
Johnson, Sylvanus, 94.
Johnson County, Mo., 125, 126.
Johnston, Pa., 209, 212.
Joliet, Ill., 99.
Jonesville, Minn., 117.
Jugtown, Ala., 65.
Junction City, Kans., 96.

SHORT-TITLE CATALOGUE

OF THE

PUBLICATIONS

OF

JOHN WILEY & SONS,

NEW YORK.

LONDON: CHAPMAN & HALL, LIMITED.

ARRANGED UNDER SUBJECTS.

Descriptive circulars sent on application. Books marked with an asterisk (*) are sold at *net* prices only. All books are bound in cloth unless otherwise stated.

AGRICULTURE—HORTICULTURE—FORESTRY.

Armsby's Manual of Cattle-feeding..............................12mo, $1 75
 Principles of Animal Nutrition.........   ....8vo, 4 00
Budd and Hansen's American Horticultural Manual:
 Part I. Propagation, Culture, and Improvement...............12mo, 1 50
 Part II. Systematic Pomology....................................12mo, 1 50
Elliott's Engineering for Land Drainage........................12mo, 1 50
 Practical Farm Drainage.......................................12mo, 1 00
Graves's Forest Mensuration..8vo, 4 00
Green's Principles of American Forestry..........................12mo, 1 50
Grotenfelt's Principles of Modern Dairy Practice. (Woll.)..........12mo, 2 00
* Herrick's Denatured or Industrial Alcohol... ....8vo, 4 00
Kemp and Waugh's Landscape Gardening. (New Edition, Rewritten. In
 Preparation).
* McKay and Larsen's Principles and Practice of Butter-making.......8vo, 1 50
Maynard's Landscape Gardening as Applied to Home Decoration......12mo, 1 50
Quaintance and Scott's Insects and Diseases of Fruits. (In Preparation).
Sanderson's Insects Injurious to Staple Crops......................12mo, 1 50
* Schwarz's Longleaf Pine in Virgin Forests.......... ....12mo, 1 25
Stockbridge's Rocks and Soils.....................................8vo, 2 50
Winton's Microscopy of Vegetable Foods............................8vo, 7 50
Woll's Handbook for Farmers and Dairymen..........................16mo, 1 50

ARCHITECTURE.

Baldwin's Steam Heating for Buildings.............................12mo, 2 50
Berg's Buildings and Structures of American Railroads...............4to, 5 00
Birkmire's Architectural Iron and Steel............................8vo, 3 50
 Compound Riveted Girders as Applied in Buildings...............8vo, 2 00
 Planning and Construction of American Theatres................8vo, 3 00
 Planning and Construction of High Office Buildings....   ....8vo, 3 50
 Skeleton Construction in Buildings............................8vo, 3 00
Briggs's Modern American School Buildings..........................8vo, 4 00
Byrne's Inspection of Material and Wormanship Employed in Construction.
                16mo, 3 00
Carpenter's Heating and Ventilating of Buildings....................8vo, 4 00

1

Freitag's Architectural Engineering.. ....8vo   3 50
   Fireproofing of Steel Buildings. 8vo, 2 50
French and Ives's Stereotomy. 8vo, 2 50
Gerhard's Guide to Sanitary House-Inspection.....................16mo, 1 00
* Modern Baths and Bath Houses...................................8vo, 3 00
   Sanitation of Public Buildings .'..............................12mo, 1 50
   Theatre Fires and Panics...................................12mo, 1 50
Holley and Ladd's Analysis of Mixed Paints, Color Pigments, and Varnishes
                                        Large 12mo, 2 50
Johnson's Statics by Algebraic and Graphic Methods 8vo, 2 00
Kellaway's How to Lay Out Suburban Home Grounds 8vo, 2 00
Kidder's Architects' and Builders' Pocket-book. ....16mo, mor. 5 00
Maire's Modern Pigments and their Vehicles 12mo, 2 00
Merrill's Non-metallic Minerals: Their Occurrence and Uses...........8vo, 4 00
   Stones for Building and Decoration.............................8vo, 5 00
Monckton's Stair-building....................................4to, 4 00
Patton's Practical Treatise on Foundations..........................8vo, 5 00
Peabody's Naval Architecture.......................................8vo, 7 50
Rice's Concrete-block Manufacture 8vo, 2 00
Richey's Handbook for Superintendents of Construction..........16mo, mor. 4 00
   * Building Mechanics' Ready Reference Book:
      * Building Foreman's Pocket Book and Ready Reference. (In
        Press.)
      * Carpenters' and Woodworkers' Edition...........16mo, mor. 1 50
      * Cement Workers and Plasterer's Edition..........16mo, mor. 1 50
      * Plumbers', Steam-Filters', and Tinners' Edition....16mo, mor. 1 50
      * Stone- and Brick-masons' Edition..............16mo, mor. 1 50
Sabin's House Painting..12mo, 1 00
   Industrial and Artistic Technology of Paints and Varnish.........8vo, 3 00
Siebert and Biggin's Modern Stone-cutting and Masonry..............8vo, 1 50
Snow's Principal Species of Wood...................................8vo, 3 50
Towne's Locks and Builders' Hardware.....................18mo, mor. 3 00
Wait's Engineering and Architectural Jurisprudence 8vo, 6 00
                                     Sheep, 6 50
   Law of Contracts.......................................8vo, 3 00
   Law of Operations Preliminary to Construction in Engineering and Archi-
      tecture..8vo, 5 00
                                      Sheep, 5 50
Wilson's Air Conditioning.......................................12mo, 1 50
Worcester and Atkinson's Small Hospitals, Establishment and Maintenance,
   Suggestions for Hospital Architecture, with Plans for a Small Hospital.
                                    12mo, 1 25

ARMY AND NAVY.

Bernadou's Smokeless Powder, Nitro-cellulose, and the Theory of the Cellulose
   Molecule..12mo, 2 50
Chase's Art of Pattern Making.....................................12mo, 2 50
   Screw Propellers and Marine Propulsion.......................8vo, 3 00
* Cloke's Enlisted Specialist's Examiner...........................8vo, 2 00
   Gunner's Examiner..8vo, 1 50
Craig's Azimuth..4to, 3 50
Crehore and Squier's Polarizing Photo-chronograph...................8vo, 3 00
* Davis's Elements of Law..8vo, 2 50
*   Treatise on the Military Law of United States..................8vo, 7 00
                                     Sheep. 7 50
De Brack's Cavalry Outpost Duties. (Carr)................24mo, mor. 2 00
* Dudley's Military Law and the Procedure of Courts-martial... Large 12mo, 2 50
Durand's Resistance and Propulsion of Ships.....................8vo, 5 00

2

* Dyer's Handbook of Light Artillery............................12mo, 3 00
Eissler's Modern High Explosives...............................8vo, 4 00
* Fiebeger's Text-book on Field Fortification.................Large 12mo, 2 00
Hamilton and Bond's The Gunner's Catechism 18mo, 1 00
* Hoff's Elementary Naval Tactics...............................8vo, 1 50
Ingalls's Handbook of Problems in Direct Fire.....................8vo, 4 00
* Lissak's Ordnance and Gunnery.................................8vo, 6 00
* Ludlow's Logarithmic and Trigonometric Tables 8vo, 1 00
* Lyons's Treatise on Electromagnetic Phenomena. Vols. I. and II.. 8vo, each, 6 00
* Mahan's Permanent Fortifications. (Mercur)..............8vo, half mor. 7 50
Manual for Courts-martial.................................16mo, mor. 1 50
* Mercur's Attack of Fortified Places..........................12mo, 2 00
*   Elements of the Art of War................................8vo, 4 00
Metcalf's Cost of Manufactures—And the Administration of Workshops..8vo, 5 00
Nixon's Adjutants' Manual....................................24mo, 1 00
Peabody's Naval Architecture..................................8vo, 7 50
* Phelps's Practical Marine Surveying...........................8vo, 2 50
Putnam's Nautical Charts......................................8vo, 2 00
Sharpe's Art of Subsisting Armies in War..................18mo, mor. 1 50
* Tupes and Poole's Manual of Bayonet Exercises and Musketry Fencing.
                                                    24mo, leather,   50
* Weaver's Military Explosives.................................8vo, 3 00
Woodhull's Notes on Military Hygiene..........................16mo, 1 50

ASSAYING.

Betts's Lead Refining by Electrolysis..............................8vo, 4 00
Fletcher's Practical Instructions in Quantitative Assaying with the Blowpipe.
                                                    16mo, mor. 1 50
Furman's Manual of Practical Assaying...........................8vo, 3 00
Lodge's Notes on Assaying and Metallurgical Laboratory Experiments....8vo, 3 00
Low's Technical Methods of Ore Analysis.........................8vo, 3 00
Miller's Cyanide Process......................................12mo, 1 00
       Manual of Assaying.....................................12mo, 1 00
Minet's Production of Aluminum and its Industrial Use. (Waldo)......12mo, 2 50
O'Driscoll's Notes on the Treatment of Gold Ores..................8vo, 2 00
Ricketts and Miller's Notes on Assaying.........................8vo, 3 00
Robine and Lenglen's Cyanide Industry. (Le Clerc)...............8vo, 4 00
Ulke's Modern Electrolytic Copper Refining......................8vo, 3 00
Wilson's Chlorination Process.................................12mo, 1 50
       Cyanide Processes.....................................12mo, 1 50

ASTRONOMY.

Comstock's Field Astronomy for Engineers.........................8vo, 2 50
Craig's Azimuth 4to, 3 50
Crandall's Text-book on Geodesy and Least Squares.................8vo, 3 00
Doolittle's Treatise on Practical Astronomy.......................8vo, 4 00
Gore's Elements of Geodesy....................................8vo, 2 50
Hayford's Text-book of Geodetic Astronomy.......................8vo, 3 00
Merriman's Elements of Precise Surveying and Geodesy..............8vo, 2 50
* Michie and Harlow's Practical Astronomy........................8vo, 3 00
Rust's Ex-meridian Altitude, Azimuth and Star-Finding Tables........8vo, 5 00
* White's Elements of Theoretical and Descriptive Astronomy 12mo, 2 00

3

CHEMISTRY.

4

CIVIL ENGINEERING.

BRIDGES AND ROOFS. HYDRAULICS. MATERIALS OF ENGINEER-
ING. RAILWAY ENGINEERING.

BRIDGES AND ROOFS.

Johnson, Bryan, and Turneaure's Theory and Practice in the Designing of
    Modern Framed Structures............................Small 4to, 10 00
Merriman and Jacoby's Text-book on Roofs and Bridges:
    Part I.   Stresses in Simple Trusses...........................8vo,   2 50
    Part II.   Graphic Statics.....................................8vo,   2 50
    Part III. Bridge Design.......................................8vo,   2 50
    Part IV.   Higher Structures...................................8vo,   2 50
Morison's Memphis Bridge..............................Oblong 4to, 10 00
Sondericker's Graphic Statics, with Applications to Trusses, Beams, and Arches.
                                                              8vo,   2 00
Waddell's De Pontibus, Pocket-book for Bridge Engineers...... 16mo, mor,   2 00
*   Specifications for Steel Bridges.......................12mo,   50
Waddell and Harrington's Bridge Engineering. (In Preparation.)
Wright's Designing of Draw-spans. Two parts in one volume.........8vo,   3 50

HYDRAULICS.

Barnes's Ice Formation...8vo,   3 00
Bazin's Experiments upon the Contraction of the Liquid Vein Issuing from
    an Orifice. (Trautwine)...................................8vo,   2 00
Bovey's Treatise on Hydraulics....................................8vo,   5 00
Church's Diagrams of Mean Velocity of Water in Open Channels.
                                             Oblong 4to, paper,   1 50
    Hydraulic Motors...8vo,   2 00
    Mechanics of Engineering.....................................8vo,   6 00
Coffin's Graphical Solution of Hydraulic Problems.............16mo, mor.   2 50
Flather's Dynamometers, and the Measurement of Power...........12mo,   3 00
Folwell's Water-supply Engineering...............................8vo,   4 00
Frizell's Water-power..8vo,   5 00
Fuertes's Water and Public Health...............................12mo,   1 50
    Water-filtration Works......................................12mo,   2 50
Ganguillet and Kutter's General Formula for the Uniform Flow of Water in
    Rivers and Other Channels. (Hering and Trautwine)....... 8vo,   4 00
Hazen's Clean Water and How to Get It.................... Large 12mo,   1 50
    Filtration of Public Water-supplies.........................8vo,   3 00
Hazlehurst's Towers and Tanks for Water-works...................8vo,   2 50
Herschel's 115 Experiments on the Carrying Capacity of Large, Riveted, Metal
    Conduits..8vo,   2 00
Hoyt and Grover's River Discharge.................. ....8vo,   2 00
Hubbard and Kiersted's Water-works Management and Maintenance.....8vo,   4 00
* Lyndon's Development and Electrical Distribution of Water Power....8vo,   3 00
Mason's Water-supply. (Considered Principally from a Sanitary Standpoint.)
                                                              8vo,   4 00
Merriman's Treatise on Hydraulics.................................8vo,   5 00
* Michie's Elements of Analytical Mechanics......................8vo,   4 00
* Molitor's Hydraulics of Rivers, Weirs and Sluices...............8vo,   2 00
Richards's Laboratory Notes on Industrial Water Analysis. (In Press).
Schuyler's Reservoirs for Irrigation, Water-power, and Domestic Water-
    supply..Large 8vo,   5 00
* Thomas and Watt's Improvement of Rivers........................ 4to,   6 00
Turneaure and Russell's Public Water-supplies 8vo,   5 00
Wegmann's Design and Construction of Dams. 5th Ed., enlarged......4to,   6 00
    Water-supply of the City of New York from 1658 to 1895..........4to, 10 00
Whipple's Value of Pure Water.............................Large 12mo,   1 00
Williams and Hazen's Hydraulic Tables............................8vo,   1 50
Wilson's Irrigation Engineering.............................Small 8vo,   4 00
Wolff's Windmill as a Prime Mover................................8vo,   3 00
Wood's Elements of Analytical Mechanics..........................8vo,   3 00
    Turbines...8vo,   2 50

MATERIALS OF ENGINEERING.

RAILWAY ENGINEERING.

Andrews's Handbook for Street Railway Engineers........3x5 inches, mor. 1 25
Berg's Buildings and Structures of American Railroads................4to, 5 00
Brooks's Handbook of Street Railroad Location................16mo, mor. 1 50
Butt's Civil Engineer's Field-book............................16mo, mor. 2 50
Crandall's Railway and Other Earthwork Tables................... 8vo, 1 50
    Transition Curve...16mo, mor. 1 50
* Crockett's Methods for Earthwork Computations....................8vo, 1 50
Dawson's "Engineering" and Electric Traction Pocket-book......16mo, mor. 5 00
Dredge's History of the Pennsylvania Railroad: (1879).............Paper, 5 00
Fisher's Table of Cubic Yards................................Cardboard, 25
Godwin's Railroad Engineers' Field-book and Explorers' Guide... 16mo, mor. 2 50
Hudson's Tables for Calculating the Cubic Contents of Excavations and Em-
    bankments..8vo, 1 00
Ives and Hilts's Problems in Surveying, Railroad Surveying and Geodesy
                        16mo, mor. 1 50
Molitor and Beard's Manual for Resident Engineers..................16mo, 1 00
Nagle's Field Manual for Railroad Engineers...................16mo, mor. 3 00
Philbrick's Field Manual for Engineers.......................16mo, mor. 3 00
Raymond's Railroad Engineering. 3 volumes.
    Vol.   I. Railroad Field Geometry. (In Preparation.)
    Vol. II. Elements of Railroad Engineering....................8vo, 3 50
    Vol. III. Railroad Engineer's Field Book. (In Preparation.)
Searles's Field Engineering.....................................16mo, mor. 3 00
    Railroad Spiral..16mo, mor. 1 50
Taylor's Prismoidal Formulæ and Earthwork........................8vo, 1 50
* Trautwine's Field Practice of Laying Out Circular Curves for Railroads.
                            12mo. mor, 2 50
*   Method of Calculating the Cubic Contents of Excavations and Embank-
    ments by the Aid of Diagrams............................8vo, 2 00
Webb's Economics of Railroad Construction................Large 12mo, 2 50
    Railroad Construction.....................................16mo, mor. 5 00
Wellington's Economic Theory of the Location of Railways.......Small 8vo, 5 00

DRAWING.

Barr's Kinematics of Machinery....................................8vo, 2 50
* Bartlett's Mechanical Drawing....................................8vo, 3 00
*   "   "   "   Abridged Ed......................8vo, 1 50
Coolidge's Manual of Drawing...............................8vo, paper, 1 00
Coolidge and Freeman's Elements of General Drafting for Mechanical Engi-
    neers..Oblong 4to, 2 50
Durley's Kinematics of Machines....................................8vo, 4 00
Emch's Introduction to Projective Geometry and its Applications.......8vo, 2 50
Hill's Text-book on Shades and Shadows, and Perspective.............8vo, 2 00
Jamison's Advanced Mechanical Drawing............................8vo, 2 00
    Elements of Mechanical Drawing................................8vo, 2 50
Jones's Machine Design:
    Part I.   Kinematics of Machinery..............................8vo, 1 50
    Part II. Form, Strength, and Proportions of Parts...............8vo, 3 00
MacCord's Elements of Descriptive Geometry.......................8vo, 3 00
    Kinematics; or, Practical Mechanism........................8vo, 5 00
    Mechanical Drawing...4to, 4 00
    Velocity Diagrams...8vo, 1 50
McLeod's Descriptive Geometry...........................Large 12mo, 1 50
* Mahan's Descriptive Geometry and Stone-cutting..................8vo, 1 50
    Industrial Drawing. (Thompson.)...........................8vo, 3 50

10

* Lyons's Treatise on Electromagnetic Phenomena. Vols. I. and II. 8vo, each   6 00
* Michie's Elements of Wave Motion Relating to Sound and Light.......8vo,   4 00
Morgan's Outline of the Theory of Solution and its Results...........12mo,   1 00
*   Physical Chemistry for Electrical Engineers....................12mo,   1 50
Niaudet's Elementary Treatise on Electric Batteries. (Fishback)..... 12mo,   2 50
* Norris's Introduction to the Study of Electrical Engineering..........8vo,   2 50
* Parshall and Hobart's Electric Machine Design.............4to, half mor. 12 50
Reagan's Locomotives: Simple, Compound, and Electric. New Edition.
                                                   Large 12mo,   3 50
* Rosenberg's Electrical Engineering. (Haldane Gee — Kinzbrunner)...8vo,   2 00
Ryan, Norris, and Hoxie's Electrical Machinery. Vol. I...............8vo,   2 50
Schapper's Laboratory Guide for Students in Physical Chemistry......12mo,   1 00
* Tillman's Elementary Lessons in Heat............................8vo,   1 50
Tory and Pitcher's Manual of Laboratory Physics.............Large 12mo,   2 00
Ulke's Modern Electrolytic Copper Refining.........................8vo,   3 00

LAW.

Brennan's Handbook: A Compendium of Useful Legal Information for
    Business Men......................................16mo, mor.   5 00
* Davis's Elements of Law..8vo,   2 50
*   Treatise on the Military Law of United States....................8vo,   7 00
*   Sheep,   7 50
* Dudley's Military Law and the Procedure of Courts-martial...Large 12mo,   2 50
Manual for Courts-martial.................................16mo, mor.   1 50
Wait's Engineering and Architectural Jurisprudence.................8vo,   6 00
                                                     Sheep,   6 50
    Law of Contracts...8vo,   3 00
    Law of Operations Preliminary to Construction in Engineering and Archi-
       tecture..8vo,   5 00
                                                     Sheep,   5 50

MATHEMATICS.

Baker's Elliptic Functions..8vo,   1 50
Briggs's Elements of Plane Analytic Geometry. (Bôcher) 12mo,   1 00
* Buchanan's Plane and Spherical Trigonometry....................8vo,   1 00
Byerley's Harmonic Functions....................................8vo,   1 00
Chandler's Elements of the Infinitesimal Calculus 12mo,   2 00
Coffin's Vector Analysis. (In Press.)
Compton's Manual of Logarithmic Computations..................12mo,   1 50
* Dickson's College Algebra...............................Large 12mo,   1 50
*   Introduction to the Theory of Algebraic Equations........Large 12mo,   1 25
Emch's Introduction to Projective Geometry and its Applications........8vo,   2 50
Fiske's Functions of a Complex Variable...........................8vo,   1 00
Halsted's Elementary Synthetic Geometry.........................8vo,   1 50
    Elements of Geometry......................................8vo,   1 75
*   Rational Geometry.......................................12mo,   1 50
Hyde's Grassmann's Space Analysis...............................8vo,   1 00
* Johnson's (J. B.) Three-place Logarithmic Tables: Vest-pocket size, paper,   15
                                                   100 copies,   5 00
*   Mounted on heavy cardboard, 8 × 10 inches,   25
                                             10 copies,   2 00
Johnson's (W. W.) Abridged Editions of Differential and Integral Calculus
                                     Large 12mo, 1 vol.   2 50
    Curve Tracing in Cartesian Co-ordinates..................12mo,   1 00
    Differential Equations.......................................8vo,   1 00
    Elementary Treatise on Differential Calculus...........Large 12mo,   1 50
    Elementary Treatise on the Integral Calculus..........Large 12mo,   1 50
    Theoretical Mechanics..................................12mo,   3 00
    Theory of Errors and the Method of Least Squares...........12mo,   1 50
    Treatise on Differential Calculus......................Large 12mo,   3 00

Johnson's Treatise on the Integral Calculus....................Large 12mo, 3 00
     Treatise on Ordinary and Partial Differential Equations. Large 12mo, 3 50
Karapetoff's Engineering Applications of Higher Mathematics. (In Preparation.)
Laplace's Philosophical Essay on Probabilities. (Truscott and Emory)..12mo, 2 00
* Ludlow and Bass's Elements of Trigonometry and Logarithmic and Other
    Tables 8vo, 3 00
    Trigonometry and Tables published separately ....Each, 2 00
* Ludlow's Logarithmic and Trigonometric Tables 8vo, 1 00
Macfarlane's Vector Analysis and Quaternions......................8vo, 1 00
McMahon's Hyperbolic Functions..................................8vo, 1 00
Manning's Irrational Numbers and their Representation by Sequences and
    Series 12mo, 1 25
Mathematical Monographs. Edited by Mansfield Merriman and Robert
    S. Woodward...................................Octavo, each 1 00
    No. 1. History of Modern Mathematics, by David Eugene Smith.
    No. 2. Synthetic Projective Geometry, by George Bruce Halsted.
    No. 3. Determinants, by Laenas Gifford Weld. No. 4. Hyperbolic Functions, by James McMahon. No. 5. Harmonic Functions, by William E. Byerly. No. 6. Grassmann's Space Analysis, by Edward W. Hyde. No. 7. Probability and Theory of Errors, by Robert S. Woodward. No. 8. Vector Analysis and Quaternions, by Alexander Macfarlane. No. 9. Differential Equations, by William Woolsey Johnson. No. 10. The Solution of Equations, by Mansfield Merriman. No. 11. Functions of a Complex Variable, by Thomas S. Fiske.
Maurer's Technical Mechanics......................................8vo, 4 00
Merriman's Method of Least Squares........................... . .8vo, 2 00
    Solution of Equations 8vo, 1 00
Rice and Johnson's Differential and Integral Calculus. 2 vols. in one.
                                       Large 12mo, 1 50
    Elementary Treatise on the Differential Calculus..........Large 12mo, 3 00
Smith's History of Modern Mathematics 8vo, 1 00
* Veblen and Lennes's Introduction to the Real Infinitesimal Analysis of One
    Variable...8vo, 2 00
* Waterbury's Vest Pocket Hand-Book of Mathematics for Engineers.
                              $2\frac{7}{8} \times 5\frac{3}{8}$ inches, mor. 1 00
Weld's Determinations..:8vo, 1 00
Wood's Elements of Co-ordinate Geometry.... ....8vo, 2 00
Woodward's Probability and Theory of Errors......................8vo, 1 00

MECHANICAL ENGINEERING.

MATERIALS OF ENGINEERING, STEAM-ENGINES AND BOILERS.

Bacon's Forge Practice...12mo, 1 50
Baldwin's Steam Heating for Buildings.............................12mo, 2 50
Barr's Kinematics of Machinery...................................8vo, 2 50
* Bartlett's Mechanical Drawing....................................8vo, 3 00
*   "   "   "   Abridged Ed......................8vo, 1 50
Benjamin's Wrinkles and Recipes.................................12mo, 2 00
* Burr's Ancient and Modern Engineering and the Isthmian Canal......8vo, 3 50
Carpenter's Experimental Engineering.............................8vo, 6 00
    Heating and Ventilating Buildings............................8vo, 4 00
Clerk's Gas and Oil Engine....................................Large 12mo, 4 00
Compton's First Lessons in Metal Working.......................12mo, 1 50
Compton and De Groodt's Speed Lathe............................12mo, 1 50
Coolidge's Manual of Drawing.............................8vo, paper, 1 00
Coolidge and Freeman's Elements of General Drafting for Mechanical Engineers...Oblong 4to, 2 50

13

Cromwell's Treatise on Belts and Pulleys..........................12mo, 1 50
    Treatise on Toothed Gearing................................12mo, 1 50
Durley's Kinematics of Machines...................................8vo, 4 00
Flather's Dynamometers and the Measurement of Power............12mo, 3 00
    Rope Driving..12mo, 2 00
Gill's Gas and Fuel Analysis for Engineers........................12mo, 1 25
Goss's Locomotive Sparks...8vo, 2 00
Greene's Pumping Machinery. (In Preparation.)
Hering's Ready Reference Tables (Conversion Factors)... ....16mo, mor. 2 50
* Hobart and Ellis's High Speed Dynamo Electric Machinery..........8vo, 6 00
Hutton's Gas Engine..8vo, 5 00
Jamison's Advanced Mechanical Drawing...........................8vo, 2 00
    Elements of Mechanical Drawing...........................8vo, 2 50
Jones's Gas Engine. (In Press.)
    Machine Design:
        Part I. Kinematics of Machinery.........................8vo, 1 50
        Part II. Form, Strength, and Proportions of Parts..........8vo, 3 00
Kent's Mechanical Engineers' Pocket-book....................16mo, mor. 5 00
Kerr's Power and Power Transmission.............................8vo, 2 00
Leonard's Machine Shop Tools and Methods.......................8vo, 4 00
* Lorenz's Modern Refrigerating Machinery. (Pope, Haven, and Dean)...8vo, 4 00
MacCord's Kinematics; or, Practical Mechanism....................8vo, 5 00
    Mechanical Drawing......................................4to, 4 00
    Velocity Diagrams.......................................8vo, 1 50
MacFarland's Standard Reduction Factors for Gases...............8vo, 1 50
Mahan's Industrial Drawing. (Thompson).... ....8vo, 3 50
Oberg's Screw Thread Systems, Taps, Dies, Cutters, and Reamers. (In
    Press.)
* Parshall and Hobart's Electric Machine Design.....Small 4to, half leather, 12 50
Peele's Compressed Air Plant for Mines...........................8vo, 3 00
Poole's Calorific Power of Fuels..................................8vo, 3 00
* Porter's Engineering Reminiscences, 1855 to 1882..................8vo, 3 00
Reid's Course in Mechanical Drawing.............................8vo, 2 00
    Text-book of Mechanical Drawing and Elementary Machine Design.8vo, 3 00
Richard's Compressed Air..12mo, 1 50
Robinson's Principles of Mechanism..............................8vo, 3 00
Schwamb and Merrill's Elements of Mechanism....................8vo, 3 00
Smith's (O.) Press-working of Metals.............................8vo, 3 00
Smith (A. W.) and Marx's Machine Design........................8vo, 3 00
Sorel's Carbureting and Combustion in Alcohol Engines. (Woodward and Preston).
                    Large 12mo, 3 00
Thurston's Animal as a Machine and Prime Motor, and the Laws of Energetics.
                    12mo, 1 00
    Treatise on Friction and Lost Work in Machinery and Mill Work... 8vo, 3 00
Tillson's Complete Automobile Instructor.........................16mo, 1 50
                    mor. 2 00
Titsworth's Elements of Mechanical Drawing.................Oblong 8vo, 1 25
Warren's Elements of Machine Construction and Drawing............8vo, 7 50
* Waterbury's Vest Pocket Hand Book of Mathematics for Engineers.
                2⅞ × 5⅜ inches, mor. 1 00
Weisbach's Kinematics and the Power of Transmission. (Herrmann—
    Klein)...8vo, 5 00
    Machinery of Transmission and Governors. (Herrmann—Klein)...8vo, 5 00
Wood's Turbines...8vo, 2 50

MATERIALS OF ENGINEERING

* Bovey's Strength of Materials and Theory of Structures. 8vo, 7 50
Burr's Elasticity and Resistance of the Materials of Engineering........8vo, 7 50
Church's Mechanics of Engineering................................8vo, 6 00
* Greene's Structural Mechanics...................................8vo, 2 50

14

Holley and Ladd's Analysis of Mixed Paints, Color Pigments, and Varnishes.

	Large 12mo,	2 50
Johnson's Materials of Construction....................................8vo,	6 00
Keep's Cast Iron. 8vo,	2 50
Lanza's Applied Mechanics...8vo,	7 50
Maire's Modern Pigments and their Vehicles.........................12mo,	2 00
Martens's Handbook on Testing Materials. (Henning)................8vo,	7 50
Maurer's Technical Mechanics..8vo,	4 00
Merriman's Mechanics of Materials...................................8vo,	5 00
* Strength of Materials..12mo,	1 00
Metcalf's Steel. A Manual for Steel-users.. ....12mo,	2 00
Sabin's Industrial and Artistic Technology of Paints and Varnish........8vo,	3 00
Smith's Materials of Machines.......................................12mo,	1 00
Thurston's Materials of Engineering... ....3 vols., 8vo,	8 00
Part I. Non-metallic Materials of Engineering and Metallurgy...8vo,	2 00
Part II. Iron and Steel. 8vo,	3 50
Part III. A Treatise on Brasses, Bronzes, and Other Alloys and their Constituents..8vo,	2 50
Wood's (De V.) Elements of Analytical Mechanics...................8vo,	3 00
Treatise on the Resistance of Materials and an Appendix on the Preservation of Timber....................................8vo,	2 00
Wood's (M. P.) Rustless Coatings: Corrosion and Electrolysis of Iron and Steel...8vo,	4 00

STEAM-ENGINES AND BOILERS.

Berry's Temperature-entropy Diagram.............................12mo,	1 25
Carnot's Reflections on the Motive Power of Heat. (Thurston)... .....12mo,	1 50
Chase's Art of Pattern Making......................................12mo,	2 50
Creighton's Steam-engine and other Heat-motors. 8vo,	5 00
Dawson's "Engineering" and Electric Traction Pocket-book.....16mo, mor.	5 00
Ford's Boiler Making for Boiler Makers.............................18mo,	1 00
*Gebhardt's Steam Power Plant Engineering.......................8vo,	6 00
Goss's Locomotive Performance.... ....8vo,	5 00
Hemenway's Indicator Practice and Steam-engine Economy..........12mo,	2 00
Hutton's Heat and Heat-engines.....................................8vo,	5 00
Mechanical Engineering of Power Plants........................8vo,	5 00
Kent's Steam boiler Economy.......................................8vo,	4 00
Kneass's Practice and Theory of the Injector........................8vo,	1 50
MacCord's Slide-valves...8vo,	2 00
Meyer's Modern Locomotive Construction...........................4to,	10 00
Moyer's Steam Turbines. (In Press.)	
Peabody's Manual of the Steam-engine Indicator...................12mo.	1 50
Tables of the Properties of Saturated Steam and Other Vapors. 8vo,	1 00
Thermodynamics of the Steam-engine and Other Heat-engines......8vo,	5 00
Valve-gears for Steam-engines...................................8vo,	2 50
Peabody and Miller's Steam-boilers.................................8vo,	4 00
Pray's Twenty Years with the Indicator........................Large 8vo,	2 50
Pupin's Thermodynamics of Reversible Cycles in Gases and Saturated Vapors. (Osterberg)..12mo,	1 25
Reagan's Locomotives. Simple, Compound, and Electric. New Edition. Large 12mo,	3 50
Sinclair's Locomotive Engine Running and Management.............12mo,	2 00
Smart's Handbook of Engineering Laboratory Practice..............12mo,	2 50
Snow's Steam-boiler Practice..8vo.	3 00
Spangler's Notes on Thermodynamics.............................12mo,	1 00
Valve-gears..8vo,	2 50
Spangler, Greene, and Marshall's Elements of Steam-engineering.......8vo,	3 00
Thomas's Steam-turbines...8vo,	4 00

Thurston's Handbook of Engine and Boiler Trials, and the Use of the Indicator and the Prony Brake. 8vo, 5 00
Handy Tables. 8vo, 1 50
Manual of Steam-boilers, their Designs, Construction, and Operation..8vo, 5 00
Thurston's Manual of the Steam-engine. ....2 vols., 8vo, 10 00
   Part I. History, Structure, and Theory. 8vo, 6 00
   Part II. Design, Construction, and Operation. 8vo, 6 00
Steam-boiler Explosions in Theory and in Practice. 12mo, 1 50
Wehrenfenning's Analysis and Softening of Boiler Feed-water (Patterson) 8vo, 4 00
Weisbach's Heat, Steam, and Steam-engines. (Du Bois). 8vo, 5 00
Whitham's Steam-engine Design. 8vo, 5 00
Wood's Thermodynamics, Heat Motors, and Refrigerating Machines...8vo, 4 00

MECHANICS PURE AND APPLIED.

Church's Mechanics of Engineering. 8vo, 6 00
Notes and Examples in Mechanics. 8vo, 2 00
Dana's Text-book of Elementary Mechanics for Colleges and Schools..12mo, 1 50
Du Bois's Elementary Principles of Mechanics:
   Vol. I. Kinematics. 8vo, 3 50
   Vol. II. Statics. 8vo, 4 00
   Mechanics of Engineering. Vol. I. ....Small 4to, 7 50
       Vol. II. ....Small 4to, 10 00
* Greene's Structural Mechanics. 8vo, 2 50
James's Kinematics of a Point and the Rational Mechanics of a Particle.
             Large 12mo, 2 00
* Johnson's (W. W.) Theoretical Mechanics. 12mo, 3 00
Lanza's Applied Mechanics. 8vo, 7 50
* Martin's Text Book on Mechanics, Vol. I, Statics. 12mo, 1 25
*   Vol. 2, Kinematics and Kinetics ..12mo, 1 50
Maurer's Technical Mechanics. 8vo, 4 00
* Merriman's Elements of Mechanics. 12mo, 1 00
Mechanics of Materials. 8vo, 5 00
* Michie's Elements of Analytical Mechanics. 8vo, 4 00
Robinson's Principles of Mechanism. 8vo, 3 00
Sanborn's Mechanics Problems. ....Large 12mo, 1 50
Schwamb and Merrill's Elements of Mechanism. 8vo, 3 00
Wood's Elements of Analytical Mechanics. 8vo, 3 00
Principles of Elementary Mechanics. 12mo, 1 25

MEDICAL.

* Abderhalden's Physiological Chemistry in Thirty Lectures. (Hall and Defren)
             8vo, 5 00
von Behring's Suppression of Tuberculosis. (Bolduan). 12mo, 1 00
* Bolduan's Immune Sera 12mo, 1 50
Bordet's Contribution to Immunity. (Gay). (In Preparation.)
Davenport's Statistical Methods with Special Reference to Biological Variations. ....16mo, mor. 1 50
Ehrlich's Collected Studies on Immunity. (Bolduan). 8vo, 6 00
* Fischer's Physiology of Alimentation. ....Large 12mo, cloth, 2 00
de Fursac's Manual of Psychiatry. (Rosanoff and Collins)...... Large 12mo, 2 50
Hammarsten's Text-book on Physiological Chemistry. (Mandel). 8vo, 4 00
Jackson's Directions for Laboratory Work in Physiological Chemistry ...8vo, 1 25
Lassar-Cohn's Practical Urinary Analysis. (Lorenz). 12mo, 1 00
Mandel's Hand Book for the Bi -Chemical Laboratory. 12mo, 1 50
* Pauli's Physical Chemistry in the Service of Medicine. (Fischer). 12mo, 1 25
● Pozzi-Escot's Toxins and Venoms and their Antibodies. (Cohn). 12mo, 1 00
Rostoski's Serum Diagnosis. (Bolduan). 12mo, 1 00
Ruddiman's Incompatibilities in Prescriptions. 8vo, 2 00
Whys in Pharmacy. 12mo, 1 00

Salkowski's Physiological and Pathological Chemistry. (Orndorff)......8vo, 2 50
* Satterlee's Outlines of Human Embryology 12mo, 1 25
Smith's Lecture Notes on Chemistry for Dental Students............. 8vo, 2 50
Steel's Treatise on the Diseases of the Dog....................... 8vo, 3 50
* Whipple's Typhoid Fever...................................Large 12mo, 3 00
Woodhull's Notes on Military Hygiene 16mo, 1 50
*   Personal Hygiene.....................................12mo, 1 00
Worcester and Atkinson's Small Hospitals Establishment and Maintenance,
    and S ggestions for Hospital Architecture, with Plans for a Small
    Hospital 12mo, 1 25

METALLURGY.

Betts's Lead Refining by Electrolysis 8vo, 4 00
Bolland's Encyclopedia of Founding and Dictionary of Foundry Terms Used
    in the Practice of Moulding 12mo, 3 00
    Iron Founder 12mo, 2 50
    "   "   Supplement.....................................12mo, 2 50
Douglas's Untechnical Addresses on Technical Subjects..............12mo, 1 00
Goesel's Minerals and Metals: A Reference Book ....16mo, mor. 3 00
* Iles's Lead-smelting 12mo, 2 50
Keep's Cast Iron 8vo, 2 50
Le Chatelier's High-temperature Measurements. (Boudouard—Burgess) 12mo, 3 00
Metcalf's Steel. A Manual for Steel-users 12mo, 2 00
Miller's Cyanide Process 12mo, 1 00
Minet's Production of Aluminium and its Industrial Use. (Waldo) ...12mo, 2 50
Robine and Lenglen's Cyanide Industry. (Le Clerc) 8vo, 4 00
Ruer's Elements of Metallography. (Mathewson) (In Press.)
Smith's Materials of Machines 12mo, 1 00
Tate and Stone's Foundry Practice. (In Press.)
Thurston's Materials of Engineering. In Three Parts 8vo, 8 00
    Part I.   Non-metallic Materials of Engineering and Metallurgy...8vo, 2 00
    Part II.   Iron and Steel.................................8vo, 3 50
    Part III. A Treatise on Brasses, Bronzes, and Other Alloys and their
        Constituents.....................................8vo, 2 50
Ulke's Modern Electrolytic Copper Refining 8vo, 3 00
West's American Foundry Practice 12mo, 2 50
    Moulder's Text Book 12mo, 2 50
Wilson's Chlorination Process 12mo, 1 50
    Cyanide Processes.....................................12mo, 1 50

MINERALOGY.

Barringer's Description of Minerals of Commercial Va ue.......Oblong, mor. 2 50
Boyd's Resources of Southwest Virginia............................8vo, 3 00
Boyd's Map of Southwest Virginia... ....Pocket-book form. 2 00
* Browning's Introduction to the Rarer Elements........ .... 8vo, 1 50
Brush's Manual of Determinative Mineralogy. (Penfield).............8vo, 4 00
Butler's Pocket Hand-Book of Minerals........................16mo, mor. 3 00
Chester's Catalogue of Minerals. ....8vo, paper, 1 00
                                                    Cloth, 1 25
* Crane's Gold and Silver. 8vo, 5 00
Dana's First Appendix to Dana's New "System of Mineralogy.."..Large 8vo, 1 00
    Manual of Mineralogy and Petrography......................12mo 2 00
    Minerals and How to Study Them 12mo, 1 50
    System of Mineralogy.................Large 8vo, half leather, 12 50
    Text-book of Mineralogy.................................8vo, 4 00
Douglas's Untechnical Addresses on Technical Subjects. 12mo, 1 00
Eakle's Mineral Tables. 8vo, 1 25
    Stone and Clay Products Used in Engineering. (In Preparation.)

Egleston's Catalogue of Minerals and Synonyms.....................8vo, 2 50
Goesel's Minerals and Metals: A Reference Book.. ....16mo mor. 3 00
Groth's Introduction to Chemical Crystallography (Marshall)........ 12mo, 1 25
* Iddings's Rock Minerals..8vo, 5 00
Johannsen's Determination of Rock-forming Minerals in Thin Sections.....8vo, 4 00
* Martin's Laboratory Guide to Qualitative Analysis with the Blowpipe.12mo, 60
Merrill's Non-metallic Minerals: Their Occurrence and Uses..........8vo, 4 00
    Stones for Building and Decoration............. .... 8vo, 5 00
* Penfield's Notes on Determinative Mineralogy and Record of Mineral Tests.
                                                            8vo, paper, 50
    Tables of Minerals, Including the Use of Minerals and Statistics of
        Domestic Production...8vo, 1 00
* Pirsson's Rocks and Rock Minerals..............................12mo, 2 50
* Richards's Synopsis of Mineral Characters....................12mo, mor. 1 25
* Ries's Clays: Their Occurrence, Properties, and Uses...............8vo, 5 00
* Tillman's Text-book of Important Minerals and Rocks...............8vo, 2 00

MINING.

* Beard's Mine Gases and Explosions.......................Large 12mo, 3 00
Boyd's Map of Southwest Virginia.....................Pocket-book form, 2 00
    Resources of Southwest Virginia.............................8vo, 3 00
* Crane's Gold and Silver 8vo, 5 00
Douglas's Untechnical Addresses on Technical Subjects..............12mo, 1 00
Eissler's Modern High Explosives...................................8vo, 4 00
Goesel's Minerals and Metals: A Reference Book..............16mo, mor. 3 00
Ihlseng's Manual of Mining...8vo, 5 00
* Iles's Lead-smelting..12mo, 2 50
Miller's Cyanide Process...12mo, 1 00
O'Driscoll's Notes on the Treatment of Gold Ores.....................8vo, 2 00
Peele's Compressed Air Plant for Mines 8vo, 3 00
Riemer's Shaft Sinking Under Difficult Conditions. (Corning and Peele)...8vo, 3 00
Robine and Lenglen's Cyanide Industry. (Le Clerc).................8vo, 4 00
* Weaver's Military Explosives......................................8vo, 3 00
Wilson's Chlorination Process......................................12mo, 1 50
    Cyanide Processes..12mo, 1 50
    Hydraulic and Placer Mining. 2d edition, rewritten 12mo, 2 50
    Treatise on Practical and Theoretical Mine Ventilation...........12mo, 1 25

SANITARY SCIENCE.

Association of State and National Food and Dairy Departments, Hartford Meeting,
    1906...8vo, 3 00
        Jamestown Meeting, 1907....................................8vo, 3 00
* Bashore's Outlines of Practical Sanitation.........................12mo, 1 25
    Sanitation of a Country House.................................12mo, 1 00
    Sanitation of Recreation Camps and Parks.....................12mo, 1 00
Folwell's Sewerage. (Designing, Construction, and Maintenance).......8vo, 3 00
    Water-supply Engineering.......................................8vo, 4 00
Fowler's Sewage Works Analyses....................................12mo, 2 00
Fuertes's Water-filtration Works...................................12mo, 2 50
    Water and Public Health..12mo, 1 50
Gerhard's Guide to Sanitary House-inspection 16mo, 1 00
*   Modern Baths and Bath Houses.................................8vo, 3 00
    Sanitation of Public Buildings..................................12mo, 1 50
Hazen's Clean Water and How to Get It. ....Large 12mo, 1 50
    Filtration of Public Water-supplies.............................8vo, 3 00
Kinnicut, Winslow and Pratt's Purification of Sewage. (In Press.)
Leach's Inspection and Analysis of Food with Special Reference to State
    Control..8vo, 7 00

18

Mason's Examination of Water. (Chemical and Bacteriological)......12mo, 1 25
  Water-supply. (Considered Principally from a Sanitary Standpoint)..8vo, 4 00
* Merriman's Elements of Sanitary Engineering.....................8vo, 2 00
Ogden's Sewer Design...12mo, 2 00
Parsons's Disposal of Municipal Refuse..............................8vo, 2 00
Prescott and Winslow's Elements of Water Bacteriology, with Special Refer-
  ence to Sanitary Water Analysis.........................12mo, 1 50
* Price's Handbook on Sanitation....................................12mo, 1 50
Richards's Cost of Cleanness. A Twentieth Century Problem........12mo, 1 00
  Cost of Food. A Study in Dietaries.........................12mo, 1 00
  Cost of Living as Modified by Sanitary Science.................12mo, 1 00
  Cost of Shelter. A Study in Economics......................12mo, 1 00
* Richards and Williams's Dietary Computer..........................8vo, 1 50
Richards and Woodman's Air, Water, and Food from a Sanitary Stand-
  point.. ....8vo, 2 00
Rideal's Disinfection and the Preservation of Food. 8vo, 4 00
  Sewage and Bacterial Purification of Sewage.................8vo, 4 00
Soper's Air and Ventilation of Subways ....Large 12mo, 2 50
Turneaure and Russell's Public Water-supplies.......................8vo, 5 00
Venable's Garbage Crematories in America...........................8vo, 2 00
  Method and Devices for Bacterial Treatment of Sewage...........8vo, 3 00
Ward and Whipple's Freshwater Biology.............................12mo, 2 50
Whipple's Microscopy of Drinking-water............................8vo, 3 50
* Typhod Fever.......................................Large 12mo, 3 00
  Value of Pure Water.................................Large 12mo, 1 00
Winslow's Bacterial Classification..................................12mo, 2 50
Winton's Microscopy of Vegetable Foods. 8vo, 7 50

MISCELLANEOUS.

Emmons's Geological Guide-book of the Rocky Mountain Excursion of the
  International Congress of Geologists.................Large 8vo, 1 50
Ferrel's Popular Treatise on the Winds..............................8vo, 4 00
Fitzgerald's Boston Machinist.....................................18mo, 1 00
Gannett's Statistical Abstract of the World.........................24mo, 75
Haines's American Railway Management. 12mo, 2 50
* Hanusek's The Microscopy of Technical Products. (Winton)..........8vo, 5 00
Owen's The Dyeing and Cleaning of Textile Fabrics. (Standage). (In Press.)
Ricketts's History of Rensselaer Polytechnic Institute 1824–1894.
             Large 12mo, 3 00
Rotherham's Emphasized New Testament....................Large 8vo, 2 00
Standage's Decoration of Wood, Glass, Metal, etc........... .....12mo, 2 00
Thome's Structural and Physiological Botany. (Bennett)............16mo, 2 25
Westermaier's Compendium of General Botany. (Schneider)...........8vo, 2 00
Winslow's Elements of Applied Microscopy......................12mo, 1 50

HEBREW AND CHALDEE TEXT-BOOKS.

Green's Elementary Hebrew Grammar.............................12mo, 1 25
Gesenius's Hebrew and Chaldee Lexicon to the Old Testament Scriptures.
  (Tregelles)...............................Small 4to, half mor. 5 00